*Library and Information Science Education:
An Intrenational Symposium*

Advisory Committee

Harris B. H. Seng
Chen-yung Fan
Lucy Te-Chu Lee
Ming-der Wu
Shiow-jyu Lu

Library and Information Science Education: An International Symposium

Papers Presented at the International Conference on Library
and Information Science Education Sponsored by the
Department and Graduate Institute of Library Science
National Taiwan University
November 29–30, 1985

Edited
by
James S.C. Hu

Department and Graduate Institute of Library Science

National Taiwan University

Taipei, Taiwan, R.O.C.

1986

Department and Graduate Institute of Library Science
National Taiwan University
1, Roosevelt Road, Sec. 4
Taipei, Taiwan, R.O.C.
Telephone: (02) 396-2859

Table of Contents

Editor's Introduction

We are undergoing an information revolution which propels us into the information age. In this age of drastic change in technology, the pace of obsolescence is accelerating as never before, and innovation becomes the only alternative for survival. Whereas the industrial revolution of the 19th century was characterized by factory machinery, the information revolution has been mainly symbolized by computer and satellite. It is common sense today that the 20 million books and the nearly 100 million items of other printed and non-printed materials in the U.S. Library of Congress can be held in a computer the size of a regular home refrigerator. Through satellite, a message, a document, or a videotaped program, can be transmitted from one corner of the world to another directly and instantly. While these changes have been so pervasive and their pace so swift that perhaps no one is able to comprehend their full range of implications at this point, it is clear and certain that they have posed a tremendous impact on the storage, retrieval and transfer of information, and challenged the established values of human individuals and institutions as well.

In response to the profound changes of technology in the information age, libraries throughout the world have since the 1970's taken various measures to accommodate the new environment, which, in turn, entails necessary adjustment in library education. How to modernize the curriculum to meet the need of the information society and to equip students with adequate competencies in order to cope with new advances in technology is the prime responsibility of library educators. The International Conference on Library and Information Science Education which was held on November 29-30, 1985 at the Department and Graduate Institute of Library Science of National Taiwan University was a direct result of this development.

The Conference was originally planned to invite one hundred domestic delegates and twenty foreign educators in the field of library and information science from ten different countries. Due to the limited funds, however, the number of foreign delegates was reduced to twelve and the countries to six. They were (at the time of invitation):

Ching-chih Chen, Professor & Associate Dean, Graduate School of Library and Information Science, Simmons College, U.S.A.

Charles H. Davis, Professor & Dean, Graduate School of Library and Information Science, University of Illinois at Urbana-Champaign, U.S.A

Harold Goldstein, Professor & Dean, School of Library and Information Studies, The Florida State University, U.S.A.

Rupert Hacker, Professor & Director, Department of Librarianship, Bavarian Civil Servants' College, Munich, Federal Republic of Germany

Peter Havard-Williams, Professor & Head, Department of Library and Information Studies, Loughborough University of Technology, England

Robert M. Hayes, Professor & Dean, Graduate School of Library and Information Science, University of California at Los Angeles, U.S.A.

Edward G. Holley, Professor & Dean, School of Library Science, University of North Carolina at Chapel Hill, U.S.A.

Norman Horrocks, Professor & Dean, School of Library Service, Dalhousie University, Canada

T. Young Lee, Professor & Chairman, Department of Library Science, Chung Ang University, Republic of Korea

Tze-chung Li, Professor & Dean, Graduate School of Library and Information Science, Rosary College, U.S.A.

Yoshinari Tsuda, Professor, School of Library and Information Science, Keio University, Japan

Herbert S. White, Professor & Dean, School of Library and Information Science, Indiana University, U.S.A.

Of the twelve finally invited, only ten could come to Taipei. Professor Charles H. Davis of the U.S.A. and Professor T. Young Lee of the R.O.K. were unable to make it because of personal reasons.   While no paper was received from Professor Lee, Professor Davis did submit a paper titled "The

Art and the Science of Library and Information Science" which was read by Professor Norman Horrocks at the first session of the Conference.

The main theme of the Conference was Library and Information Science Education. Participants were invited either to present papers or to enter into discussions on the following topics:

1. The Present Role of Library and Information Science in the Information Age
2. Current Status and National Trends in Library and Information Science Education in the East and the West
3. Assessment of Current Library and Information Science Curricula
4. The Integration of Library Science and Information Science
5. Future Trends in Library and Information Science Education

A total of seventeen papers were presented at the Conference, which are collected in this volume. Since the papers are difficult to group according to the five areas listed above, they are arranged in the order of presentation. Because we have no plan to publish the complete proceedings, these papers are preceded by the welcome address of the university president and followed by the Conference Program.

At an international conference like this, uniformity in viewpoint is neither sought nor desirable. Therefore, as we move from one paper to another, disagreements as well as overlapping will be occasionally noted. Needless to say, each author is responsible for the contents of his or her paper and the accuracy of its citations. However, since an attempt has been made to follow the *Chicago Manual of Style* as much as possible for their bibliographies and footnotes, the editor alone is responsible for those parts.

It is generally agreed that the Conference was a success, which was due to the contributions of many people and agencies. I wish to take this opportunity to express my sincere thanks to the three funding agencies outside the university, namely, the Ministry of Education, the National Council for Cultural Planning and Development, and the China Foundation for the Promotion of Education and Culture, without whose generous grants this fruitful Conference would not have been possible.

My deep gratitude is due to Dr. Chen Sun, President of the National Taiwan University, who not only encouraged us to initiate the Conference but also provided needed financial support; to Dr. Tung-bin Lo, Dean of Academic Affairs, who gave us a substantial portion of the university's teaching and research fund at his command; and to Dr. Yen Chu, Dean of the College of Liberal Arts, who rendered necessary assistance in obtaining funding for us from the university administration.

I am indebted to Professors Harris B. H. Seng, Lucy Te-Chu Lee, Chen-yung Fan, Ming-der Wu, and Shiow-jyu Lu.   Their professional experiences, thoughtful ideas, and creative suggestions greatly contributed to the almost flawless completion of the Conference.

Finally, my appreciation goes to the three former teaching assistants of our department, Misses Fuh-hwa Wang, Hweifen Weng, and Jing-huei Huang, who offered timely help in one way or another; and to the three present assistants, Misses Shiuann Tang, Pao-naun Hsieh, and Ren-kuang Lu, who did all of the administrative chores relative to the publishing of this work.

James S. C. Hu
Chairman & Editor

Department & Graduate Institute
  of Library Science
National Taiwan University
Taipei, Taiwan, R.O.C.
November 1, 1986

INTERNATIONAL CONFERENCE ON LIBRARY AND INFORMATION SCIENCE EDUCATION

Welcome Address
by
Dr. Chen Sun
President, National Taiwan University

Distinguished Guests, Honored Delegates, Ladies and Gentlemen:

On behalf of the university administration and the faculty of the Department and Graduate Institute of Library Science of the National Taiwan University, I would like to formally welcome you to the International Conference on Library and Information Science Education. To those who have travelled many thousands of miles from the other parts of the world to attend this Conference, we wish to express our special thanks and appreciation. We realize that all of you in this room are taking valuable time from your busy schedules to share in these proceedings. We thank you all for your kind participation.

The Conference's theme is Library and Information Science Education. Participants at this Conference are to present papers and to enter into discussions concerning:

1. The Present Role of Library and Information Science in the Information Age
2. Current Status and National Trends in Library and Information Science Education in the East and the West
3. Assessment of Current Library and Information Science Curricula
4. The Integration of Library Science and Information Science
5. Future Trends in Library and Information Science Education

Our presence here today testifies to the timeliness of these topics. It has been recognized that nations of the world are faced with the need both to supply traditional library services to their citizens, and to keep pace with the ever increasing technical advances being made in the areas of information storage and retrieval. In order to accommodate the changing environment, library science educators throughout the world, particularly those in the West, have adopted various measures. Some schools of librarianship, if I may be permitted to use somewhat old-fashioned terminology, add courses in information science to their curricula and change their names to schools of library and information science. Other schools divide the areas of library science and information science into two departments, and even grant separate degrees. Still others keep their old names but offer new courses in information science.

We in the Republic of China are confronted with the same situation. To keep abreast of the trends in the information age, our Government has, in recent years, stressed the importance of automation in library and information management and the need to train specialists in this field. Schools of library and information science here in Taiwan must keep up with these trends and prepare to assume the new responsibility of training the next generation of professional librarians. But how? What are other nations doing in this regard? How are our schools to reset their educational goals and curricular standards in order to meet the new requirements encountered in the information age? How can we best improve and update our educational programs of library and information science in the light of international experience and the needs of our own students and fellow citizens? It is our hope that this Conference will not only provide some answers to these and other questions, but will also make a significant contribution to the promotion of international academic and cultural interchanges.

We thank you for coming here to participate in this Conference and to share your ideas with us. We hope that you find this Conference as valuable as we expect it to be.

I hereby declare the International Conference on Library and Information Science Education of the National Taiwan University officially open.

Thank you.

The New Technology and Its Potential for Information Professionals and the Effects on Library and Information Science Education*

Ching-chih Chen
Professor and Associate Dean
Graduate School of Library and Information Science
Simmons College
Boston, Massachusetts, U.S.A.

It is a cliche to say that we are in an "information age." The 1980's are a period of rare and special promise. We have endured perils and an era of stressful change brought on by convulsive waves of shifting values on every front in technology and economics, in view of the world and of ourselves, in the ways and means of our growing society.

TECHNICAL REVOLUTION

Looking back in historical perspective, in the 1950's two major revolutions burst upon us: television and the electronic computer. These two advances have fundamentally altered the communications systems in every part of the world, and in the last two or three decades had an irrevocable impact on our libraries and information services. As a result, we have witnessed an information age culminating in the quick disappearance of the traditional "gate-keepers" role of libraries and the transformation of our contemporary culture from the traditional print orientation to an expanding, resplendent visual culture in which McLuhan's dictum, "the medium is the message," is a constant reality. The new media compete with word-based materials. The information is generated and produced faster than libraries can organize, store, and disseminate it. Thus, we have experienced the birth and transformation of a highly competitive information industry that flourishes on an ability to do things that libraries cannot do, such as repackaging information tailored to the information consumers' specific needs.

In the Spring of 1980 when we entered a new decade, I was fortunate to be asked to receive the Distinguished Alumnus Award at the University of Michigan's Library School, and gave a convocation talk entitled "Golden Opportunities in the 80's for Information Professionals." I said at that time, "The 1980's represent a frontier of further development and rapid expansion in electronic and telecommunication technologies. In the area of information sciences, the intelligent terminals, fiber optics technology, direct broadcast satellite transmission through digital links, electronic mail, facsimile transmission, computerbased message systems, large-scale data base storage, video disc technology, high speed printing, and photography offer us all outstanding, ever-expanding opportunities in the coming decade..." "Thus, in the 1980's we can expect a dramatic change in the mode of information production, transfer, and delivery. Due to the advent of a low-cost, distance-insensitive, wideband satellite network, both local television stations and cable systems may be partially supplemented by direct home-to-satellite broadcasts; home televisions can be used to display text from central online data bases; small, inexpensive-but-powerful computers will provide a means of access to machine-readable data bases at home and in small businesses. Real-time online conversations with consultants, colleagues of the invisible college, and information specialists are well within our technological capabilities."

"There can be a sharp increase of remote library browsing, remote literature searching, and remote interlibrary loans. Real-time hard copy reference and document delivery will also be possible. The 'electronic library' and/or 'telelibrary' awaits in the not-too-distant future; sooner than many of us would like to imagine. The rate of technological change created by television and mass media in the past two decades was so stunning that many librarians have been unable to assess clearly the farreaching effect it has had on the world of their services and operations. The pace of change brought on by the telecommunication technology of the 1980's will surely be far greater in the years ahead. Each of us must ponder deeply the role of new technology as a powerful change agent in the information field. We must understand fully the profound and permanent implications of technology in the future role of libraries and information professionals. Our continued relevance and usefulness depend on it."[1]

These were my predictions in early 1980 and seemed to be rather mind-boggling at that time, yet, only half a decade later, in 1985, not only has everything which I mentioned then become reality but also we have come of age in such a high-tech world that many of today's firsts, a mere decade ago, would have been labeled science fiction. One recent article which I read on a plane flight, cited a few examples to illustrate this point:

"the first student to enroll in a new ' electronic university ', a 25-year old double amputee who is earning his college degree at home by computer; the first soldier who never sleeps, a mobile defensive robot capable of guarding perimeters, patrolling wooden areas and doing various jobs too dangerous for humans; the first car in which the clutch is worked and the gears shifted by a miniature robot – an innovation which lets drivers enjoy the ease of an automatic while preserving the greater fuel savings of a manual transmission ..."

And now, to look at something less science fiction-like: travelling internationally many, many times in the last few years, I have progressively noticed how the general public's attitude toward the use of high technologies has changed – and rapidly so. Computers are no longer being viewed as a menace, but as a positive extension of human ingenuity; the general public have become much more computer-literate, therefore, they can use and/or understand computers; "user-friendly" has become less an advertising slogan and more a reality as hardware and software developers and producers have rushed to compete with credible products; and more and more professionals and organizations in every field have relied on new technologies to increase productivity and efficiency.

TRENDS IN INFORMATION TECHNOLOGY AND ITS IMPACT ON THE LIBRARY COMMUNITY IN THE FUTURE

It has been said that the amount of new computing power installed in the world is doubling every two years. To put it another way, the computers purchased in the next two years will have a total processing power greater than all computers purchased since the beginning of time. Why is this happening? And where is it taking us? The following are a few random observations:

Since the late 1970's, the microprocessing industry has been developed at such an unprecedented pace that in less than a decade, microcomputers/personal computers have developed from the simple 4-bit Atari for game use and the 8-bit Apple II to the powerful 32-bit micros such as MacIntosh and IBM AT with processing power rivaling mini-computers. Thus, in the last few years, computer processing costs have been decreasing by more than 20% per annum, while personnel costs have been increasing by 7% per annum. This means that relative to the cost of computer processing power, people are now at least 20 times more expensive than they were 10 years ago and 400 times more expensive than they were 20 years ago. As electronic breakthroughs have continued their whirlwind pace in all related areas, we have witnessed that system software has become easier to use and more reliable, application software packages have greater functionality and with more flexibility, end-users have many more alternatives; and hardware improvements have brought more processing power to the users.

As end-users become more sophisticated and technology more complex, the market need will prompt the design of fifth-generation computers-machines that incorporate artificial intelligence which will allow them to understand natural language, make deductions, draw inferences and solve problems.   This is where we will see the shift from information processing to knowledge processing.   On the subject of artificial intelligence, the library community has begun to perceive the potential application of artificial intelligence in many areas, such as cataloging and indexing, by incorporating AI into a public online catalog, and database retrieval.

The birth and proliferation of personal computer have helped create different types of information systems.   We will see the greater trend in treating information itself as a commodity.   For example, we have witnessed a great proliferation of machine-readable databases.   According to Carlos Cuadra, the number of online databases available to the public has grown more than 500 percent in the past five years.   In 1979, its *Directory of Online Databases* identified 400 online databases of all kinds, offered on 59 online services. Today a total of 2453 online databases developed by 1189 producers and are being offered on 362 online services.   Similarly, the number of online users has grown from an estimated 50,000 in 1975 to over 400,000 in 1983.

As the number and variety of electronic databases increase sharply, so have the speed and mode in the flow of information increased greatly — communication via text, voice, and image provide effective solutions to the problems of information flow.   For example, one can have voice communication by using an inexpensive microcomputer, such as IBM PC, with a communication modem at less than $600.   The use of audio synthesizers to create voice messages from a machine-readable database is in general use throughout the microcomputer and this technology has a great deal to offer for libraries in providing information services, and also particularly to special populations, such as the handicapped and others.

As the technology progresses dynamically, so do the electronic information delivery and distribution media change greatly in format.   While the traditional printed information entails a fixed format, the electronic information can be delivered and distributed in many options, such as videotex, audiotex, digital voice mail, interactive video-audiotex and many, many others.

Telecommunications – there is considerable evidence that the technologies used in telecommunications will continue to provide multiple alternatives to the traditional paired-wire, leased-line mode presently in place. Fiber optics, satellites, microwave, cable television, local area networks, etc. all have implications for telecommunications in libraries and libraries to home and office.   Local area networks for the PC have come of age in 1985. With the release of the broadband PC Newtork, IBM has conferred needed legitimacy on local networking, an area of personal computing that has until recently suffered from a lack of discernible hardware standards and appropriate software.

Micro-mainframe link has been another buzzword since 1984. Microcomputers are no longer used as single workstations only, but are clearly integrated into the whole system in a workable, cohesive configuration. Micros have become so powerful and versatile that they should not be used for simple functions only.   How can they be tied in with the existing and/or new library computer systems?   How can they be adapted to library operations? These questions deserve to be seriously explored.

Robotics – as I mentioned earlier, it is certainly feasible to use robots to shelve books, to deliver items within a building, to check out books, and to perform other repetitive tasks.

Other emerging technologies which should have an impact on the library community in the future include artificial intelligence, expert systems, management systems such as the energy management systems which can be used to control and reduce energy consumption in library buildings.   These also include distributed systems, bionics which could enhance the library's utility, say, for the handicapped, computer translation, computer graphics, such as the use of pictographs on computer systems with the MacIntosh, which would require less training for the use of a library catalog or other kinds of bibliographic instruction, and chemical technologies in the preservation of material on paper and film.   Smart cards with memory that can contain all kinds of information about users can certainly be used for services requiring a fee such as the photocopier, circulation fines, etc.   Electronic publishing and books on chip have great potential for information dissemination both now and in the future.

Storage media technologies have had rapid development as well. One of the biggest problems faced by libraries is "space," be it library space or system storage space.   In fact, this was one of the greatest criticisms on the earlier use of microcomputers for library applications because of the storage capacity on floppy discs.   Recent strides in storage technology portend lower cost and greater capacity systems for all computers.   In the past few years, the cost per MB of large disc storage has been falling by 22% per year, thus the effective cost of data storage is now only eight percent of what it was 10 years ago. This has encouraged users to keep more and more data online concurrently for data analysis and other purposes. It has also encouraged new applications such as electronic mail, electronic filing, and other applications.

The tremendously increased market potential in the microcomputer arena has served to accelerate the development and availability of the low cost and small size mini-(5 1/4-inch) and micro-(less than 4-inch) products. These present and soon to be available products span an impressive spectrum of technologies and technological improvements that are not always evident to the consumer. The products employing these technologies include magnetic tapes, floppy disks, removable hard discs, and non-removable Winchester discs. The fast developments in these peripheral areas have helped to overcome a great deal of the problems in the use of microcomputers for substantial applications in library and information work. For example, it is possible to have a microcomputer hooked up with 30MB of hard disc.

Laser optical storage and retrieval technology, including CD-ROM, in my view, hold great promise for libraries. In the area of library and information services, earlier applications were only possible for large national libraries, such as the Library of Congress, which started its three-year Optical Disc Pilot Program in 1982, exploring the use of optical disc technology for both information preservation and management. The widespread use of this technology in libraries began in mid-1984, when Library Corporation introduced its Bibliofile on CD-ROM for libraries to use with IBM PC's with added CD-ROM Drive in order to have access to approximately 500,000 machine-readable MARC catalog card data. Since then, CD-ROM and optical videodisc technology have begun to mushroom into a great variety of library and information related projects, ranging from Gaylord's full MARC database on laser readable disc to OCLC's experimental project in subject access and document delivery, from Information Access Company's InfoTrac project to Grolier's CD-ROM version of *Academic American Encyclopedia*, and it becomes obvious that a new form of electronic publishing is spreading rapidly.

So, what do these technologies portend for microcomputer-based information management? Very simply, the spectrum of storage technologies available for microcomputer systems today should be sufficient to make most applications of interest feasible. That is, within the limits of microcomputers themselves, storage should not be a constraint. While the cost of some technologies, Winchester and optical disc in particular, may still be too high for the personal computer market, they are certain to open up an increasing number of professional applications for distributed, microcomputer-based systems.

Yet, the real potential lies in the interactive nature of using these video/optical discs with microcomputer devices. The potential for information retrieval and education and training is indeed unbound. This is the area where one can create the demand for a technology that can reshape the world of learning and information retrieval for the society. For precisely this reason, a research and development project, entitled "PROJECT EMPEROR-I: China's Treasure Revealed via Videodisc Technology," is currently ongoing at Simmons College under my general supervision, and funded by the Humanities in Libraries Program of the National Endowment for the Humanities, in order to demonstrate how interactive videodisc technology can, indeed, revolutionize our whole concept of information storage, processing, retrieval, dissemination and provision.

In such a high-tech world, what does the future hold? No one dares to predict the long term prospects, which are simply mind-boggling and frankly out of this world. However, even the short-term prospects are no less exciting.

What do all these developments mean to us as information professionals, and how is the profession itself changing as a result of the new technology? Yes, in the last few years, there has been a dramatic change in the mode of information production, transfer, and delivery. The information consumers are much more sophisticated, and many of them have become either effective and frequent end-users of information systems themselves or have become information producers. Can libraries afford to provide their information services in their traditional mode? Have libraries learned fast to use technology as an ally rather than view it as a threat? Do informational professionals continue to educate themselves through various avenues in order to make themselves new technology literate and thus understand the new technologies well enough to utilize them to the best advantage or do they, instead, spend plenty on new technology with little substantial benefit? Does this development have any effect on the library job market? Is the new technology introducing and/or widening the gap between librarians and information scientists? What is the profession doing to cope with the new technology? These are essential questions for all of us to ponder deeply. While no simple answers exist, it is clear nonetheless that there is a need for a fundamental change in our professional education. Throughout my research and activities, I have stressed the fact that the library is only one of many viable information providers and, most frequently, not the most important one.   In order to increase the library's relevance and its role in the present information environment, our professional education must shift focus to include the following directions in addition to our basic functions:

--From library-centered to information-centered;

--From the library as an institution to the library as an information provider, and the librarian as a skilled information specialist functioning in an all related information environment;

--From using new technology to automate library functions to utilizing technology to enhance access to information not physically contained within the four walls of the library;

--From library networking for information provision to area networking for all types of information source providers.

You will notice my use of the term "information specialists," rather than "librarians" or "information scientists."   The reason for this is my firm belief that the library is only one component among many which comprise the total information environment.   In the emerging information world of the 1980's, all of those who are engaged in the fields and professions where "information" is a common word should work together, in harmony, rather than in isolation or competition in order to construct a unified and effective information service network.

Persuant to this, there are tremendous challenges in every aspect of our work — education, research, continuing education, management, staff development, communication, marketing, public relations and legislation, etc.   In the increasingly difficult and complex years ahead, we must collectively reset our goals and objectives, rearrange our priorities, re-examine our mode of operations, reinvest our energy and resources in new areas of development, and recommit ourselves to a new and more exact set of responsibilities.

EDUCATION AND RESEARCH

The broadening of the field must have serious consequences for education and training.   We discussed the need of a theoretical base of innovation. It is high time for professional training to move beyond a heavy emphasis on practice at the "how" and "what" levels of education to that of theory: our educators must also ask "Why?"   Only by probing the "why" will we be able to generate innovation and ideas, and evolve new systems to meet new challenges.   The broadening of the information field requires us continuously to alter and expand our curriculum and broaden our knowledge base through the study of other fields.   The knowledge base of information professionals should include greater attention to management, communication and behavioral sciences, to computer sciences and new technology, to problem-solving tools such as statistical methods and problem-oriented research methodology. Our library school curriculum must be the result of a constant change and evolution.

There is a need for information practitioners to pursue continuing education. Educators will undoubtedly carry a heavy burden in this area. While the expanded curriculum and program can always be considered opportunities for continuing education, short-term offerings (ranging from a one-day workshop to a multi-week course) should be planned on pertinent topics for a homogeneous target group, utilizing experts from diversified fields and disciplines. The development in this area is the joint responsibility of educators, information professionals and their organizations. The open opportunities are plentiful for those with innovative ideas and true conviction. We need vision, innovation and leadership.

Research creates new knowledge. It is, consequently, one of the most effective ways to advance and enlarge the knowledge base of a profession. The sophistication in research activities in a field is also a major criterion used to judge the maturity of a profession. There are plentiful indications that the library profession is rather immature in its developmental stages. Because of this, there are excellent opportunities for those with research capabilities and interests.

The library and information profession is full of basic problems requiring rectification that have been completely neglected. The new dynamic information environment has compounded the complexity and scope of many researchable problem areas. It is time for concrete research plans and actions. Let me conclude with an example. In the foreseeable future, possibly sooner than we expect, most information sources will be in electronic form. Concurrently, the development of a new generation of software, based on artificial intelligence, will be ready for us to assimilate information in an unstructured way with the ability to draw inferences. We will no longer speak of databases, but of a new type of information source, the knowledge base. Knowledge bases will totally revolutionize our information services. In other words, instead of doing a computer search of a database by using keywords, the computer will review the information contained and make inferences based on our requests and provide us with a synthesized answer not explicitly visible in any text.

This vividly illustrates again how information technologies have had, and will continue to have, a fundamental impact on the manner in which information can and will be used. While it is easy to witness a realization of all these new technologies as time progresses, it is important to keep in mind that the whirlwind pace of new technological developments have generally greatly outpaced our ability and effort to conceptualize and develop new appropriate educational programs and curricula for preparing our information professional for the efficient, full and productive use of these new technologies. Thus, the challenge to us as educators in restructuring our educational conceptual model, in continuously updating our curriculum, in offering continuing education opportunities, and in conducting research, is, indeed, great. It is an understatement to say that we live in an interesting time!

FOOTNOTES

* This paper is based partially on several invited speeches on the related subject delivered at the Quebec Library Association's Annual Meeting, Montreal, Canada on April 26, 1985; Royal School of Librarianship, Copenhagen, Denmark on September 11, 1985; the Swedish School of Library and Information Science, Boras, Sweden on September 13, 1985; and the University of Lund, Lund, Sweden on September 16, 1985.

1. Ching-chih Chen, "Golden Opportunities in the 80's for Information Professions," a special publication for the Alumni-in-Residence Program. (Ann Arbor, MI: School of Library Science, The University of Michigan, 1980). Also reprinted in *Journal of Library & Information Science* (圖書館學與資訊科學)8 (April 1982):1-19.

Professional and Academic, The Recognition of Library and Information Science Education

Josephine Yu Chen Sche
Associate Professor
Department of Educational Media & Library Sciences
Tamkang University
Taipei, Taiwan, R.O.C.

A social system could exist for decades without major changes under the cover of ageing and tradition, even if it can no more satisfy the needs of that society or its development. This kind of situation can very often be found in a society which tolerates a lot of traditions, such as in our Chinese society. Many traditions have their historical fragrance which constitutes the major part of our culture and pride. In the development of an educational system, a tradition could be a milestone in the history of that past development. It could also be, however, a stumbling block for the future development. The social system has operational functions serving the current needs of the society, which may have been changing continuously due to the effect of different social factors.

This international conference on library and information science education offers us the opportunity to exchange ideas, experiences, and insights on the educational problems of the library and information science profession internationally and comparatively. For the problems which occur in our country could also be identified in many other countries of the world, at least comparatively though maybe not identically.

THE PROBLEM

From the paper of Prof. Huang on the state of the art of continuing education for librarians in the Republic of China, you will notice that there is already a six-week summer program held by the Chinese Library Association, offered to library practitioners who have no formal library and information science education background. Most of these participants are taking professional responsibilities in various libraries.   This summer program has been held continuously since its inception in 1956, except for a one-year interruption in 1963.[1]   Courses are fundamental in nature, including: Introduction to Library Science; Classification and Cataloging (Chinese and Western); Book Selection and Acquisitions; Audio Visual Materials; and a Choice of courses focusing on different types of libraries – academic, public, school, or special.[2]   Upon the completion of the six-week summer program and the passing of a final examinations, a certificate will be granted to the participants.

We also have formal library and information science education programs offered in four universities and one college.   Every year we have about three hundred students completing their B.A. degree, three-year diploma, or Master's degree in library and information science from these institutions.   Their LIS programs began separately in 1955 (National Taiwan Normal University), 1961 (National Taiwan University), 1964 (World College of Journalism), 1970 (Fu-Jen University), and 1971 (Tamkang University).[3]   Up to 1980, 2503 graduates completed their degrees and diplomas from the above mentioned library education programs.   In the same year, however, there were only a total of 620 library practitioners in the Republic of China holding the B.A., Master's degree, or the three-year diploma from the library and information science education programs.[4]   More than seventy-five percent of the graduates of the formal LIS education programs are not working in the profession.

Based on a survey conducted in 1981, forty percent of the special libraries have no personnel with formal library and information science education background;[5] sixty-two percent of high school libraries have no formally trained library and information science personnel; and among the 124 school libraries that have personnel with LIS education, 107 of these libraries are serviced by personnel who have completed only the six-week summer program courses held by the Library Association of China.[6]   In the university and college libraries, where the qualifications of library personnel are superior to those of the other types of libraries, 51 out of 130 of these academic libraries have no personnel with formal library and information science education background; although among the rest of the academic libraries, 28 of them, over fifty percent of their library staff have completed the formal library and information science education.[7]

Where do these library personnel who have had no formal LIS education background but have professional responsibilities, come from?   And, how have they been recruited?   These questions touch the vital problem of the R.O.C. library and information science education namely, the value and meaningful existence of the formal LIS education programs.

In most of the libraries, the recruitment of new library personnel is not based on their library and information science education background. The general situation is that anyone with either general high school education, college education, or graduate education, could find a job in a library as a librarian, depending on the types of libraries.

There are two levels of civil service examinations held by the central government every year for various civil service positions in many public- and government-supported institutions. Library personnel is one of the categories to be recruited through the national civil service examinations. Anyone who holds a high school diploma could take the General Civil Service Examinations. Among the seven examination subjects for the library personnel, three are LIS related: Introduction to Library Science, Chinese Cataloging and Classification, and Chinese Reference Materials. For the Higher Civil Service Examinations for library personnel, five subjects are LIS related: Library Administration, Bibliography, Cataloging and Classification, Reference Work and Reference Materials, and Introduction to Electronic Data Processing. The qualification for taking the Higher Civil Service Examinations is a college degree or its equivalent.

There is no difference made between the graduates of the formal library and information science education programs and of other subject fields. Since the positions guaranteed by these civil service examinations in library and information science profession are limited (10 to 20 openings in each of the general and higher examinations) this can not be the main stream of recruiting library personnel for public services.

There is no official regulation to define the library and information science profession or the professional qualifications of personnel. In most public service institutions the library personnel are classified under the category of general administration. The lack of recognition of its professional value and status from society, from the library and information science profession, and even from the higher education institutions which offer the formal library and information science education programs has become a serious problem of the formal library and information science education in the Republic of China.

WHAT SHOULD BE RECOGNIZED?

Most of us who are participants in this conference probably would admit that library and information science education is a kind of professional education for educating the practitioners of the LIS profession. Therefore the LIS education programs and courses should consist of professional knowledge, competences, and techniques as the main content to be taught to the current and future LIS professional practitioners.

Some of us, however, may be considering library and information science education as a part of liberal arts or social education within the higher education, because in many universities the library and information science education is given in the College of Arts or the College of Education. In such an environment, the professional nature of LIS education is de-emphasized; such is the situation in the Republic of China.

In many countries, however, a university setting for LIS education is still far out of reach, due to the tradition that librarianship has been considered as a technical profession rather than an academic discipline.

Academic or professional, what should be recognized? The history of formal library education already exceeds or approaches one-hundred years.[8] The contents of the library education courses have been developed from purely technical library work to the most sophisticated information processing and services, including research and development. The limited traditional library techniques can no more satisfy most of the library and information services of today, due to the evolution of society, information needs, communication processes, and technological availability. The pressure of information needs has pushed the library and information science profession to accept a more responsive role on information processing and transfer work of the information communication chain. The role of library and information science education has become much challenging than ever. Professional excellence and academic research are compatible and necessary to professional library and information science education and also to the profession.

The recognition of library and information science education, therefore, should be placed on its dual functions, professional and academic. To recognize it as a professional education means to admit the value of library and information science education in transmitting general and systematic knowledge that will serve as the foundation of professional performance.[9] A refined recognition of professional education could distinguish the different programs of library and information science education in relation to the different levels and types of professionalism in the professional work. These distinctions are necessary when a profession matures and grows more complex.

The different levels of LIS education could be recognized according to the different levels of professional qualifications, such as: para-professional, first professional, and senior professional. The different types of LIS education could be based on the types of professional specializations, such as: subject specialist, administration and management specialist, reader services specialist, technical services specialist, etc.

To recognize it as an academic discipline will encourage the placement of LIS education in a university setting.   In such an environment, the responsibility of library and information science education should not only transfer human knowledge and techniques which we have accumulated for the library and information science profession, but also create new knowledge and new techniques for future development.   The prime advantage of placing the library and information science education in a university setting, as professor Saunders indicated, would be "the opportunity it presents for associating with, contributing to, and drawing on a whole range of scholarly discipline."[10] Because of such an environment, research in library and information science becomes necessary and possible.   Most of the research in our field has been done on an interdisciplinary basis.   To most professions, academic research has been one of the symbolic steps which serves to raise its status from an occupation to a more fully professional standing.[11]   The library and information science profession is now about to approach the steps which the well developed professions, such as medical science, engineering, etc., have experienced several decades ago.   The speed and level of this progress towards a full professional standing, however, is conditioned by the methods and phases of the recognition of library and information science education.

HOW TO ACHIEVE TOTAL RECOGNITION?

According to the experience from the countries represented by the participants in this conference, the attainment of recognition of the LIS education can be identified in three different phases.   However, none of our countries has achieved the total recognition in all three phases, professionally and academically.

1. The Recognition from LIS Education Institutions

When the schools and departments which have library and information science education recognize the professional and academic nature of the LIS education which they provide, their recognition will result in their accepting a responsibility to provide suitable professional education to the professional practitioners of the LIS community, and their engagement in the academic research and development of the LIS discipline.   The actions of this recognition are demonstrated in two ways: firstly, to establish professional and academic goals and objectives publicly, and to achieve these goals and objectives through their educational programs. Secondly, to undertake responsibility for placement and to ensure professional status for their graduates to enter the library and information science profession.

The schools of library and information science education in the United States of America have exemplified such recognition. Since 1972, most of prestigious schools with library and information science education have reviewed their programs according to the new set of accreditation standards adopted by the American Library Association for the first professional Masters programs. The very first one of these standards states:

> The library school should have clearly defined, publicly stated goals. It should also define explicit objectives for its specific educational programs, stated in terms of the educational result to be achieved.[12]

A further comment explains:

> If the school offers more than one program leading to the first professional degree, the scope and nature of each should be clearly defined. Each program should qualify the graduates to contribute to the advancement of the profession, rather than to serve only the purposes of one institution or locality.[13]

Based on this minimum standard, many library schools have established the statements of goals and objectives for not only the first professional Master's program, but also the post-Masters and doctoral programs. The following are a few examples which we may identify from the library school bulletins which are the means for announcing their public statements.

The goals of the first professional library education program from Indiana University are stated as:

> To educate the librarian to assume a responsible, professional role by providing him with (a) an understanding of the library and information center in society; (b) an appreciation of its role in the history of the communication of recorded ideas; (c) a knowledge of the principles and practices of library and information center organization and administration; (d) the ability to evaluate, interpret, and stimulate use of all types of materials, print and nonprint; and (e) a basic competence in the application of research methods.[14]

The goals of their doctoral program are:

> To provide for the advanced education of library administrators, research personnel, and library and information science teachers by means of a program leading to the Ph.D. degree. The doctoral program in librarianship and information science offers an opportunity to acquire (a) a broader understanding

of librarianship and information science; (b) an understanding of the purpose and process of education for library and information science; (c) through knowledge of a special area within these fields and further study in a related discipline; and (d) an ability to identify problems and conduct research concerning them.[15]

In general, the goals and objectives of the U.S. graduate library and information science education programs are threefold, such as those stated for the programs in the State University of New York at Buffalo:

> A primary aim of the School of Information and Library Studies is to educate men and women to be knowledgeable in the theories and practice of library and information science and in the intricacies of the information-processing world.　We expect that our graduates will be effective practitioners in information-transfer processes in a wide variety of contexts.
> ...another aim ... is to educate specialists in research and development needed to advance information and library science.
> ...A third aim ... is to educate leaders for the future development of the profession of librarianship.[16]

These purposes aim to educate three different levels of professional personnel: practitioners, specialists, and leaders for the library and information science profession.

Most of the library and information science education institutions in many countries, including the Republic of China, are aware of the professional function of the library and information science education but fail to take any action indicating the acceptance of their professional and academic responsibilities.　Students coming to these programs have no idea what objectives their education are supposed to achieve.　The only hints are the titles of the LIS education institutions and that of the program courses.　This is especially true when the students are recruited through a general entrance examination for university studies, and their becoming a LIS education student is mainly because of the fact that their final grades happened to match that required for the library and information science education programs.

2. Recognition from the LIS Profession

This phase of recognition will be achieved when the various types of libraries, information centers, and LIS professional associations can distinguish the differences between the professional and non-professional (Including para-professional) personnel, in terms of their positions, responsibilities, and salary grades based on their library and information science education background.

There should be a better relationship between LIS education and the LIS profession. The several education programs should be designed according to the current and future manpower needs of the profession. The profession should care about the quality of LIS professional education through the setting of the standards for the acceptance of the graduates from the LIS education programs to the profession as professional practitioners. Feedback on the professional needs and expectations from the profession could also be reflected for the innovations of the library and information science education curriculum. The means used to evaluate and recognize the professional library and information science education programs could also be used as an instrument to warrant the qualification and competence of the professional practitioners who complete their professional education from the qualified LIS education programs.

In the United States of America, the standards for accreditation of library and information science education programs, adopted by the American Library Association, also become a means of quality control in the professional staffing of libraries by the profession. Through the accreditation processes, LIS education programs are evaluated according to the set of standards by the Committee on Accreditation of the ALA. The qualified programs are recognized as accredited programs. As a consequence, graduates of the accredited programs are recognized as professionally qualified librarians.

The adoption by the American Library Association of the manpower policy "Library Education and Personnel Utilization"[17] is a further recognition of the various levels of library and information science education programs from the American LIS professional associations and the professional institutions. The categorization of the senior professional, first professional, para-professional (associate, assistant), and non-professional (clerk) personnel requires the following compatible education background: post-Master's, Master, Bachelor, Two-Year College, and High School. In order to be classified as a professional librarian, the practitioners will need to have library and information science education from an accredited program with a post-Master or Master degree as the basic qualification for the first two categories of the manpower policy.

The endeavours of the British Library Association in library education in the past one hundred years have exemplified a strong quality control of the professional association on professional librarians.[18] Since 1885, the British Library Association has held numerous professional examinations for granting professional qualifications and registration which have established the prestige and authority of the British Library Association in various non-formal library education programs.   Within the last two decades, academic degrees and diplomas of formal LIS education have been replacing the former Library Association's examinations as requirements for professional qualifications.   Today, the Library Association no longer holds professional examinations, but still keeps the professional registration for the junior and senior professional qualifications: the Associate of the Library Association and the Fellow of the Library Association.   These qualifications are granted to the graduates of the various library and information science education programs of the universities and polytechnics where they have earned their academic degrees and diplomas.   The professional registration of the graduates from the LIS education programs is also a kind of recognition of these education programs given by the British Library Association. The granting of these professional titles through registration requires several years of successful professional experience in addition to the former LIS education the graduates received from the educational institutions.   Through the cooperation of the LIS education institutions and the professional association, the professional and academic quality of library and information science education is quaranteed.   The professional status of the graduates of the LIS education programs is also recognized and protected.

Based on experiences from the U.S.A. and the U.K. we may realize that the library and information science professional associations should have a strong organization, including an adequate budget, an official building and offices with sufficient full time staff to operate the various functions of professional associations.

3. Recognition from the Government

Through the issue of legislation, a much firmer professional status could be established.   A professional personnel policy adopted by legislation is much more powerful than that adopted by the professional associations alone.   Supervision of professional examinations and establishment of regulations for the placement of public and civil service positions for the profession are also means of recognition given by the government.

In the Federal Republic of Germany, state decrees establish admissions requirements, length of programs, content of curriculums, and requirements of professional examinations for the professional library education programs in each state.   The state government authorizes the professional qualifications of graduates of its own library education programs, and acknowledges the professional status of librarians graduated from the LIS education programs of other states.

Graduates of the educational programs supported by the state are qualified to take library positions in public service and many of them join a civil service career as a librarian if they make a contract with the government at the beginning of their library education program.   Through the contract, various library and information science education programs become the preparatory tracks for different levels of library and information service positions in civil service.[19]   Because of the close relationship of the library education institutions and the state governments, manpower planning and control is much more easily implemented in the Federal Republic of Germany.

However, due to the strong protection of its professional status by government legislation, there is a great shortcoming in the German professional library education programs— a lack of academic research and status, because the traditional professional library education is given by the professional library institutions which are independent from the universities.   In the State North Rhein-Westphalia, the traditional professional education institutions are under the supervision of the State Minister of Culture and Education (Kultursminister) which is responsible for cultural affairs and general education; higher education institutions and universities are under the supervision of the State Minister of Scholarship and Research (Minister für Wissenschaft und Forschung).[20]   Under the current situation, professional status is not compatible with academic status for the library and information science education.   An academic LIS education was initiated at the University of Köln in 1977.   This academic library and information science education institute, however, does not provide any professional qualifications to their graduates because of the lack of recognition of their professional status from the state legislation.[21]

To achieve both academic status and professional qualification for the professional LIS education provided in the university setting is desirable and possible in the Federal Republic of Germany, for many of the full professions already have such a standing there.   Such an achievement will require our German colleagues' effort in solving the problems of gaining recognition from the government.   However, the total effort of LIS education over the world on the enrichment of professional content and the advancement of library and information science knowledge will be indispensable requirements for such an achievement in the Federal Republic of Germany, and in the other countries of the world.

CONCLUSIONS

Library and information science education will be meaningless without recognition of its professional status and academic value in a given country.

Recognition of LIS education will not only benefit the LIS profession, but also profit the user, the society, and the government. Due to the recognition process, close cooperation among the LIS professional education institutions, the profession, and the government become possible. Graduates of the LIS education programs are prepared to meet the manpower needs of the nation; the waste of LIS education could be reduced to the minimum.

Standards and other means of recognition of LIS education ensure also the quality of the professional library and information science manpower. Distinctions between the professional personnel and the para-professional or the non-professional worker are made based on their LIS education background.

A rise in the quality of professional manpower will result in an excellence of professional performance for the library and information services for a given country, which is the responsibility of the profession and the ideal objective of the library and information science education.

FOOTNOTES

1. 王振鵠，「三十年的台灣圖書舘教育」，中國圖書舘學會會報，第35卷（民國72年12月）：頁16-17.

2. 同前註，頁17.

3. 同前註，頁9.

4. 雷叔雲等撰，台閩地區圖書舘現況調查研究（台北：國立圖書中央圖書舘，民國71年），頁126.

5. 同前註，頁142.

6. 同前註，頁137-138.

7. 同前註，頁135.

8. First library education institution established in the U.S. at Columbia College in 1887; first professor chair established in Germany at Göttingen University in 1886; first British Library Association examination held in 1885.

9. Martha Boaz, "Managing the Library School," in *Current Concepts in Library Management*, ed. Martha Boaz (Littleton, Colo. :Libraries Unlimited, 1979), p.163.

10. W. L. Saunders, "The Library School in the University Setting," in *Li-*

brary Education: An International Survey, ed   Larry Earl Bone (Champaign, Ill.: University of Illinois, 1968),p.95.

11. Martha Boaz, "The Need for Research in a Young Profession," in *Current Concepts in Library Management*, ed.   Martha Boaz (Littleton, Colo.: Libraries Unlimited, 1979), p. 249.

12. "Standards for Accreditations, 1972," in *The Administrative Aspects of Education for Librarianship: A Symposium*, ed.   Mary B. Cossata and Herman L. Totten (Metuchen, N.J.: The Scarecrow Press, 1975), p. 384.

13. Ibid., p. 385.

14. Indiana University, *Graduate Library School Bulletin, 1977-78* (Bloomington, Ind.: Indiana University, 1977), pp. 11-12.

15. Ibid., p. 12.

16. State University of New York at Buffalo, School of Information and Library Studies, *Program of Study, 1973-1975* (Buffalo, N.Y. : SUNY at Buffalo, 1973), p. 11.

17. "Library Education and Personnel Utilization: A Statement of Policy Adopted by the Council of the American Library Association, June 30, 1970" (Chicago: American Library Association, 1970).

18. Gerald Bramley, *Apprentice to Graduation: A History of Library Education in the United Kingdom* (London: Clive Bingley, 1981).

19. Gisela von Busse and Horst Ernestus, *Libraries in the Federal Republic of Germany* (Wiesbaden: Otto Harrassowitz, 1972), pp. 244-255.

20. Paul Kaegbein and Dianne D. Rusch, "Library and Information Science Education in West Germany,:" *Journal of Education for Librarianship* (Winter 1982) : 163.

21. Paul Kaegbein,: Neuere Tendenzen der Bibliothekarischen Ausbildung in der Bundesrepublik Deutschland," *Archieves et Bibliotheques de Belgique* 48 (1977); 578-579.

The Art and the Science of Library and Information Science

Charles H. Davis
Professor and Dean
Graduate School of Library and Information Science
University of Illinois
Urbana, Illinois, U.S.A.

INTRODUCTION

At approximately the time that UNIVAC I was first made commercially available (ca. 1950), the graduate schools of librarianship in the United States coincidentally decided that the master's degree would be the "first professional degree" in library science.   Canada followed suit some years later.   For the past 35 years the ALA's Committee on Accreditation (COA), acting under the authority of the Council on Post Secondary Accreditation has maintained that only those individuals well grounded in the arts and sciences would be admitted to these master's degree programs.   The purpose has been to defer the teaching of professional matters involving library and information science until after students have majored in traditional disciplines.   The principal models that inspired this approach were medicine and law.

From time to time, other professional associations and societies in information processing have expressed an interest in accrediting programs or certifying individuals, but the Council on Post Secondary Accreditation has ruled that the COA would have sole authority for accrediting professional programs in librarianship and closely related areas.   To its credit, the COA has sought input from sister societies such as the American Society for Information Science (ASIS) and the Special Libraries Association (SLA), and members from these and other associations serve both on COA and on site teams that visit and assess graduate programs throughout the United States and Canada.

Some science graduates subsequently enter programs in computer science; however, the majority of scientifically trained librarians and information specialists are graduated from schools of library and information science, the best of which encompass both computer-based systems and traditional methods of information handling.   While departments of computer science sometimes have courses or programs in information retrieval, the majority continue to address problems of hardware and/or applied mathematics – usually depending on whether the parent unit is an engineering school or a department of mathematics.   Not to be overlooked in all of this is the simple fact that many employers insist on a degree from a school whose program has been accredited by the COA.

A complete account of the historical reasons for the existing situation in education for information science is clearly beyond the scope of this paper.   However, those readers interested in pursuing the topic are referred to Shera's classic work entitled *The Foundations of Education for Librarianship*, in which he discussed the interrelationships between and among traditional librarianship, documentation, and information science.[1]

STRUCTURE OF THE PROGRAMS

One of the best examples of a scientific field that has recognized the importance of educating its members in information retrieval is chemistry, and therefore it is probably profitable to examine how it has approached the matter of integrating library and information science.   Herman Skolnik, the first and long-time editor of the *Journal of Chemical Information and Computer Sciences*, once wrote that chemical information science "...is without a bridge to academic chemistry departments."[2]   And it is true that few of the master's level programs described permit a real major in chemical information science, choosing rather to concentrate on scientific literature, science documentation, and general theoretical and practical matters of concern to everyone involved in information retrieval.

At least one notable exception has evolved at Indiana University, where extensive cooperation has taken place between chemistry librarians, the chemistry faculty, and specialists in data processing.   This program has been described in an interesting paper by Wiggins.[3]   Nevertheless, the assertion by Skolnik is essentially accurate and represents a challenge to scientists and information specialists alike, who must cooperate if the special problems of information retrieval are to be addressed properly and in depth.   What is the nature, then, of these other graduate programs that obviously address at least some of the problems faced by specialists in chemical information science?

In the first place they are definitely generalist programs requiring all students to know the fundamentals of both traditional and contemporary techniques of information organization, storage, retrieval, and dissemination. Specialization comes afterwards. It has been fairly well established that there is a core of intellectual problems that must be addressed regardless of the devices one employs to perform this set of tasks, and dealing with such matters is definitely the long suit of these master's degree programs. These intellectual problems include, but are certainly not limited to: establishing authorship of works, classifying and determining the subject content of documents, providing satisfactory physical descriptions of items for identification or archival purposes, determining the optimum method for storing and retrieving materials, performing question negotiation to determine the actual (as opposed to the stated) needs of clients, planning search strategies (often involving a mix of media such as print, audio-visual, and computer-based materials), and implementing techniques permitting evaluation of the services provided.

This turns out to be a non-trivial assignment. In fact, many schools are now exploring means of lengthening their programs so that these fundamentals can all be covered, and so that a decent measure of specialization can be provided as well. The traditional length has been one full year, typically consisting of two semesters and a summer session, or else four quarters, depending on the calendar of the parent university. Within the last few years, some schools have elected to require a two-year master's degree program, while others have chosen to provide an optional second year and a second credential, often called a Certificate of Advanced Study. In any case, even though the curricula may differ in some ways, all of the master's programs accredited by the ALA provide an introduction to the foundations of library and information science, to the techniques related to the organization and storage of materials, and to information retrieval and the provision of traditional and contemporary information services.

SPECIALIZATION IN SCIENCE AND TECHNOLOGY

Although specialization in chemical information science *per se* is rare, specialization in the literature and information services of science and technology assuredly is not. In fact, because of its long history and reputation for excellence, chemical documentation usually represents a major component of such areas of concentration. Time did not permit a survey of all the schools; however, the University of Illinois course entitled "Scientific and Technical Literature and Reference Work" (LIS 412) is probably representative. Its stated aims are (a) to acquaint students with typical library materials in science and technology, and (b) to develop proficiency in their selection, evaluation, and use for reference work. A prerequisite to this course is LIS 320, "Introduction to Information Sources and Services," a course required of all students that introduces information referral techniques, reader's advisory and online information services, and that examines representative printed and online sources as well as developing question negotiating skills and search strategies.

The text for LIS 412, which is recommended rather than required, is *Science and Engineering Literature: A Guide to Reference Sources*, 3d edition, by Malinowski and Richardson.[4] Assignments include evaluating encyclopedias and dictionaries as well as indexing and abstracting serials, tracing the scientific publication cycle, performing literature searches in three of six areas such as chemistry, a case study, an online search, and a term project.

For the field of chemistry alone, the current *Study Guide* for the course lists six articles or journals for background reading, nine bibliographies or guides to the literature, fourteen encyclopedias, nine dictionaries, nineteen handbooks, one special set of chemical tables, six directories, four abstracts or abstracting services, *Chemical Titles*, the American Chemical Society Primary Journal Database, CHEMDEX, CHEMLINE, and CHEMNAME. A number of other elective courses are usually recommended to individuals expressing an interest in information science. Typical of these are courses dealing with automation or data processing, government publications, information storage and retrieval, online information systems, library service to specialist users, medical literature and reference work, advanced bibliography, measurement and evaluation of library services, telecommunications, research methods, information management, bibliometrics, and techniques for managerial decision-making in library and information science. Students are also counseled to take cognate courses in other schools and departments as appropriate – typically in computer science, business administration, communications, and linguistics.

DOCTORAL PROGRAMS

Thus far, the programs described have been designed primarily for practitioners − those destined to work in government, business and industry, abstracting and indexing services, or a variety of special libraries and technical information centers. Some graduates, especially those with substantial prior experience, may also choose consulting or some kind of entrepreneurial venture.

For those interested in research or teaching at the university level, there are over 20 schools in North America that offer the Ph. D. in library and information science.   In addition, one or two offer the D. L. S. (Doctor of Library Science) or the D. A. (Doctor of Arts).   The D. L. S. is technically a professional rather than an academic degree, but it often has quite similar requirements; the D.A. is intended primarily for those wishing to pursue careers in administration, and it may therefore have a less rigorous research component.   In any case, entrance to such advanced programs normally entails the possession of an accredited master's degree (or its equivalent in a closely related field) and sometimes suitable professional experience as well.

Given the highly eclectic backgrounds of those drawn to library and information science, dissertation projects range from traditional historical and bibliographic works through social and behavioral studies to systems − analytic projects involving operations research.   Depending on the strength of an individual's background and the nature of the dissertation project, approximately three to seven years are required to complete most doctoral programs.

A NOTE ON THE NEED FOR INFORMATION SPECIALISTS

Most people are smart enough to do much of their own information retrieval.   However, everyone reaches that famous point of diminishing returns − the point at the which any individual, particularly a person doing scholarly research, will be spending too much time searching the literature. Information specialists save time and provide more thorough service precisely because they know more about information sources and systems and how to use them.   They are trained to get things done efficiently that others might accomplish only after an inordinate amount of "hacking".   Moreover, the problems are not limited to understanding hardware or system protocols; they also include intellectual challenges such as those involving nomenclature, vocabulary control, and the intelligent selection of search strategy to optimize retrieval performance.

Scientists on the cutting edge of research may also become arrogant. This is implicit in what the late Derek Price called the "invisible college," that group of scholars to be found in most scientific fields − perhaps all fields − who typically satisfy their information needs by consulting each other.   It is asserted that their knowledge of the literature is so great that they have no need for it whatsoever.[5]   Regrettably, experts in one field are often little better than laymen in others − including some which may be highly pertinent to the research in question, especially in this era of interdisciplinary work. Moreover, the experts' dependency on the literature, whether in machine-readable form or not, becomes proportionately higher the farther they stray from their original areas of expertise.[6,7]   Good information specialists also have a way of capitalizing on serendipity.   They have wide-ranging interests and are sensitive to the relevance of seemingly unrelated facts and materials. They are pattern-recognizers who put together pieces that others might ignore, and they provide themselves with a wide array of source materials — in short, they browse.

Insufficient information can be dangerous.   Especially serious are the consequences when scientists perform incomplete searches of the literature, a situation exacerbated by having substantial newer material in machine-readable form while much older and still valuable documents remain in printed form.   The temptation is to assume that only the most current information is of value, and scientists may content themselves with online searches when they should also examine older sources for the sake of thoroughness.

This point was driven home by Nair in a recent letter to the editor of *Chemical & Engineering News*, in which he responded to earlier warnings about the danger of acetone peroxides:

> [T]he apparent reluctance to do thorough literature surveys to discover safety considerations is quite pertinent. This is one aspect of research that the younger generation... may easily neglect.   ...Given the track record of the chemical industry on safety of chemicals or at least the public perception of it, neglect of older literature can lead to unfavorable consequences when least anticipated. Modern investigators need an awareness that chemical safety data do not always lie in the modern computer data banks; if you don't find [them], do not assume all is well, that no safety data had ever been developed. It takes a little longer to do it the old-fashioned way, but the results may be valuable and future mistakes may be avoided.[8]

As more and more data are converted to machine-readable form, our data bases will of course become more reliable. For the time being, however, one would probably be well advised to enlist the help of a professional chemical information specialist when doing such crucial searches of the literature.   Moreover, it is highly probable that such an individual will do a better job than the average researcher even when the stakes are not so high, and the researcher will have more time to spend on those things for which he or she may be uniquely qualified.

INFORMATION RESEARCH AND DEVELOPMENT

On the other hand there is considerable hope for the future in designing systems that are more user-friendly, and that will allow the end users to do more of their own information work if they wish to do so.   Changes in hardware and software − especially hardware − hold out the prospect for faster machines with remarkable storage capacity.   We have already seen the introduction of microcomputers that have gone from eight − to sixteen − and even thirty-two bit words, thus blurring the distinctions between and among micros, minis, and mainframes.   Among other things this means that we can already have personal computers for home, school, and business that represent most of what we need for stand-alone jobs, and which can also be used as intelligent terminals for interfacing with other computers through existing networks.   Many of the inconveniences associated with complicated protocols and sign-on procedures can be eliminated by using these micros intelligently.   The gradual replacement of copper wire with fiber optics will allow us to transmit vastly greater quantities of data while providing greater security for the transmitted messages.   And laser disks hold out the promise of extremely dense storage for both pictorial and textual material, perhaps permitting us to download entire sections of online encyclopedias or other information sources.

In addition, there is hope emanating from the field of artificial intelligence, which has already introduced so-called "expert systems" into a number of areas − including medicine, where routine preliminary diagnoses can now be initiated by computers. And there is also progress in voice recognition, which would release us from the constraints imposed by keyboards − still the most efficient and cost-effective method for communicating online with computer-based systems.

These and other exciting possibilities are being explored by a variety of people in a number of settings, sometimes in industry, but often in our universities, where those teaching information science at the graduate level are also engaging in research.

REFERENCES AND NOTES

1. Jesse H. Shera, *The Foundations of Education for Librarianship* (New York: Wiley, 1972).
2. Herman Skolnik, "Chemical Information Science in Academe," *Journal of Chemical Information and Computer Sciences* 20 (1980): 2A.
3. Gary Wiggins, "The Indiana University Chemical Information Specialist

Program: Training the Library User and the Librarian," *Science and Technology Libraries* 1 (1981): 5–11.

4. H. R. Malinowski and J. M. Richardson, *Science and Engineering Literature: A Guide to Reference Sources,* 3d ed. (Littleton, CO: Libraries Unlimited, 1980).

5. Derek J. de S. Price, *Little Science, Big Science* (New York: Columbia University Press, 1963), pp. 90–91.

6. Charles H. Davis and James E. Rush, *Information Retrieval and Documentation in Chemistry* (Westport, CT: Greenwood Press, 1974), pp. 9–10.

7. Charles H. Davis and James E. Rush, *Guide to Information Science* (Westport, CT: Greenwood Press, 1979), pp. 7–14.

8. J. H. Nair, "Chemical Safety Literature in Data Banks," *Chemical and Engineering News* 63 (1985): 4.

Library Education in the Republic of China

James S. C. Hu
Professor, Chairman and Director
Department and Graduate Institute of Library Science
National Taiwan University
Taipei, Taiwan, R. O. C.

I. INTRODUCTION

It may be a surprise to learn that the shaping of the educational system in modern China was influenced by America, and that American missionary schools and colleges in the three decades before the Second World War made special contributions in this regard. During this period, educational standards set by American missionary secondary schools were unsurpassed by Chinese middle schools, while missionary-sponsored institutions of higher learning, such as Yenching, Nanking, Lingnan, and the Catholic University of Peking, were the equal of the best Chinese national universities.[1] Moreover, these missionary colleges and universities had developed a number of professional schools in such fields as nursing, medicine, law, journalism, and library science, which broke new ground for the training of Chinese professionals.[2]

The first educational program for librarianship in Republican China was initiated in 1920 by an American, Miss Mary Elizabeth Wood. Born in Batavia, New York, on August 22, 1861, Miss Wood came to China in 1899 to visit her missionary brother Robert and to teach in a missionary school. Educated at the Pratt Institute in Brooklyn, N.Y. and graduated from the library school at Simmons College in Boston, she managed to found a library school in 1920 at Boone University, an American Episcopalian institution located in Wuchang of Hupeh Province in Central China. In 1928, when Boone University was merged with several American Episcopalian missionary colleges to form the new Huachung University (Central China University), Miss Wood dissociated her school from the CCU and reorganized it into an independent professional institution known as the Boone Library School. Miss Wood died on May 1, 1931,[3] and the school was continued by her student, Professor Samuel T.Y. Seng,[4] who headed the school until 1950, when the Chinese communist government forced it to close and to become a department of library science at Wuhan University. For 30 years (i.e. 1920-1950) the school remained the only professional library school in China and its graduates made great contributions to Chinese libraries and library education, and to the East Asian libraries in the United States as well.[5]

The formal educational program for training professional librarians here in the Republic of China on Taiwan was started in 1955 as a division of the Department of Social Education at the Taiwan Provincial Normal College (now the National Taiwan Normal University). Prior to that, in 1954, a one-year and six-credit course titled *Library Science* taught by Mrs. Marian Orgain was offered at the Department of Foreign Languages and Literature of the National Taiwan University.[6] It was, perhaps, the first such course ever offered in a university in Taiwan.

In 1961, the National Taiwan University established the ROC's first Department of Library Science in its College of Liberal Arts. Three years later, in 1964, a library education program at the junior college level was founded at the World College of Journalism. A third library science program at the university level was added in 1970 at Fu Jen Catholic University, followed by the fourth in 1971 when Tamkang University established its Department of Educational Media Science (now the Department of Educational Media & Library Sciences) with the dual purpose of training librarians and A-V personnel.[7]

The first graduate school of library science in China (in either the ROC or the PRC) to offer a program leading to the Master's degree was approved in 1980 by the Ministry of Education of the Republic of China as the Graduate Institute of Library Science at the NTU's College of Liberal Arts. While some library-related courses at the graduate level are also available elsewhere,[8] the NTU's Graduate Institute remains the only program that offers the M.A. degree in library science here in Taiwan.

With regard to library education on the other side of the Taiwan Strait, there were only two such programs before the end of the 1970's, located at Wuhan University and Peking University. Since the 1980's, however, educational programs for librarians on the mainland have expanded rapidly. To my knowledge, the PRC has at present some 50 such programs in various colleges and universities throughout the country with a total of five to six thousand students.[9] Meanwhile, a recent report shows that the PRC has established a number of information science programs at universities and institutes. The Sci-Tech Information Program founded in 1978 at the Department of Library Science of Wuhan University is the oldest of such programs in the PRC.[10] According to the same report:

Both undergraduate students (4 years) and graduate students (3 years) are enrolled in information science in formal universities and institutes. There are programs at Wuhan University, Ji Lin Industrial University, Nan Jing University, Shan Dong University, The North-West Electrical-Communication Engineering Institutes, and the People's University. In addition, there is a teaching-research group in the Library Science Department of Beijing University. Altogether there are over 400 undergraduate students and more than 40 graduate students.[11]

The purpose of this paper is to provide an overview of the current status of the six library science programs in the Republic of china. Materials and figures in the following pages were primarily based upon a survey conducted in August 1985.[12] Before we go to the professional aspects of these programs, however, it seems appropriate to provide a brief profile of their parent institutions which, I believe, will enable us to have a better understanding with respect to the present situation of higher education in this country.

General Profile of Parent Institutions of ROC's Library Science Programs

NTU = National Taiwan University
NTNU = National Taiwan Normal University
Catholic = Fu Jen Catholic University (private)
Tamkang = Tamkang University (private)
WCJ = World College of Journalism (private, junior)

Entries	Institutions				
	NTU	NTNU	Catholic	Tamkang	WCJ
Year founded	1945[a]	1946	1950[b]	1950	1955
Academic status	univ.	univ.	univ.	univ.	junior college
No. of colleges	6	4	6	6	
No. of departments	47	20	31	32	8
No. of doctoral programs	41	3	1	3	
No. of Master's programs	53	17	15	14	

No. of faculty	2,011	1,066	1,357	1,483	449
full-time	1,486	770		588	187
part-time	525	296		895	262
No. of students	15,248	7,417	14,077	17,031	5,813
male	9,387	3,142	5,559	8,898	3,084
female	5,861	4,275	8,518	8,133	2,729
Bachelor's	13,099	6,800	13,778	16,547	
Master's	1,727	514	299[c]	456	
Doctoral	422	101		28	
Library holdings(vols.)	1,584,052	629,797	427,584	372,604	56,285

a. The university was originally established by the Japanese government in March 1928 as the Taihoku (Taipei) Imperial University. After the conclusion of the the Second World War in 1945, Japan retroceded Taiwan to China, and the university was renamed the National Taiwan University on November 15, 1945. It remained the only university in Taiwan until 1954.

b. The university was first founded by American missionaries in 1929 as the Fu Jen Catholic University of Peking.

c. The figure includes both Master's and doctoral students.

II. LIBRARY SCIENCE PROGRAMS IN THE REPUBLIC OF CHINA

1. National Taiwan University
College of Liberal Arts
Department and Graduate Institute of Library Science

As of today, NTU is the only university in the ROC that has both a department and a graduate institute of library science.

(1) Department of Library Science

Year established: 1961

Degree awarded: B.A.

Present enrollment: 235 undergraduate students (30 males, 205 females).

Curriculum: Basic structure of the curriculum consists of five parts :[13]

1) 6 general courses of 28 credits, such as Chinese, English, General History of China, etc. which are required by the Ministry of Education for all freshman classes in colleges and universities.

2) 14 professional courses of 50 credits which are required by the MOE for all undergraduate library science programs.[14]

3) 10 courses of 35 credits, such as Mass Communication, General Psychology, Logic, Research Methods, Second Foreign Language, etc. which are required by the Department.

4) 7 courses of 15 credits are electives. More than 40 courses are currently offered by the Department for this purpose.

5) A minor of at least 20 credits in a subject area other than library science to be selected by students.

A minimum of 148 credits is required for the
B.A. degree in library science at NTU.

Library and Information Science Courses Offered in the NTU Program

Course Title	Credit	Required	Elective	Remarks
Introduction to Library Science	2	x		Required by MOE
Introduction to Information Science	2	x		do.
Introd. to Computer Science	4	x		do.
Chinese Cataloging and Classification	6	x		do.
Western Cataloging and Classification	6	x		do.
Chinese Reference Sources	4	x		do.
Western Reference Sources	4	x		do.
Bibliography	4	x		do.
Building Library Collections	4	x		do.
Non-Book Materials	2	x		do.
A-V Materials	4	x		do.
Library Management	4	x		do.
Library Automation	4	x		do.
Library Field Work	0	x		2 hrs. per week for seniors
History of Libraries	2	x		Required by Dept.
Special Topics in Library Science	2	x		do.
Mass Communications	4	x		do.
Research Methods & Thesis Writing	2	x		do.
History of Books	2		x	do.
Introduction to Reference Service	2		x	

Course	Units	Offered	Notes
Library Service for Special Readers	2	x	
Literature of the Humanities	4	x	1 of the 3 is required by the Dept.
Literature of Social Sciences	4	x	
Literature of Science & Technology	4	x	
Literature for Young Adults and Children	4	x	
Western Literature for Children	4	x	
Collection Development	2	x	Offered for both graduate and under-graduate students
Issues in Modern Librarianship	2	x	
Evaluation of Library Operations	2	x	
Chinese Collectanea	4	x	
Study of Classification Systems	2	x.	
Cat. and Classification of Materials in Japanese Language	2	x	
Japanese Reference Sources	3	x	
Government Documents	3	x	
Study of Government Publications	2	x	
Printing and Publishing	2	x	
College and University Libraries	2	x	1 of the 4 is required by the Dept.
Public Libraries	2	x	
School Libraries	2	x	
Special Libraries	2	x	
Children's Libraries	2	x	
Selected Readings on Library Science in English	2	x	
English for Librarians	2	x	
Introduction to A-V Materials	3	x	
Planning & Producing A-V Materials	3	x	
Library Statistics	6	x	
Introduction to File Design	2	x	

Applications of File Design	2	x	
System Analysis	3	x	
Introduction to Data Processing for Libraries	3	x	
Computer Programming	3	x	
Application of Computer in Libraries	3	x	
Application of Microcomputer in Libraries	3	x	
Indexing and Abstracting	3	x	
Information Storage and Retrieval	3	x	Graduate courses open to senior under-graduate students
Thesaurus Construction	2	x	
Information Systems	3	x	
Information Management	3	x	
Information Policy	3	x	
Online Information Searching	3	x	
Introduction to Database Manag.	2	x	
Library Resource Sharing	2	x	

(2) Graduate Institute of Library Science

Year established: 1980

Degree awarded: M.A.

Admission requirement:[15]   Pass the entrance examination for graduate students conducted by the University which is highly competitive. According to the records of the past few years, only one tenth of those who took the examination passed it.

Graduation requirements:[16] Requirements for the M.A. degree include:

1) 2 to 4 years of residence.
2) Completion of a minimum of 24 graduate credits
   Those students who possess a B.A.

degree in a subject other than library science must take an additional six remedial courses of 20 credits, namely Chinese Cataloging and Classification (4 credits), Western Cataloging and Classification (4), Chinese Reference Sources (4), Western Reference Sources (4), Book Selection and Acquisitions (2), and Library Administration (2). These credits can not be counted toward the 24 graduate credits required for the M.A degree.

3) Fulfill second foreign language requirement.
4) Pass graduation examination.
5) Pass oral examination on thesis.

Present enrollment:

32 graduate students are currently enrolled in the program, of which 5 are foreign students including 1 from the United States and 4 from the Republic of Korea.

Curriculum:

5 courses of 10 credits are required of all graduate students. 14 of the required 24 credits for graduation may be taken from the electives. Three courses are offered for both graduate and undergraduate students. Eight of the information science courses are primarily offered for graduate classes, but are open to senior undergraduate students.

List of Courses Offered by the NTU Graduate Institute of Library Science

Course Title	Credits	Required	Elective	Remarks
Research Methods	2	x		
Seminar in Library Administration	2	x		
Seminar in Reader Services	2	x		
Seminar in Technical Services	2	x		
Seminar in Information Science	2	x		
Education for Librarianship	2		x	
Comparative Librarianship	2		x	
Special Topics in Chinese Bibliography	2		x	
Study of Chinese Block Editions	2		x	
History of Chinese Printing	2		x	
Chinese Biographical Literature	2		x	
Study of Chinese Rare Books	2		x	
Chinese Classical Reference	2		x	
Cataloging for Chinese Classics	2		x	
Theory of Classifications	2		x	
Seminar in Public Libraries	2		x	
Seminar in Academic Libraries	2		x	
Thesis Writing	2		x	
Operations Research	4		x	
Study of Chinese Computer	2		x	
Seminar in Computer Science	2		x	
Computer Data Structure	2		x	
Management of Computer Centers	2		x	
Information Science Education	2		x	
Study of A-V Education	2		x	
Collection Development	2		x	Open to senior under-graduate students
Evaluation of Library Operations	2		x	
Issues in Modern Librarianship	2		x	
Indexing and Abstracting	3		x	
Introduction to Database Manag.	2		x	
Information Storage and Retrieval	3		x	
Online Information Searching	3		x	
Thesaurus Construction	2		x	
Information Management	3		x	
Information Policy	3		x	
Library Resource Sharing	2		x	

(3) Faculty

26 persons are currently on the faculty of the Department and the Graduate Institute, of which 11 are part-time.   16 of the 26 received graduate education in the United States, including 9 PhDs, 1 PhD candidate, and 6 MLSs.

(4) Facilities and equipment

1) Departmental Library

NTU houses the largest library in the Republic of China.   As of September 1985, its collections numbered 1,584,052 volumes. While a substantial portion of these materials is available for teaching library courses, the Department maintains a special library of professional materials.   Present holdings and budget of this library are as follows:

Library & Information Science Books: 15,510 volumes
Professional Periodicals: 187 titles
1985/86 Budget: For Books: NT $600,000.00
or U.S. $15,000.00
For Periodicals: NT $240,000.00
or U.S. $6,000.00

2) A-V and other equipment

In addition to facilities and equipment at the University Computer Center and the A-V Center at the College of Liberal Arts that are used for teaching A-V and computer courses, the Department has the following equipment for its own convenience: 50 typewriters (4 of them are electronic), 7 microcomputers, 10 terminals, 3 copy machines, 4 printers, and one each of the following: tape recorder, transparency maker, slide projector, overhead projector, opaque projector, 16mm film sound-slide projector, front-rear sound projector, sound-filmstrip projector, 26"AV monitor, sound sync recorder, Betamovie, stereo video cassette recorder, Multibliz, ELMO GS-800 projector, Nikon camera, and Nikon camera FM2.

(5) Observations

1) To our Knowledge, NTU is the first university in China (in either the ROC or the PRC) to have a graduate program leading to the M.A. degree in library science. While graduate library programs have been set up in the PRC in recent years, the Graduate Institute of Library Science at the National Taiwan University remains the only such program in the Republic of China.

2) In order to cope with the changing environment in library education, the Department has been planning for some time to change its name from the present Department of Library Science to the Department of Library and Information Science.

3) A total of 19 courses in information science has been offered in the two programs, including five which were taught during the past academic year by a visiting associate professor from the United States. Whenever necessary, more visiting faculty from abroad will be invited to teach in this field.

4) Courses in special librarianship, such as law, medicine, music, journalism, will be added to the curriculum as soon as qualified faculty can be appointed.

5) To provide teaching faculty for library science programs and to supply candidates for directorship of college and university libraries, the Graduate Institute of Library Science has submitted a proposal to the Ministry of Education to establish a Ph.D. program in 1988.

6) A new university library building is presently at the planning stage. The university library and the Department have been charged by the university president with the responsibility of working out a preliminary plan for the construction of this building which will house the university library and the Department and Graduate Institute of Library Science. Once the new library is completed, the Department and the Graduate Institute will have a modern and functional home for their proper operation.

7) Approximately NT$1,000,000, or US$30,000, were spent annually for library and information science books and periodicals in the past three years. We believe a comparable amount for professional materials will be allotted for each of the several years ahead.

2. National Taiwan Normal University
College of Education
Division of Library Science, Department of Social Education

Year established: 1955

Degree awarded: B.Ed.

Present enrollment: 48 students (6 males, 42 females)

Faculty: 11 of the 36 faculty members in the Department of Social Education are teaching library science courses; 4 of the 11 are on part-time basis.   7 of the library science faculty received their professional library education in the the United States.

Curriculum: The main concern of this program is twofold, education and school librarianship.   They are reflected in the curriculum which consists of 5 components:

1) 6 general courses of 28 credits for all college freshman classes are required by the Ministry of Education of the Central Government.

2) 9 courses of education of 26 credits are required for all students at normal colleges and university.

3) 5 courses of 13 credits are required by the Department of Social Education which include: Social Education, Introduction to Library Science, Introduction to Journalism, Introduction to Social Work, and Social Education Administration.

4) 14 courses in library science of 39 credits are required by the Ministry of Education. Another 12 courses of librarianship of 31 credits are offered for electives.

5) A minor of at least 20 credits in a subject area other than library science is also required.

A minimum of 154 credits is required for the B.Ed. degree which is a 5-year program, including 4 years of course work and 1 year of field work.

Library and Information Science Courses Offered in the NTNU Program

Course Title	Credits	Required	Elective	Remarks
Introduction to Library Science	2	x		Req. by MOE
Introd. to Information Science	2	x		do.
Bibliography of Literature	3	x		do.
Chinese Catalog. and Class.	4	x		do.
Chinese Reference Materials	4	x		do.
Introd. to Computer Science	2	x		do.
Sel. & Acq. of Lib. Materials	3	x		do.
Western Catalog. & Class.	4	x		do.
Western Reference Materials	4	x		do.
Non-Book Materials	2	x		do.
Library Automation	2	x		do.
Library Administration	2	x		do.
Library Field Work	3	x		do.
School Library Administration	2	x		Req. by Div.
Young Adult & Children's Reading Materials	3		x	
Library History	2		x	
Organization of Documents and Archives	4		x	
Museum Organization and Administration	3		x	
Information Processing	2		x	
Public Service in Libraries	2		x	
Literature in Social Sciences	3		x	
Study on the Problems of Library Science	2		x	
Public Library Administration	2		x	
College & University Library Administration	2		x	
Literature in the Humanities	3		x	
Science Literature	3		x	

Departmental library: The program maintains a special collection of professional materials in library and information science. It presently holds 7,912 volumes of books (4,560 in Chinese and 3,352 in foreign languages) and 81 periodicals.

A-V & other equipment: The program has fair/good facilities and equipment for teaching A-V and computer courses, including online searching practice on DIALOG.

Observations:

1) Since the prime mission of normal university and colleges in the ROC is the provision of education for secondary school teachers, the purpose of this program is mainly school librarianship.
2) Because it is a unit of a teachers college, its curriculum comprises a substantial number of education courses. Of all the required courses, 11 courses of 33 credits are in this category.
3) Students enrolled in this program must spend five years to complete the B.Ed. degree. After the completion of all course work at the end of the 4th year, each student is assigned by the university administration to a one year of field work at a secondary school or a social institution.
4) Like other students at normal colleges in the Republic of China on Taiwan, all students at this program are given free room, board, and tuition by the Government. Because of this special treatment, graduates are required to provide professional service at a designated institution for at least two years before they are permitted to accept other employment or to pursue advanced studies.

3. **Fu Jen Catholic University**
College of Liberal Arts
Department of Library Science

Year established: 1970

Degree awarded: B.A.

Present enrollment:	521 students are currently enrolled in the Department, including:

254 in the regular undergraduate program (26 males, 228 females);

267 in the evening school (29 males, 238 females), which requires 5 years to complete the B.A. degree

Faculty:

Some 30 persons are presently on its faculty, of whom more than half are on part-time basis. Almost two thirds of the faculty were professionally educated in the United States.

Curriculum:

Components of its curriculum include five categories:

1) general courses which are required by the Ministry of Education;

2) professional courses in library and information science which are required by the Ministry of Education;

3) courses which are required by the College of Liberal Arts;

4) required and elective professional courses offered by the Department;

5) a minor of no less than 20 credits in a subject other than library science or a concentration on information science courses offered by the Department.

A minimum of 148 credits is required for the B.A. degree.

Library and Information Science Courses Offered in the FJCU Program

Course Title	Credits	Required	Elective	Remarks
Introduction to Library Science	4	x		Only 2 credits req. by MOE
Introd. to Information Science	4	x		do.
Chinese Cat. and Class.	6	x		Required by MOE
Western Cat. and Class.	6	x		do.
Chinese Bibliography	4	x		do.
Non-Book Materials	2	x		do.
A-V Materials	4	x		do.
Chinese Reference Sources	6	x		Only 4 req. by MOE
Western Reference Sources	6	x		do.
Building Library Collections	6	x		do.
Library Automation	4	x		Req. by MOE
Library Administration	2	x		4 credits Req. by MOE
Library Field Work	3	x		zero credits Req. by MOE
Introd. to Computer Science	6	x		Only 4 req. by MOE
Information Services	4	x		Req. by Dept.
Data Processing	3		x	
Date Structure	3		x	
Databases	3		x	
Operations System	3		x	
Information Storage and Retrieval	4		x	
Abstracting and Indexing	4		x	
Literature of the Humanities	4		x	
Literature of Social Sciences	4		x	
Literature of Science and Technology	4		x	
Reference Work	2		x	
Management of Archives	2		x	

Introduction to Children's Literature	4	x
Children's Libraries	2	x
Public Libraries	2	x
Musical Librarianship	3	x
Medical Librarianship	3	x
College and University Libraries	2	x
Special Libraries	2	x
School Libraries	2	x
Serial Publications	2	x
Seminar in Special Topics	2	x

Departmental library: The program has a special collection of professional materials which include 7,000 volumes of books (4,500 in Chinese and 2,500 in foreign languages) and 50 periodicals (18 in Chinese and 32 in foreign languages).

A-V & other equipment: The Department maintains an A-V classroom containing various equipment for the teaching of A-V courses. In addition to the facilities at the University Computer Center that may be used for the practice of computer courses, the Department possesses 4 microcomputers and related equipment to support the teaching of information science courses.

Observations:

1) This is the only B.A. program of library science in the Republic of China that presently maintains an evening school which requires five years to receive the Bachelor's degree.

2) Although a minor is required of all B.A candidates, the requirement can be fulfilled by taking courses either in a subject area outside the Department, or in information science offered by the Department.

3) While it offers all of the 14 professional courses required by the

Ministry of Education, many of them are given particular emphasis by adding more credits. For example, Chinese and Western Reference Sources as well as Introduction to Computer Science have been increased from 4 to 6 credits.

4) The program offers a course in medical librarianship and a course in musical librarianship. The latter is at the moment the only such course offered in Taiwan.

5) Though more courses in information science will be added to meet the needs of students, the Department has no immediate plan to change its present name.

6) The Department intends to establish a graduate program leading to the M.A. degree in library science.

4. Tamkang University
College of Liberal Arts
Department of Educational Media & Library Sciences

Year established: 1971

Degree awarded: B.A.

Present enrollment: 477 students (100 males, 377 females).

Faculty: 33 faculty members, of which 23 are part-time. 14 of the 33 received their professional library education in the United States.

Curriculum: The curriculum comprises five categories:

1) 6 general courses of 28 credits required by the Ministry of Education.

2) 25 required and elective courses in library science of 77 credits, 9 of which are required by the MOE.

3) 6 A-V courses of 15 credits, 4 of which are either required by the Ministry of Education or by the Department.

4) 5 required courses of 18 credits in information science, 3 of which are required by the MOE, and 2 by the Department.

5) 4 supplementary courses of 14 credits, namely, Research Paper Writing (2 credits, required), Statistics for Educational Materials (4, elective), Social Education (4, elective), and Social Psychology (4, elective).

A minor of 20 credits in a field other than library science is encouraged but not required.

A minimum of 128 credits is required for the B.A. degree.

Library and Information Science & A-V Courses Offered in the Tamkang Program

Course Title	Credits	Required	Elective	Remarks
Chinese Reference Sources	4	x		Required by MOE
Chinese Cat. and Class.	6	x		do.
Western Reference Sources	4	x		do.
Western Cat. and Class.	6	x		do.
Building Library Collections	4	x		do.
Introd. to Library Science	2	x		do.
Bibliography	4	x		do.
Library Management	4	x		do.
Library Field Work	0	x		do. 2 hrs. per week for seniors
Government Publications	2	x		Req. by Dept.
School Libraries	2		x	Elect 3 of the 5
Public Libraries	2		x	Elect 3 of the 5
College & Univ. Libraries	2		x	Elect 3 of the 5
Special Libraries	2		x	Elect 3 of the 5
Medical Librarianship	2		x	Elect 3 of the 5
Literature of the Humanities	4		x	Elect 2 of the 3
Literature of Social Sciences	4		x	Elect 2 of the 3
Literature of Science and Technology	4		x	Elect 2 of the 3

Course	Credits		
Literature for Children and Young Adults	4		x
Management of Archives	2		x
History of Libraries	3		x
Comparative Librarianship	4		x
Introd. to Computer Science	4	x	Req. by MOE 4 credits
Library Automation	2	x	Req. by MOE only 2 req. by MOE
Introduction to Info. Science	4	x	
Computer Programming	4	x	Req. by Dept.
Information Center and Its Services	4	x	do.
Indexing and Abstracting	2	x	do.
Library System Analysis	4		x
Non-book Materials	2	x	Req. by MOE
A-V Materials	4	x	do.
A-V Education	2	x	Req. by Dept.
Photography	3	x	do.
Basic TV	2		x
TV Production	2		x
Motion Picture	2		x

Departmental library:
There is no departmental library for this program. Professional materials in library and information science and in the A-V area are housed in the University's Chueh Sheng Memorial Library. As of 1984, some 16,000 monographs and 88 periodicals relative to these subjects were reportedly recorded.

A-V & other equipment:
A-V and computer equipment of this program are relatively strong. In addition to the University Computer Center that can be used for teaching related courses, the Department has a well-equiped A-V Center for the teaching of

A-V courses and for the production of non-book materials.

Observations:

1) One of the special features of this program is that it offers more courses in the A-V area than any other library science program in Taiwan.
2) This is one of the two programs (the other being the program at the Fu Jen Catholic University) that currently offers a course in medical librarianship.
3) This is the only B.A. program in library science in the ROC that requires no minor in a subject other than library science.
4) Compared to similar programs in other universities, this program requires the least credits (128) for the B.A.degree.   128 is the minimum number of credits required by the Ministry of Education for any Bachelor's degree in the ROC.
5) While more courses in information science are being planned for the curriculum, the Department has no intention to change its present name.
6) The Department intends to inaugurate a graduate program leading to the M.A. degree in educational media and library sciences.

5. World College of Journalism
Department of Library Science

Year established: 1964

Degree awarded: Non-degree program at a junior college

Present enrollment: 420 students:

259 in day-time program (132 males, 127 females;
161 in evening school (24 males, 137 females).

Faculty: This program is primarily taught by part-time teachers.

Curriculum: A total of 120 credits is required for graduation from this program. Its curriculum comprises four categories of courses:

1) 6 general courses of 26 credits, such as Chinese, English, Chinese History, etc. which are required by the Ministry of Education.

2) 19 professional library courses of 54 credits which are required either by the MOE or by the College.

3) 13 field work courses of 28 credits which are required by the College.

4) 12 credits of elective courses to be chosen by students from among 15 courses offered by the College.

Following are professional library and information science courses offered at this program:

A. *Courses required either by the MOE or by the College*

Library and Mass Communication (2 credits)
Introduction to Library Science (4)
Library Administration (2)
History of Book Printing (2)
Introduction to Chinese Literature (4)
Chinese Bibliography (2)
Chinese Cataloging and Classification (4)
Western Cataloging and Classification (4)
Chinese Reference Sources (2 credits)
Western Reference Sources (2)
Building Library Collections (2)
Practical Computer Science (2)
Application of Microforms (1)
Management of Materials (4)
Management of Archives (4)

B. *Field work courses required by the College*

Field Work in Library Administration (2 credits)
Field Work in Chinese Cataloging and Classification (4)

Field Work in Western Cataloging and Classification (4)
Field Work in Chinese Reference Sources (1)
Field Work in Western Reference Sources (1)
Field Work in Management of Materials (4)
Field Work in Management of Archives (2)
Field Work in Book Selection and Acquisitions (2)
Field Work in Computer (2)
Field Work in Application of Microforms (1)

Observations:

1) This is the only library science program presently offered at a junior college in the Republic of China.

2) Most of the required courses in library and information science are similar to those offered in the four university programs, at least in name if not necessarily in content.

3) Field work is strongly emphasized and is required for all major professional library courses.

4) The Department offers no professional elective courses. All elective courses are general in nature and are provided by the College.

5) A great majority of courses are taught by part-time faculty who are either teaching in other library science programs or working as major administrators at university, college, or public libraries.

6) Facilities and equipment for teaching are generally poor. They need to be improved and strengthened, if the program is to operate properly.

III. SUMMARY

1. As of today, there are six library science programs in the Republic of China, including one M.A. program at the National Taiwan University, four Bachelor's programs located in NTU, NTNU, Fu Jen Catholic and Tamkang universities, and a 3-year non-degree program at the World College of Journalism which is a junior college.

2. Like library and information science programs in most other developing countries,[17] the Bachelor's degree in library science is at present the professional library degree recognized in the ROC not only by the Government but by the library profession as well.

3. Each of the four Bachelor's programs carries a set of core courses in library and information science required by the Ministry of Education. They are: Introduction to Library Science, Introduction to Information Science, Chinese Cataloging and Classification, Western Cataloging and Classification, Chinese Reference Sources, Western Reference Sources, Building Library Collections, Bibliography, Introduction to Computer Science, Non-Book Materials, A-V Materials, Library Management, Library Automation, and Library Field Work. As far as contents of these courses are concerned, most of them are rather traditional, particularly in terms of technical services and reference services.

4. Some 20 courses in information science are currently offered in these programs, three of which, namely, Introduction to Information Science, Introduction to Computer Science, and Library Automation, are required by the Ministry of Education. These courses are summarized as follows:

Course Title	NTU	NTNU	Catholic	Tamkang
Application of Computers in Libraries	x			
Appl. of Microcomputers in Libraries	x			
Computer Programming	x			x
Data Structure	x		x	
Indexing and Abstracting	x		x	x
Infor. Center & Its Service				x
Information Management	x			
Information Policy	x			

Information Storage and Retrieval	x		x	
Information Systems	x			
Introduction to Computer Science	x	x	x	x
Introduction to Data Processing	x	x	x	
Introduction to Databases	x		x	
Introduction to Information Science	x	x	x	x
Library Automation	x	x	x	x
Management of Computer Centers	x			
Online Information Searching	x			
Operations Research	x			x
System Analysis	x		x	x
Thesaurus Construction	x			

Presently, National Taiwan University has the largest number of courses in information science (19); about half of them are offered for both graduate and undergraduate students.

5. Only a few courses in special librarianship are currently available. NTU has a course for special readers, Fu Jen Catholic University offers a course in music librarianship, and medical librarianship is being taught at both Tamkang and FJCU.

6. In terms of special features, Tamkang is strong in A-V program, NTNU emphasizes school librarianship, NTU has a wide variety of course offerings, and FJCU provides a minor in information science.

7. With regard to student enrollment, Fu Jen Catholic University has the largest number (521), followed by Tamkang (477), NTU (267, 235 undergraduate students and 32 graduate students), and NTNU (48). Similar to the situation in other countries throughout the world, library science students in Taiwan are also predominantly female.

8. Due to the fact that over 60% of the teaching faculty at these programs received their professional library education in the United States, it is no surprise to find that many aspects of these programs, such as curriculum structure, course contents, teaching methods, etc., are patterned after American library schools.

9. While Tamkang and FJCU intend to establish Master's programs in librarianship, the National Taiwan University is planning to inaugurate a Ph.D. program at its Graduate Institute of Library Science.

10. Although the library science program at the World College of Journalism is a non-degree program, its students are regarded as library

professionals. To operate properly and to maintain professional standards, the entire program needs to be improved and strengthened.

NOTES

1. Kwang-ching Liu, *Americans and Chinese: A Historical Essay and a Bibliography* (Cambridge, Mass.: Harvard University Press, 1963), pp. 16-18.

2. John K. Fairbank, *Chinese-American Interactions: A Historical Summary* (New Brunswick, N.J.: Rutgers University Press, 1975) , p.50.

3. A brief biography of Miss Wood can be found in, among others, Wen-yu Yen, "Miss Mary Elizabeth Wood and the Boxer Indemnity Fund," in *A Collection of Library Science Essays by Professor Wen-yu Yen* (Taipei: Fu Jen Catholic University Department of Library Science, 1983), pp. 247-252.

4. For a brief description of Professor Seng's life, see Wen-yu Yen, "Professor Samuel T.Y.Seng: the Father of Library Education in China," in *ibid.*, pp.253-258.

5. *Ibid.*

6. This course was listed in the 1954 class schedule of the NTU's Department of Foreign Languages and Literature.

7. A history of library education in the Republic of China during the period 1954-1983 can be found in Cheng-ku Wang, "Thirty Years of Library Education in Taiwan," *Bulletin of the Library Association of China* 35 (December 18,1983): 9-19.

8. The Graduate Institute of History at the Chinese Culture University offers such courses as Comparative Librarianship, Management of Documents and Archives, and Bibliography. The newly established Graduate Institute of Social Education at the National Taiwan Normal University offers three elective courses in library and information science, namely, Seminar in Library Science, Seminar in Library Automation, and Comparative Study of Library Science.

9. Information concerning library science programs in the PRC was provided to me by a well-informed source when I was attending the 51st Annual Conference of the International Federation of Library Associations and Institutions (IFLA) in Chicago, August 18−24, 1985.

10. Fan Chu Shu, "Information Science Education in China," *Journal of Education for Library and Information Science* 25 (Winter 1985): 226-227.

11. *Ibid.*, p. 227.

12. A questionnaire including five areas, namely, curriculum, facilities, faculty, students, and future plans, was sent to each of the five library science programs in July 1985.   All of them responded and returned by the end of August.

13. For the rationale and discussion of the NTU's undergraduate library science curriculum, see James S.C.Hu, "Major Considerations in the 1983 Curriculum Revision for the Department of Library Science at the National Taiwan University," *Shu-fu* (Bulletin of Librarianship) 5 (June 11, 1984): 32-39.

14. The reasoning as to why these professional library courses are required by the Ministry of Education can be found in Chien-chang Lan, "An Evaluation on the Newly Revised Required Courses in the Library Science Curriculum," *Bulletin of the Library Association of China* 35 (December 18, 1983): 67-73.

15. For details of the admission requirements, see James S.C. Hu, "Admission and Graduation Requirements of the First Graduate School of Library Science in Republican China," *Shu-fu* (Bulletin of Librarianship) 6 (August 31, 1985): 2-12.

16. *Ibid.*

17. Tefko Saracevic, et al., "Issues in Information Science Education in Developing Countries," *Journal of the American Society for Information Science* 37 (May 1985): 195.

Problems Confronting Library Science Education
in the Republic of China

Harris B.H. Seng
Professor
Department and Graduate Institute of Library Science
National Taiwan University
Taipei, Taiwan, R.O.C.

On the surface, education for librarianship in this country can be neatly divided into two phases: What we did during our Mainland days and what we have been doing on the soil of Free China.

This kind of division is neither natural nor logical, however, for these two phases are inseparable. Each is an integral part of the whole. The common belief is that the Chinese people tend to look back and that historical method is the approach constantly employed by Chinese research workers. Even though there are some merits in such a statement, I can assure my colleagues here that is not the case in my writing this paper. I go back to the past only to explain why we are where we stand today.

One of the chief characteristics of the modern Chinese library movement is its orientation to the West. It all started when Miss Mary Elizabeth Wood (1861-1931) of the United States of America went to China in 1904 and discovered that there was not a single modern library in China at the time. She returned to America and received her library education at Simmons College. She came to China again and started the first library school (The Boone Library School) and the first modern public library (The Boone Library) in China. Until the end of World War II, Boone monopolized the supply of library personnel. It also monopolized library research work. In addition to the publication of the *Boone Library School Quarterly*, Boone must have published more than 30 titles in the field.

As I examine some of the publications today, I cannot help but feel that they are like American meals prepared by Chinese chefs. The following two examples are used to explain my point; perhaps one of the most important books in the Boone Library School Library Series was *A List of Subject Headings* compiled in 1937 by Professor Samuel T.Y. Seng.   The list was based upon the third edition of the *Library of Congress Subject Headings*.   Its size is about three times that of the *Sear's List*.   On classification schemes, the influence of Melvil Dewey was even more apparent.   Again Professor Seng led the field by compiling the first modified *Dewey Decimal Classification*.   During the time between Seng's scheme and 1944, there were several schemes published by Boone Alumni.   Each one was a satellite of Dewey.[1]

It is not my intention to undermine the great contribution that was made by the Boone Library School in the advancement of librarianship in China. I merely report a library science education situation of my country at a particular period of time.   I am a Boone alumnus and the late Professor Samuel T.Y. Seng was my beloved father.

What were the problems of education for librarianship at that particular period of time as the Chinese librarians saw it themselves?   Some of the problems were stated by Professor Samuel T.Y. Seng, the then Director of the Boone Library School.   In this paper, *Library Education in China*,[2] he mentioned the following points:

"First, whatever training the library school may offer, it must fit its graduates for library service in college libraries as well as in public libraries. Because most of the public libraries have collections of Chinese Books only, but the college and university libraries have foreign books... not only English and Japanese, but also German, French and... other languages.   Library school graduates must be prepared to catalog and classify all these languages and at the same time must be well grounded in Chinese culture.   It is difficult for the library school to carry the burden of so much language training. English is the only language taught in most schools and colleges in China.

The second difficulty is that library schools in China have to give two courses for many of the subjects; one in Chinese and one in English.   No Western professor can teach book selection, book reviews, reference work or bibliography for Chinese books.   Neither can a Chinese scholar teach adequately these courses for Western books.   Hence, two courses must be offered in each of these subjects.   Chinese students must be thoroughly versed in Chineses subjects, yet they must be prepared to work in libraries where there are bi-lingual or multi-lingual collections and catalogs.

Third, the students must be taught of the subject peculiar to China. At one time, the students must study stone and bronze inscriptions in addition to manuscripts and rare books.   This means a combination of museum and library work.   Thus it is not only difficult to find suitable professors to teach all these subjects, but also difficult for the students to find time to study them all."

Professor Samuel T.Y. Seng's observations were made fifty years ago. Are we better off today?

The present situation of library science education is stated clearly and precisely by Dr. James Hu.   There is no need for repetition.   This paper, in fact is an appendix to Dr. Hu's brilliant presentation.   My assignment is an easier one.   I merely raise questions.   I count on your expertise to provide us with answers.

In Professor Whitbeck's paper— *Comparative Study of Education for Librarianship and Information Science*, he mentioned five Library Science Departments, namely:[3]

        National Taiwan University

        National Taiwan Normal University

        Fujen Catholic University

        Tamkang University

        World College of Journalism

The list is correct.   However, it didn't state that N.T.U. and Chinese Culture University also provide graduate program.   And a new graduate program at N.T.N.U. will pretty soon be established.

He further mentioned a comment from Chinese librarians that weaker schools were producing the largest number of graduates.[4]

Consider the size of Taiwan (0.3% of Mainland China and about 0.4% of U.S.) and population (7.6% of U.S. and 1.8% of Mainland China); and yet we have so many library schools.   Allow me to borrow Prof.   Herbert White's question: "Is there a surplus?   Was there a shortage?"[5]   Should we have less schools so that we could pull our resource together or in Dr. White's words: "The best way to insure quality in library education, as in anything else, is to encourage healthy competition between existing programs."[6]   This is precisely our intention.   But how successful are we?

The relationship between quality and quantity is intertwined.   Some scholars are very much concerned with the quality of library science education.   According to Professor Laracevic,"... a good number (if not even the majority) of library schools are of no quality whatsoever as graduate professional schools."   "Only a few schools have a full quality program."   He estimates not more than ten.[7]

What is wrong?   What is the library school for?   Again I quote Pauline Wilson.   In a paper entitled *Taking the Library Out of Library Education*, she writes "Library school is where the formal process of becoming a librarian begins, and where signs of fundamental change in the profession can be expected to occur first."[8]   Does that mean library science education is a life long process?   Library schools are only the starting point of education for librarianship?   Professor Herbert White, the winner of ASIS award of merit, suggested that we are preparing students for work next year, but also forty years from now.   He writes "Plan and implement a curriculum that stresses the overriding values of the profession at large, as best we can see them developing and changing."[9].

In other words, stress education, even at the expense of training.   Training is best given on the job, anyway.   I think to separate education and training is an excellent idea.   Professor White's idea of long range plans of education for librarianship has now support from many scholars.   Professor Martha Boaz feels that plans for libraries and library/information science education should include both immediate (and perhaps radical) innovations as well as continuous and long range plans.[10]   Professor K.J. McGarry of Polytechnic of North London endorses the idea from a different perspective. He says that the curriculum planner has to base the curricula on issues and problems that will still be important at the end of the century.[11]

What should the curriculum be?   Even though that the students who now enter schools of librarianship can be expected to remain active in the profession for the next 30-35 years, Professor K. Subramanyam thinks that library and information science faculty cannot clearly forsee all the changes and prepare the students to meet changes with confidence.[12]   Perhaps so.   But to try to forsee is the least we should do.

To prepare future professionals, Dr. Hwa-wei Lee suggests the following competencies:[13]

1. The foundations of librarianship (including information science).
2. Subject specialization and language facility.
3. Human relations and communication.
4. Information technology and application.
5. Management theory and practice.
6. Business knowledge and marketing.
7. Fund raising and grantsmanship.

He further states the challenges that lie ahead are the following:

1. The challenge of information explosion and pollution.
2. The challenge of new information technology.
3. The challenge of the changing roles of libraries (and information centers).
4. The challenge of new professional competencies required.
5. The challenge of global interdependence.

Then, what should be included in our curriculum?   In this paper *Implications for Library and Information Science Education*, Professor Lancaster makes the statement: "It seems likely that the information professionals of the future must be specialized in terms of the subject matter they deal with."[14] This I whole-heartily agree with. He also says "The fact is that computer and telecommunication technologies are making it increasingly feasible for librarians to perform their professional tasks outside of the library." This I also agree with. He further says that "What goes on in a library is still the principal focus of our collective curricula." and "the librarians have traditionally been more dependent on the library than physicians have been on the hospital, pharmacy on other facility." "This overdependence on a physical facility has had undesirable consequences." Professor Lancaster is a great scholar. And I really respect him for his tremendous scholarship. He seems to move ahead from "paperless" to "libraryless." This is a pretty heavy dose of prescribed medicine for a library patient like me to take. We Chinese invented paper. The "paperless" idea makes us feel sad. Professor McGarry, on the other hand, suggests the "professional curricula have traditionally been centered on the document—more specifically on the book.[15] He divides the traditional core studies into three parts: indexing, management and bibliographical studies. The views are echoed by Professor Subramanyam.[16] He says: "It will be a mistake to neglect entirely such 'traditional' courses as classification and cataloguing; after all, organization of materials and information is the backbone of all library service, and the advent of the machine has hardly had any effect on the basic principles of organization. Professor Boaz also suggests that education of the future "be less concerned with the development of specific work skills which may become obsolete and more concerned with learning how to acquire and organize knowledge which enable people to learn, unlearn, and relearn."[17] And "It is important that the library profession plan to manage the future, not be managed or overwhelmed by it."

What should the product of professional library school look like? In Professor Pauline Wilson's words "A librarian is a specialist— a library expert, one who knows how to create, operate and maintain libraries. A librarian understands that institution called a library, know its place in society, and knows how to make it perform to meet society's expectations."[18] Librarians are expected to be knowledgeable not only regarding librarianship but also the literature of various academic disciplines.[19]

By definition, a librarian is a person in charge of a library or part of a library, or a person trained to work in a library, according the *World Book Dictionary*. The *World Book Dictionary* is my favorite reference tool. Still I dislike the definition. I think a librarian is a custodian of culture. Mr. Sweeney[20] writes that there have been three technology revolutions of such moment that they have changed libraries forever.

>   1. the invention of writing
>   2. the invention of printing
>   3. the development of remote electronic access and delivery of information.

That means a librarian has to deal with human cultural development of the past, present and the future.   This is a pretty big order for librarians.

My humble suggestion is that the prospective librarian should be equipped with:

>   1. A solid subject background.
>   2. A thorough knowledge of library science.
>   3. A workable knowledge of information science.
>   4. A fundamental knowledge of psychology.
>   5. An understanding of environment and ergonomics.

Item 1, 2 and 3 speak for themselves.   Since basic human information needs will remain practically unchanged and so will human motivation; future curricula will have to include the study of human information processing and human creativity.   Item 4 is inspired by the idea of Professor McGarry.[21] The environment of library education is advocated by Professor Lundu.[22] He is of the opinion that library education ought to fulfil special needs at each particular point in time.   According to him, the two environments of library education are:

>   1. The needs of the country of region as a whole.
>   2. The library and information infrastructure of the country or region.

It is not our intention to design a permanent new curriculum.   And our curriculum is not a temporary one either.   It lies somewhere in between. We have plans for evaluating and renovating our curriculum periodically, about every five years.   In a year or two the Ministry of Education of this country will appoint a team to evaluate our library schools.   As hosts of this conference, we would appreciate it very much if our colleagues, particularly our distinguished guests from abroad could contribute their expertise to help us in solving problems confronting library science education in this country.

FOOTNOTES:

1. Harris B.H. Seng, "Research in Librarianship in the Republic of China," *Research in Librarianship* 3(17): 133-6.
2. Chinese Library Association, *Libraries in China*, Peiping, the Association, 1935, pp.   59-65.

3. George W. Whitbeck, "Comparative Study of Education for Librarianship and Information Science in the Republic of China and North America," *Journal of Library and Information Science* 10 (April 1984): 42.

4. Ibid., p. 55.

5. Herbert White, "Library Education: a Strategy for the Future," *Wilson Library bulletin* (October 1981): 105.

6. Ibid., p. 108.

7. Pauline Wilson, "Impending Change in Library Education: Implications for Planning," *Journal of Education for Librarianship* 18 (Spring 1983):161.

8. Bill Katz, and Kathleen Welbel, *Library Lit. 12 - the Best of 1981* (London: the Scarecrow Press, 1982), p. 69.

9. White, op. cit., p. 108.

10. Martha, Boaz, "Readers Comment," *Journal of Education for Librarianship* 24 (Winter 1984): 215.

11. K.J. McGarry, "The Influence of Technology on Professional Curricula," *ASLIB Proceedings* 35 (Feb.   1983): 102.

12. K. Subramanyam, "Current Concerns in American Library Education," *International Library Review* (1983): 303.

13. Hwa-wei Lee, "Challenge for the Library and Information Profession," *Bulletin of the Library Association of China* No. 35 (December 18, 1983): 259.

14. F.W. Lancaster, "Implication for Library and Information Science Education," *Library Trend* (Winter 1984): 343.

15. McGarry, op. cit. p. 103.

16. Subramanyam, op. cit. p. 300.

17. Martha Boaz, "The Future of Library and Information Science Education," *Journal of Education for Librarianship*(Spring 1978) : 319.

18. Wilson, op. cit. p. 71.

19. Maurice P. Marchant, and Carolyn F. Wilson, "Developing Joint Graduate Programs for Librarians," *Library Trend* (Summer 1983) : 30.

20. Richard Sweeney, "The Role of the Library in the Information Age: Will it Be Human?" *Journal of Educational Media and Library Sciences* 21(3) (Spring 1984): 240-41.

21. McGarry, op, cit., p. 104.

22. M.C. Lundu, "Library Education and Training; at Home or Abroad? a Personal Assessment and Impressions," *International Library Reviews* (1982): 365-67.

BIBLIOGRAPHY

Boaz, Martha.   "The Future of Library and Information Science Education." *Journal of Education for Librarianship* (Spring 1978): 315-23.

Colson, John Calvin.   "Professional Ideals and Social Realities: Some Questions About the Education of Librarians."   *Journal of Education for Librarianship* (Fall 1980).

Lancaster, F.W.   "Implication for Library and Information Science Education."   *Library Trend* (Winter 1984)

Lee, Hwa-wei.   "Challenges for Library and Information Profession."   *Bulletin of the Library Association of China* 35 (1983): 99-106.

Marchant, Maurice P. and Wilson, Carolyn F.   "Developing Joint Graduate Programs for Librarians."   *Journal of Education for Librarianship* 24: 1 (Summer 1983): 30-37.

McGarry, K.J.   "The Influence of Technology on Professional Curricula."   *ASLIB Proceedings* 35:2 (Feb. 1983): 99-106.

McGarry, Kevin.   *"Progress in Documentation."*   vol.39 no.2.

Morehead, Joe.   *Theory and Practice in Library Education.* Colo.: Libraries Unlimited, 1980.

Seng, Harris B.H.   "Research in Librarianship in the Republic of China." *Research in Librarianship* vol.3 no.17.

Whitbeck, George W.   "Comparative Study of Education for Librarianship and Information Science in the Republic of China and North America: a Survey" *Journal of Library and Information Science* 10 (April 1984): 40-62.

White, Herbert.   "Accreditation and the Pursuit of Excellence." *Journal of Education for Librarianship* 23 (Spring 1983).

White, Herbert.   "Library Education: a Strategy for the Future."   *Wilson Library Bulletin* (Oct. 1981): 105-9.

Wilson, Pauline.   "Impending Change in Library Education: Implications for Planning."   *Journal of Education for Librarianship* 18 (Spring 1983): 159-74.

APPENDIX

HISTORY AND BACKGROUND OF BOONE LIBRARY SCHOOL

The Boone Library School was founded by Mary Elizabeth Wood (1862-1931), in Wuchang, China.   Possessed by the desire to see popular libraries in China, she devoted her life to the realization of her dream.

She raised enough money in the United States, when she was there on leave of absence, to build the Boone Library, which was opened in 1910. Later, in 1917, she was able to secure sufficient funds to send two university graduates to the United States for library training.   The present director, Professor Samuel T. Y. Seng, was one of them.

Consistent with her progressive idea was the realization that modern libraries required trained administrators; so she founded the Boone Library School to provide this professional training and to satisfy a very definite demand by educators, librarians, and prospective students desiring this special education.

In the beginning the school was a department of Boone University, now Central China University, and its courses were of three years duration beyond the second year of college.[1]   In 1926 it terminated its university connection with Boone University and registered with the Ministry of Education as an independent professional library school having a college status.

As a Christian Institution, it is under the authority of the Bishop of the Hankow Diocese of the Church of China, affiliated with the Protestant Episcopal Church in the U.S.A

Boone, as the first and only full-fledged library school in China, has played a leading role in the Chinese library field, especially during the years when Boone Library served as the center of such activities.   A nationwide campaign for arousing interest in libraries by means of lecture tours, personal visits, and correspondence, was carreied on from the Boone Library School. Miss Wood was instrumental in the return of the remaining portion of the American Indemnity Fund to China, and in the securing of Arthur E. Bostwick, as delegate from the American Library Association, to survey the library field in China.   As a result of these efforts there came into being the China Foundation For the Promotion of Education and Culture, the National Library of Peiping, and the Chinese Library Association.   The contribution of the Boone Library School to the Chinese library field has been mainly the train-

---

[1] Ruth A. Hill, "The Training of Librarians in China," *Library Journal*, Feb. 1, 1937, p. 109.

ing if librarians and the publishing of library literature.   Since its inception in 1920, the training activities of the school have made continuous progress, despite changing political and economic conditions of the country.   Its graduates have filled not a few of the responsible positions and practically all the technical posts in the Chinese library field.[2]

During the Sino-Japanese war (1937-1945), the school with its staff and students was moved, according to the Chinese government instructions, to Chungking campus was completely destroyed by incendiary bombs from enemy planes.   The school then bought a new site in Kiangpei, directly across the Kialing River from Chungking, where six more buildings were erected. The school went through this crisis and emerged even more vigorous than ever before, because K. C. Wu, the Governor of Formosa, its Board Chairman, secured from the Nationalist Government a substantial amount of the fund for the purchase of the new site and the erection of these new buildings, while the students then under training (and the alumni) raised enough money for the school to build an assembly hall and the library.   It was also at this most difficult time that the Rockefeller Foundation, through the Regional Director of the Far East Office, made a generous grant annually over a six-year period, and two years later the United China Relief, now United Service to China, included the school as one of its beneficiaries.   This made it possible for the school to carry on its work without interruption.[3]

As soon as the war was over, the school was ordered to move back to its old site in Wuchang, Hupeh province.   At present the school has two divisions: Namely, Library Service and Archival Service.   Both offer a two-year general course in their respective fields, with the purpose of training such librarians and archivists or custodians of government files as are needed in China.   The Archival was first opened in 1940, with the sanction of the Ministry of Education, in response to the demand for workers in records, in the government bureaus and commercial concerns.

The school is open to young men and women on equal terms.   In 1914, the requirement for admission was lowered to high school graduates, at the request of the government.

The student is required to take all the courses prescribed and choose certain electives in his two-year study at the school, making a total of eighty-eight credits.   A term course is equivalent to two credits and a year course

---

[2] Samuel T.Y. Seng, "Library Schools and Librarians in China," *Library Journal*, Nov. 1944, p.933.

[3] Boone Library School Catalog,1949,pp. 3-6.

four credits.   One credit means one recitation period each week throughout the term, that is eighteen weeks each semester.

The students carry twenty-five or twenty-six hours a week, under the the direction of six full-time professors and eight part-time instructors.

Description of courses.   According to the Announcement of the Boone Library School, 1949, the courses offered are designed to train China's future librarians and archivists, giving a survey of the ideals, functions, and efficient o-peration of modern public and college libraries, and the care, preservation, and use of the records in the archival offices.

1. Courses of instruction for the Division of Library Service.

LS 101 Library Economy   4 credits

A general review of the field of librarianship and a study of the library processes, mehtods, and records.   Subjects like cataloging and classification taken up in special courses receive slight mention.

LS 102 Library Administration   4 credits

A continuation of LS 101.   A consideration of the principles of library organization and adminmistration, and an inquiry into the pro-blems of personnel, government control, finance, centralization and departmentalization and extension in library service.

LS 103 Book Selection and Acquisition   4 credits

A detailed discussion of the principles of book selection and of methods and records used in ordering books, and a system of book-keeping for order work.

LS 104 Classification   4 credits

Principles and practice of classification of books, history of Chi-nese classification systems and the organization of knowledge in Chi-nese studies; the Dewey Decimal classification is taken as a basis of study, and the ability to use it thoroughly in classifying Chinese and foreign books is required of every student.

LS 105 Comparative Classification   4 credits

A comparative study of the principles of Western classification systems, such as the Dewey and the Library of Congress classification schedules, and their uses in classification work in Chinese libraries.

LS 106 Chinese cataloging   4 credits

A study of cataloging of Chinese Books.   Topics for discussion include Chinese pseudonyms and spurious books.

LS 107 English cataloging   8 credits

A general course in the cataloging of Western books, based on A. L. A cataloging rules.   Specific topics included for class recitation are: The making of the unit card, the ordering and use of the Library of Congress cards, book numbers, subject headings, and filing. Each student is required to make a model catalog on cards, and either a union catalog or a list of periodicals as they are found in modern public library.

LS 108 Chinese bibliography   4 credits

History of Chinese books and book collecting in China, public and private types of Chinese bibliographies, history of Chinese printing, chinese bibliographical method, including textual criticism.

LS 109 Western bibliography   4 credits

An introduction to Western bibliography, practical and historical, emphasis being placed on such topics as will prove suggestive for similar studies in the field of Chinese bibliography.

LS 110 Chinese and English reference books   8 credits

A study of important Chinese and English reference books, both general and special, with practice in their use. Students are required to make a special study of some of the introductions and prefaces of such works, so as to give some knowledge of the subjects and of the handling of reference questions.

LS 111 Elements of Archive Ecomony   4 credits

A brief course in the care of records in government archive offices, or bureaus, designed to train library students in the fundamentals of archive work.

LS 112 Practice in Library Work   4 credits

A systematic study of library organization and routines. Topics included are: planning and organization, rules and regulations, schedule making, records, statistics, building and equipment, shelving and inventory taking, and charging systems.

Courses listed above are required. Total credits, fifty-six.

2. Courses of instruction for the Division of Archival Service.

AS 101 Archive Economy   4 credits

A general discussion of the principles and techniques involved in the work of custodians of public records in current use, archival service in relation to efficiency in government administration being emphasized as the essential approach to the subject.

AS 102 Archive administration   4 credits

A continuation of AS 101. A discussion of the principal European and American archives; the laws concerning archives, the administration of personnel in an archive division, and the making of surveys.

AS 103 Materials and methods in Chinese archives   4 credits

A course attempting to make a survey of the literature bearing on this subject, with the ultimate aim of working out an outline for a Chinese system of archive science along the lines of its counterpart in the West. This is done because heretofore the subject of historical records has been a special field of study in China, and since such Chinese documents as are extant are only of comparatively recent date.

AS 104 Cataloging and classification of records   4 credits

A critical analysis of the prevailing methods employed by governmental archive bureaus or record offices, in the listing and arranging of current records, and a study of ways and means of improving them.

AS 105 Filing system   4 credits

A study of various filing systems, and the tools and techniques of Western vertical filing systems and their adaptation for Chinese archive bureaus and documentation offices.

AS 106 Care of personnel records   2 credits

A discussion of the principles of personnel administration and the keeping and managing of such records.

AS 107 Western archives   4 credits

An introduction to the history and methods of the Western organization and management of archives, and a discussion of how the official documents have come to the present form, thus giving the students a foundation for further study.

AS 108 Care of minor reference material and newspaper clippings   2 credits

Training in the care of pamphlets and newspaper clippings.

AS 109 Elements of historical methods   2 credits

A discussion of the nature and use of source materials and the place of historical record.

AS 110 Organization and administration of the Chinese government   2 credits

The organization and administration of the present government system, considered in relation to its administrative history and relationship with archival service.

AS 111 Elements of library economy   4 credits

A brief course in library work for students of archival service, so that they will have some fundamentals in running a library.

AS 112 Fundamentals of library classification   4 credits

A discussion of the principles and technique of library classification and their application in archival classification, the vital difference between the two being stressed.

AS 113 Practice in archival work   4 credits

A systematic assigning of topics to students for practice in the care of records.   Processes involved include accessioning, abstracting classifying, cataloging, binding, filing storing, circulating, weeding.

Courses listed above are all required for a student's major in Archival Service.   Total credits, forty-eight.

3. Curricula for both Divisions of Library Service and Archival Service.

LA 101 typewriting   2 credits

ving them.

AS 105 Filing system   4 credits

Instruction in the use of the English typewriter by the touch system.   A reasonable rate of proficiency in this skill is expected of every student.   Instruction in the use of the Chinese typewriter is also offered.

LA 102 Chinese filing and indexing   4 credits

Discussion of and practice in the leading systems of Chinese filing.   Principles of indexing are studied.   Students are asked to compile and index to periodicals.

LA 103 Elements of museum economy   4 credits

A general course in museum work, materials and equipment for modeling, taxidermy, arranging of exhibits.

LA 104 Document writing   2 credits

A course designed to give archival students the necessary knowledge and analysis of the forms of Chinese document writing of today.

Total credits, twelve.   For both division.

4. Linguistic courses.

LA 201 Chinese   4 credits

Reading in Chinese classics and practice in the literary style of Chinese composition.   Papers on suggested topics handed in monthly.

LA 202 English   8 credits

A course in two parts, first to make up deficiency in English and, second, to enable students to acquire a greater mastery of the language.

LA 203 French   8 credits

An elementary course in French, to enable students to read titles and to determine the scope of books in the French language.

LA 204 German   8 credits
    An elementary course in German, similar to LA 203 but in the German language.
LA 205 Japanese   8 credits
    An elementary course in Japanese, similar to LA 203 but in the Japanese language.
LA 206 Russian   8 credits
    An elementary course in Russian, similar to LA 203 but in Russian language.
La 201, 202 are required for all students.   Students may elect one from LA 203 to LA 206.   Total credits, twenty.

    Reprinted in part from Harris B.H. Seng.   "A Suggested Curriculum for Boone Library School".   Ed.D. Dissertation, University of Denver, 1953.

Library and Information Education Today: From the British Point of View

Peter Havard-Williams
Professor and Head
Department of Library and Information Studies
Loughborough University
Loughborough, Leicestershire, England

Libraries in Britain are not the outcome of an overall governmental policy, but have arisen from specific needs for books, serials and other documents and for information at different times and in different clienteles. Moreover, they have arisen over a long period – manuscripts from the sixth century, college libraries from the fifteenth century, university libraries from the seventeenth century, national libraries and subscription libraries from the eighteenth century, special and public libraries mainly from the nineteenth century, each overlaying the already existing provision.

Information has of course existed since the beginning of communication-information as a concept – organised information – has arisen with the development of complex industrialised societies, and particularly with that of the last hundred years of scientific and technological innovation. This latter development, begun in the seventeenth century, has seen an acceleration with the development of science and technology and this has been accentuated with the technologies of war (hot and cold) in the twentieth century.

The invention of the computer has made possible the manipulation of data in ways inconceivable forty years ago. The application of computer methods, too, has broadened so as to make computerised information both feasible and easily accessible. This has revolutionized information handling and processing. Perhaps even more important is the extensive development of satellite communication and telecommunication generally. These facilities allow for an international, regional and national interchange of information on a scale unperceived by many scientific workers in the world. Another important element in the change of 'climate' in the information world is photocopying. The bane of publishers, photocopying has made possible the dissemination of information on a relatively cheap, easy and widely diffused scale impossible before World War II.   Though microfilming has not proved to be the panacea forecast by Fremont Rider in 1940 it also has had a considerable influence on the diffusion of information, and must not be underestimated.   Lastly, within the last ten years or so, we have seen the 'convergence' of technologies in which there can be computer input to the television screen, where audio-visual methods relatively unsophisticated in themselves can be transferred too to the television screen, where computer graphics can be developed, where optical discs can produce text and graphics, and so on.

It is not only the processes, and the information produced by them that matter.   It is the climate of opinion that is produced by them that is affecting the information world.   The way has already been prepared by the progress of radio and television and the resulting fact that the majority of the population accepts as a part of everyday life that it receives not only entertainment through the medium but also world and local news, and a good deal of explicit or implicit educational material – in terms of world politics, history, technical and scientific information (including information on agricultural, medical and health and welfare and industrial and commercial information).   All this alters attitudes to the book and printed materials in general, and places them in the category of being one means among others of obtaining information.

Printed matter itself has also contributed to the change.   The past forty years has seen a vast change both in the technology and in the cost of printing.   The period has seen a change, too, in where the printing is done. Economic considerations have played a major part in new developments both in publishing and printing, where new adjustments have had to be made to keep these activities within the scope of profitable business.   There are those who consider that the publishing and printing of much scholarly, scientific and technological information will become so expensive and uneconomic by the turn of the century that much of the secondary material (abstracts and indexes) now available on-line and in hard-copy (book form) will be available only on-line.   This is because the major market for this material is in industrialised countries, and it will be the major market that will dictate publishing policies.

Consider, for instance, the following example of information technology applied to the realm of books.   Since a library can be reproduced on an optical disk and a book on a card the size of a credit card, it is not difficult to imagine taking such a card to bed with you providing you have a reader the size of the currently available Sinclair television set.   If an optical disk or disks can reproduce the content of a reference library, and there is telex or facsimile communication readily available, the information officer and reference librarian can work at home, and communicate with his or her clients without coming near an institutional building.   An ever more pressing issue is the possibility that clients could by-pass the traditional information stores — and in particular libraries — altogether: changes in the role of librarians and information scientists must be anticipated in the evolution of curriculum development.   The technology for these developments is already there, what is needed is the necessary commercial breakthrough, and the marketing to persuade people to use the new methods.

This may seem a far cry from library education, but in fact this kind of background is influencing current thought on curriculum development.   To understand current trends in Britlsh library and information science education, it is important to appreciate the changes in attitudes to libraries and information work which are taking place rapidly in the United Kingdom.   It is, in fact, difficult to present a view precisely because change is so rapid.   There are other influences.   The whole attitude to purveying information is affected by TV with sophisticated methods of production and presentation.   Education in the United Kingdom is being affected: children expect the same kind of expertise shown in the classroom as they see on the television screen, or they become bored, according to a recent interview with a secondary school teacher. This also must affect their attitude to the effort of understanding the printed page, and the whole *ambiance* of information/library services, and educational method.

The world-wide recession is resulting in a constant search for economies. This affects commerce, industry, government and the community at large. Since libraries in particular have traditionally been a government concern, and government economies are affecting libraries both nationally and locally. These economies also affect international provision, since financial retrenchment cuts services which in turn limits scope for international action to the detriment of international cooperation.   The British Library Lending Division is no longer searching for 'not in stock' material on the scale it has done in the past, according to a librarian in a country not too far away.

While, overall, public libraries have managed to retain a small increase in their budgets they have also sought to widen their readership by producing better services to a greater proportion of their potential readership and so, in real terms, their moneys are less than they were.   While a reading public of 25% using public libraries was considered a remarkably high figure twenty years ago, a figure of 50% is now regarded as a maximum figure in Britain.   Hence, libraries have services ranging from special collections for a limited clientele (the Shakespeare collection at Birmingham, the Henry Watson Music Library at Manchester, the Roscoe Collection at Liverpool) to services for the aged, ethnic minorities (Leicester, Derby, the London boroughs for instance) prison services (Nottingham and others) also serving specific sectors of the population but with a different philosophy of provision, *viz.* to serve not the few but the many.   All this has affected general book provision, has tended to reduce stocks and made public libraries turn to low-cost books, and not least to move to paperbacks.   From the library educator's point of view, it has limited recruitment, too, for economies have had to be made in personnel as well as materials. In university libraries, cuts in personnel have been even more severe and few posts are advertised each year (for which there may be too many candidates), though there is a dearth of candidates for posts at the top (e.g. directors of university libraries).   In college libraries, there are also few openings, though in schools more posts are becoming available, because of an awareness of the need especially in large schools to develop school library resource centres with appropriate professional staff.   Openings are also increasing in the private sector, with advertisements for librarians/information officers in industrial libraries, professional offices (architects, lawyers, construction firms).   There are also opportunities for graduates in broadcasting, education, management, marketing, database production and educational technology.

It is against this background of
a) increased information flow;
b) increased facilities for information handling;
c) a widening of career opportunities;
d) the problems of recession, and a consequent limitation of the traditional openings for students

that present changes in curricula are being considered.   Currently, there is a national committee considering the teaching of library and information science in both universities and polytechnics in Britain.   Its role is

> To advise on the current provision of, and likely needs for, library and information courses at institutions within the areas of responsibility of the University Grants Committee, the National Advisory Board (for Polytechnics and Institutes of Higher Education) and the Welsh Advisory Board, taking account also of institutions within the responsibility of the Scottish Education Department and the Department of Education, Northern Ireland, and to make recommendations for action.   This will involve a review of likely future demand (both in terms of numbers and of expertise) for library and information professionals and of the courses provided by each of the library and information science schools, bearing in mind the changing nature of library and information work.

There is widespread belief that it has also been established to recommend a reduction in student numbers, and therefore staff numbers and resources, though this is denied by the committee's chairman, Professor Brian Morris. The Committee's concern will be to consider quality *versus* quantity in the production of librarians/ informatists. Currently, there are seventeen schools or departments of library and information science. There are university departments at Queen's University, Belfast, Northern Ireland, London (City University and University College London), Loughborough, Sheffield (in England) and Strathclyde University, Glasgow, Scotland. There is a hybrid 'College of Librarianship, Wales' a public sector college which conducts courses for the degrees of the University of Wales. There are polytechnic departments at Birmingham, Brighton, Leeds, Liverpool, London (Polytechnic of North London), Manchester and Newcastle. There is one each at Aberdeen (Robert Gordon's Institute), London (Ealing College of Higher Education), Loughborough (Technical College). There is a proposal before the Morris Committee to reduce the number of departments in the United Kingdom to six or seven.

Once the opportunities for students are broadened, it is difficult to determine the job opportunities. My colleague, Dr. J.M. Brittain, with a grant from the British Library, is trying to determine future opportunities for student employment and lay the foundations for curriculum development of a very different kind from the traditional 'library and information science' pattern. This was begun in our own departmental interest as part of the assignment of a Task Force we set up early in 1984, to consider the future of our curriculum and its effectiveness in preparing students for wider opportunities. But it has taken on a national significance with the appointment of the Transbinary (national) committee on library and information science with an interest in looking at the effectiveness of current educational patterns in the subject. The future that lies ahead therefore seems, at the present time, both uncertain and challenging.

It would, however, paint a false picture if one gave the impression that we now face sudden change.[1] In most departments of library and information science in Britian, there is continuous revision of syllabuses depending not only on the changing nature of the subject, and the changing demand, but also in response to staff changes, and hence changes in expertise. With the retirement or resignation of staff, opportunities are created of introducing new subjects, as staff teaching the traditional subjects of the curriculum are replaced by staff specialising in information technology, reprography, non-book media, computing or ergonomics. But the changing scene of professional practice also impels a compulsive urge to revision. At Loughborough, which is not atypical, the staff reckon to be engaged in continuous revision from year to year in response to perceived needs, changes in staff offerings and expressed student opinion.   But we also reckon to make a major revision every three to four years or so.   With so much change in the air, one must also be conscious of the importance to the student of continuity.   Students need a balance between change and stability, and the effect of change on the social stability of the department has to be taken into account.   Change to be effective must not be too drastic, must be well planned, and announced in advance, if students are to have confidence in the management and administration of the department.

Moreover, what is so difficult about curriculum development in library and information science is the problem of seeing it as a whole, and achieving for the student a coherent whole.   Politely, the subject is considered to be 'interdisciplinary': in fact, this means that it is an amalgam of subjects – logic, linguistics, systems analysis, indexing, information sources, management, psychology, bibliography, collection management and development, literature, history, etc.   Since it is, as yet, an unstable discipline, it is subject to fashion. The difficulty about fashions is that a sudden insertion of a new subject arising from a new fashion can result in a distortion of the syllabus.   What then is one to put in, what to leave out?   What is the core curriculum?

In a document produced by Unesco in 1974 for the NATIS Conference, there was a statement of the core curriculum as seen at that time;[2]   this was updated in a volume published to celebrate the centenary of the British Library Association in 1977:[3]

A core curriculum in documentation, library and archives studies

Courses	Information Science	Library Studies	Archives Studies
Foundations (Masonry)	Sociology of information	Library in society	Economic
		Library legislation	Legal history
	History of science	History of libraries and library education	Social
	Scientific communication	User research	Genealogy, heraldry
	Theory of communication		
	Research methods	Research methods	Research methods
Materials	Various formats— reports, documents data (ideas)	Various formats books, serials, new media	Various formats manuscripts, maps letters

	Information services	Reference sources Bibliographical tools History of book arts	Registers, inventories, etc. Bibliographical tools
Methods	Indexing, contents analysis Documentary languages Storage & retrieval Data organisation Information dissemination Systems analysis	Indexing, contents analysis Reader services Organisation of knowledge Reference processes Systems analysis Preservation and restoration	Registry systems Paleography Museum techniques Records management Library techniques Preservation and restoration
Management	Management and administration Personnel Systems organisation and planning Legal aspects	Management and administration Personnel Systems organisation and planning Type of library operation Legal aspects	Management and administration Personnel Systems organisation Type of archives operation Legal aspects
Mechani— sation	Computer and reprographic technology	Computer and reprographic technology	Computer and reprographic technology
Men	Educating the user	Educating the user	Educating the user

A curriculum statement which has influenced leading library and information departments in the United Kingdom is that published by the Institute of Information Scientists.   This includes —

1. Nature of information and its uses
2. Sources of information
3. Theory and practice of information storage and retrieval
4. Systems for informaion storage and retrieval
5. Analysis of information
6. Dissemination of information
7. Management
8. Technology and its applications
9. Ancillary skills – research methods, mathematics and statistics,linguistics
   and foreign languages.

The core curriculum, in my view, still exists though its expression in principle has become simplified while the content has become more varied and more specialised to cater for wider employment opportunities.

> Management
> Indexing
> Sources of Information
> Information Technology

The intellectual content has been very considerably developed. Logic and systems analysis lie at the heart of the discipline which has been interestingly expressed and elaborated recently in an 'Online curriculum for a postgraduate training course for information specialists in the field of social sciences'.[4] This includes

1. General theoretical fundamentals of information and documentation work.
2. Methods and techniques of information processing.
3. Special problems of the development of information retrieval systems and dissemination of information.
4. Survey of national and international information systems and their management and planning.
5. Problems of relationship between information and documentation and librarianship.
6. Further problem areas (languages, copyright, communication science, etc.).

   – to be added: organisational, resource and personnel management.

Another formulation, much older but still valid is that given by Schur and Saunders in 'Education and training for scientific and technological library and information work'.[5] This proposed

1. Scientific and technological communities and their information and library needs;
2. Sources of information;

3. Techniques (by which 1 and 2 are brought together):
   a) The organisation of knowledge: principles and techniques of information storage, retrieval and dissemination.
   b) Techniques of library/information unit organisation and management.
The notion of the 'community' which exists around information and library services is important.   Pioneered by the Department of Information Studies at Sheffield, it emphasizes the fact that, whatever the kind of service it is set in the community for which it provides-educational, institutional, industrial concern, professional practice, national, business, or local community. Too often in the past, libraries (particularly) and information units, have been regarded by the professionals working in them almost as closed systems, whereas they are service units to a larger organisation or community.   Their operration must therefore be seen in terms not only of the efficiency of the system but also in terms of the effectiveness of their operation i.e. providing the best and most appropriate service to the greatest number of users within their community at the lowest cost.   For this reason, university libraries must be considered, analysed, organised and managed in the context of the university systems as a whole – and likewise for documentation centres, special libraries, college, public and school libraries.   It remains true, as the NATIS conference affirmed eleven years ago that information is central to modern community development –

> Information is an essential part of a nation's resources and access to it is one of the basic human rights.   The formulation and implementation of a national information policy is the only way to ensure that those who engage in administrative, educational, scientific and cultural activities have access to the information they need.   Priorities in the national planning must, therefore, be reflected in specialized information sub-systems.
>
> Information is not only a national resource vital for scientific and economic progress, but also the medium of social communication.   The personal, vocational and social development of the individual depends on the amount, quality and accessibility of information to such a user.   The ultimate aim of an information policy must, therefore, be an informed society.[6]

A further point to make about the development of the curriculum is that a world perspective is now essential.   It has been stated many times that no library 'is an island of itself' and that even the great national libraries in Britian, France, the United States and Russia, for instance, can no longer attempt to maintain world coverage of publications and documents.   They never have, but they imagined they did.   With the development, for instance, of Unesco/IFLA programmes such as Universal Bibliographical Control, the Universal

Availability of Publications, the Transborder Transfer of Information and Conservation, and the activities of FID and the International Council on Archives, no educational programme can either confine itself to consideration of services within its own borders, or, equally significantly, omit to evaluate these services against world standards and world practice.   The latter requires perception, courage, powers of analysis, a faculty for positive action to influence the limited community of practitioners, government, and the wider community at large.   (As a colleague said to me thirty years ago when I became a university librarian, 'Librarians are known and remembered for what they do, not what they say!   I took that to heart then, and as a library and information educator still do today.)   No less important is the world perspective given by technology.   This applies particularly to international data bases and data stores at the present time, though the technology of facsimile reproduction, optical disks, other new technologies, reprography and non-book media generally must not be ignored.   Indeed, the ability to absorb different technologies in the service of information, and to use them appropriately is part of the intellectual effort required in studying the subject at a professional level.

We have, then, a curriculum, at this stage of the argument, with a world perspective both in general conception of information and library services and in techniques, a community perspective with consideration of the place of the information service or library service within the community it serves (industry, education, the public at large) and connecting the two, of course, a national perspective within which practical planning and a philosophy of service must exist.   This must rest on appropriate management teaching, the sources of information, and its organisation, and the required techniques, whether traditional and manual, or *via* other technologies.

This brings me back to thinking about the curriculum as a whole.   The danger currently is that computers will dominate the scene.   Professor Saunders, in a paper to the Irish Library Conference in Cork in 1980 stated

> I think those of us concerned with education and training have a duty to overcome... 'the fear of the machine' while at the same time avoiding... 'the worship of the machine'.[7]

You will note, I am sure, that I group the computer with other technologies. That is deliberate.   It is important to consider the aims the 'ends' of the service rather than the means.

If you think the argument is too information science oriented, do not be deceived.   What about the recent flavour of the month, 'conservation'?   When we thought, at least at Loughborough, we had got the balance of the curriculum just about right, we heard of the concern of the British Library about conservation and the consequent investigation and report of Dr. F. Ratcliffe, Librarian of the University of Cambridge and Visiting Professor at Loughborough, on the importance of conservation.[8]   I have written at some length elsewhere on conservation[9] (and indeed we had already been thinking about it at Loughborough), so it is not proposed to deal with it again here.   It is, however, important to point out that conservation is no longer a matter concerning old books alone, but it is relevant to most of the publications of the last 150 years, i.e. since the invention of chemical paper and, more recently, new methods of binding.   It is relevant to the books we buy today.

Why conservation is important in the context of this paper is that it underlines the fact that, while we must pay due attention to developments in information technology, we cannot afford to neglect the book.   This will still remain even if, as Professor Lancaster thinks, most, if not all, publications of a learned nature will not be in book-form by the end of the century, but will be on-line, or on optic disk or in a form of technology about which we do not as yet even know.   Books will remain, and will still be actively used (even if used differently) because we have five hundred years of them in a relatively consistent and modern format, and more than a thousand years of them in the West in other forms, and for yet a longer time in the East.   The danger, today, is indeed that we are all too prepared to wipe away history, and to neglect or to forget what has happened in the past.   There is a danger of this happening among librarians in Britain at the present, and it tends to be happening elsewhere.   While it is important to teach about computers, it is equally important to convey the significance of the development of culture, and its organisation and preservation in durable form.

How then do we achieve a balanced curriculum?   We must provide, it seems to me, a core curriculum as outlined above.   This must be angumented with options which students can choose.   This is perhaps a coward's way out of a difficulty.   The danger is that we *think* we are giving an overall rounded education, when in fact we are giving bits and pieces of education.   The student is choosing for himself, and we may be abrogating our duty to see that he/she has everything necessary for his or her professional career.   In a perfect world, this might be so, but it is my view that students are best motivated when they have control over what courses they wish to pursue.   We thus (like most department or schools in Britain and, even more, in the U.S.) offer alternatives within the core course-specialisations in management, computer applications, sources of information.   Within this, the student has a further choice since he or she has a considerable say in the topics of his or her coursework.   In other words, there is a basic structure, within which students can choose and specialise.   Moreover, while, in general, it is useful to undertake studies which will be appropriate to their careers, I still hold the view (old-fashioned though it may be) that within limits it is not so important as to what they study, but how well they study.   The relevance considered so necessary today may be given not only strictly in connection with the subject-matter, but in the theoretical plus practical orientation of the studies involved.   This will vary according to the age and cultural development of the student: the many experienced students we receive from other countries are encouraged to undertake projects directly relevant to their country and their needs.   The fine library building planned by James N'ganga, Librarian of Kenyatta University of Nairobi, for instance, was planned during his year at Loughborough – tangible enough evidence of what a mature student can achieve within a master's programme.

There is a view that we should be able to send out the 'complete informatist'.   This is based, in my view, on a mistaken view of what university education is.   It must be emphasied that we can introduce students, even at the postgraduate stage, to a subject, we can make them think, introduce them to problem solving methods, and we can try to give them a professional orientation-this is at least as important as the subject-matter.   But we cannot hope to teach them everything.   No student of mathematics, physics, English or history, management or sociology knows everything about his subject when he leaves university, and professional practitioners should not expect more of library and information studies.   We need to teach principles not practice, though principles cannot be divorced from practice.   Nor do I think that we should expand into two year postgraduate courses – certainly not in the United Kingdom.   This is because the subject is as yet insufficiently developed though it now has a strong intellectual content, demanding capacities both for literary and numerate expression.   It is only within the last five to ten years that it has offered an interdisciplinary study that is intellectually demanding – in indexing, management, information technology and sources of information. A two-year course would bore students to death, because they are looking for a practical orientation and application already in the United Kingdom after a three or four year intensive honours degree and a year's practical experience.   Two programmes are now being planned, first, are an MSc in Information Science and Drug Chemistry, Materials Technology, Ergonomics, and other subjects.   These aim to aid in producing specialists in a specialised field with particular information expertise in their own subject.   One of the complaints of scientists is that information scientists do not really understand the information problems in their field.   Dr. Brittain's recent volume reporting the proceedings of a seminar concerned with medical information[10] points this up, and tends to show that where information is most difficult for the specialist to find, it is even more difficult for the information scientist. The kind of course now envisaged will go some way to meeting this problem. Secondly, plans are afoot for an MSc in Information Resource Management to meet the demand for graduates to manage the information resources of organisations in the context of information technology. This will include courses in the information environment, information studies, management studies, information technology and computing.

So far, I have assumed that we are considering primarily a postgraduate programme, normally of one calendar year, with taught courses. This is undertaken after the successful completion of a specialised 'honours' degree in another subject (e.g. history, mathematics, modern languages, zoology) and our candidates are selected from the top 30%-40% of the national output of graduates. I would add that I think a well-developed dissertation is essential, and gives students a real opportunity to learn about research methods within the subject, and provides them with the basis of a useful completed project with which to begin their careers.

This approach, however, neglects a number of problem areas. The first is that the profession as a whole has concentrated far too much on professional education and not enough on education for professionals. By this, is meant the necessity to see professional development as a whole: this includes
1. general education (a degree in a specialised subject)
2. a period of pre-professional training
3. professional education
4. pupillage period in practice

We should not state that information/library education lasts a year, but that it takes, say, three plus three years, i.e. six years, including 1-4 above. As ever, we underestimate ourselves. This *schema* emphasises, too, the importance of training *versus* education. There must be a partnership between teaching institutions and the profession to provide programmes combining both education and training, and this will depend on the practices evolved in different countries. As employment opportunities widen, and employers are found to be organised in very different professional societies in the United Kingdom, this of course becomes more difficult. But the basic problem cannot be ignored: the more highly developed the education, the greater necessity for adequate training. In this connection the Library Association has published a series of guidelines for training programmes, for example 'The establishment of local cooperative training schemes', which deals with cooperative efforts in training.

This partnership in education and training also involves graduates at bachelor level in library and information science, and para- professionals.

The primary education for professional workers in the information and library world must be at the postgraduate level, since a degree in a subject specialisation is required in most senior posts, and all of them in national, tertiary education, and special libraries.   What is then the place of the graduate (BA or BSc) in library and information science?   Currently our graduates with BA or BSc degrees are getting posts in public libraries, polytechnic libraries, small special libraries, and junior posts in academic libraries, where subject specialisation is not required.   A few have been promoted to senior jobs. In the future, it is likely that the BA's or BSc's will do more of the basic library work, while the major information and library posts will go to postgraduates. However BA's and BSc's do have their advantages, which must not be ignored: they are much better trained as librarians, because they have greater time to learn about library and information problems over three years, and do not suffer the intensive education received by postgraduates.   They do not, however, have the same range of subject knowledge, and this tends to be a disadvantage in the contemporary specialised information oriented world in which we live.   However, Leeds, has maintained a BSc in Information Science since 1968 (with some difficulty in attracting students) but with the tremendous development in information technology and a change in student attitudes, there is room for a new look at an information science degree.   A new generation of students is appearing who seek education leading to careers in a wide spectrum of information activities, and will include computer studies. Alternatively, it may well happen that bachelor's degrees will become subject degrees like any other, i.e. not solely vocational-indeed, it is already happening – and students will expect to add a vocationally oriented master's degree in information science, computer science, management, etc.   Departments of library and information science are currently producing about equal numbers of both, though at Loughborough we are producing twice as many postgraduates as graduates.

Where Britain has fallen down is in the education for para- professionals. Since the 1960's[11] we have had a 'library assistant's certificate' of a relatively elementary character, organised not by the Library Association, but by the Royal Society of Arts.   The Paulin Committee[12] in 1978 recommended para–professional certificates in library work at OND and HND level, but instead of doing the work themselves, they left it to the Business Education Council, and the results have not been very successful.   There is still a vacuum here that needs to be filled.   For them and the graduates the total preparation for work at an appropriate level too needs to be considered.   For graduates, the content of the degree must be more general in character 'giving a liberal education through a vocational subject', and for para-professionals, it is necessary to have a general education at least to the 16 year old level, and preferably a little more. Both require pre-professional pre-para-professional training (of perhaps a more limited kind and for a shorter period), both require pupillage period on acquiring their qualification.

H. Schur,[13] in an important contribution in 1972 outlined different levels of performance for which different educational programmes were necessary-technical assistant; first level professional; second level professional; advanced professional,*or*, in terms of qualification, para-professional, graduate, post-graduate, and further degree. So far I have dealt only with basic qualifications, but advanced masters' degrees (the equivalent of Advanced Certificates in the US) have been offered for some time at London, Loughborough, Sheffield as well as at some of the Polytechnics (Leeds, Manchester) and the College of Librarianship Wales. Recently, however, the desire for a further degree has received considerable impetus from senior librarians, and we at Loughborough (aided by a grant from the British Library) are having discussions with the Open University and others on an MSc in Library and Information Management by distance learning for full-time senior librarians in post, who feel they need some further education, particularly in management. The University of Wales also has a degree in management for librarians, and the degrees at Manchester and Leeds include a management content. This is, of course, part of the concern for continuing education, a great need in a profession (or a group of profession) which is/are growing so fast. At Loughborough, for twelve years or so we have had a master's degree for qualified, non-graduate, librarians which provided for the needs of 'middle management' librarians, and other schools have provided more conventional offerings (as mentioned above). The professional associations (Aslib, the Library Association, SCONUL, the Institute of Information Scientists), the departments and schools of library and information science and the British Library have all been active in organising courses and conferences, seminars and workshops at various levels, and on a large variety of subjects to meet the needs of developing professional interests. Further, the elaboration of MPhil and PhD programmes (by thesis alone) has provided an additional means of giving an opportunity for research effort on the part of a small but select group of librarians and information officers who have wished to pursue their studies further.

One cannot omit a mention of the influence of the British Library Research and Development Department on the development of professional education. It is with assistance (financial, intellectual and moral) from the British Library that schools and departments have been able to build up their research potential and their information technology teaching. Much of the teaching of computer applications has resulted from grants from the British Library R & D Department to individual institutions.   Moreover, the Department has supported Centres(including LMRU/CLAIM at Loughborough) which have added to publication in the subject and helped to transform practice.   The Library and Information Services Council (and its predecessor, the Library Advisory Council) has also produced a number of reports which have influenced national policy for the better, and helped top clarify the minds of practitioners, administrators, teachers and students, alike.   One has also to pay tribute to international government (Unesco, Unido, WHO, FAO, etc.) and non-governmental (IFLA, FID, ICA, IFIP, WIPO) organisations which have also over the years provided a considerable number of publications. These have broadened the scope of library and information science education, and made our students less insular in outlook.

Last, but not least, one must mention the British contribution to overseas library and information education.   This contribution has been effective for the past thirty years at least, and many librarians and information workers in Africa, Asia, Latin America and Oceania owe some, or all, of their expertise to British library schools.   Aberystwyth, Leed, London, Loughborough, Sheffield are towns well known to the world-wide library community (particularly in the Commonwealth, but also elsewhere).   At Loughborough, many well-known librarians were trained in the Loughborough College school in the 'fifties and 'sixties and, since the establishment of the university department, we have received over 450 students from other countries [14]   and are still receiving about fifty overseas students a year.   About half come back with the financial aid of the British Council, which has been responsible not only for bringing students from other countries for training in Britian over the past forty years, but has also made possible British expertise in library and information education in many countries.   This has included academic link schemes, the appointment of British contract staff, and expert visits.   It has also included, not least, the work of permanent British Council staff in building up fine collections in British Council, and other, libraries which has provided useful collections of British books and non-book media in countries where it has not always been possible to obtain them.   Moreover, the libraries have served as models of practice in countries where libraries and information services have not been equally developed and their example has encouraged professionals whose resources have been scarce, and where difficulties of implementation have been great, to apply methods appropriate to their countries, often with the advice of British Council librarians, book development officers, and others, who have also been able to drawn on the Council's accumulated wisdom.

The picture is that of a very highly developed system, with seventeen library schools (plus an excellent school in Dublin, in the Republic of Ireland, making eighteen members of the Association of British Library and Information Studies Schools-ABLISS).   Each of these have their individual programmes, but all in the United Kingdom are overseen by national professional associations (especially the Library Association and the Institute of Information Scientists).   The programmes of the polytechnics are also approved by the Council of National Academic Awards.   Many of the schools have relationships with outside bodies – British Library, British Academy, the Research Councils, government departments, trusts and foundations, industry and commerce, country seats – and with institutions in other countries.   Currently examined by a national 'trans-binary' committee, they face an exciting future, and their future well-being will influence library and information education and practice not only in Britian, but also to some degree worldwide educational philosophy, principle and practice in the field of library and information science.

FOOTNOTES

1. See, for instance, A. Day, *Library Association Record* 86 (1984) : 15-24.
2. Planning Information Manpower, Paris: Unesco, 1974.
3. K.C. Harrison, ed., *Prospects for British Librarianship*, Library Association Centenary Volume, 1976, p. 35.
4. Published by the European Coordination Centre for Research and Documentation in Social Sciences, Vienna.
5. London, HMSO, 1968.
6. NATIS, *Objectives for National and International Action* (Paris, Unesco, 1975), p. 10.
7. Irish Library Conference, Cork, 1980.   *An Leabharlann,* 9 (1980): 85-90.
8. F. W. Ratcliffe, *Preservation Policies and Conservation in British Libraries*, Library and Information Research Report, 25 (London: The British Library, 1984).
9. P. Havard-Williams, Library Association Conservation Seminar, "Education for Conservation in Library and Information Studies," *Journal of Librarianship* 17 (1985): 100-105.
10. J. M. Brittain, ed., *Consensus in the Medical Sciences: Implications for Information Transfer*, London: Taylor, Graham, 1985.
11. See David Baker in *Education and Training* 2 (1985): 42-49.
12. Library Association, *Report on the Working Party on the Future of Professional Qualifications*, London, 1977.

13. K. Schur, Education and Training of Information Specialists for the 1970's (DAS/STINFO/72.9) PGSLIS, Sheffield, 1972 (for the OCED) 114P.
14. P. Havard-Williams, "Overseas Students as a Resource," *Information Development* (1985): 100-102.

The First Professional Step: The MLS in Library and Information Science in the United States

Harold Goldstein
Professor and Former Dean
School of Library and Information Studies
The Florida State University
Tallahassee, Florida, U.S.A.

INTRODUCTION

The beginning of library science education, rather than training, can be said to have started with the opening of Melvil Dewey's School of Library Economy in 1887 at Columbia College.   Precedent to this major focus, much concern had been expressed at various American Library Association conferences about the scope, role, location, and purpose of training personnel for the rapidly expanding field of librarianship in the United States.

Between 1853 and the establishment of the American Library Association in 1876, attempts were made to promote discussion about the training of librarians; for the most part, this concern focused on personnel for public libraries.   The meeting of "eminent librarians" and persons interested in libraries, held in New York City in May, 1853, included some discussions of library training.[1]

The thirty years following this landmark conference did not highlight much concern for the education of future librarians beyond that of on-the-job training.   No plan for library education was presented at the Conference of Librarians of All Nations in London, 1877, although references were made to needed qualifications.[2]   In 1883, Samuel Swett Green wrote Justin Winsor, librarian at Harvard College and a leader in the profession, about the need for a formal training program; Green received no encouragement from Winsor at that time.

In the early 1880's on several occasions Dewey wrote of the "need for a training school for preparation for the special work (librarianship)"[3]   for those who had necessary general education (preferably a college degree).

In May, 1883, Dewey became chief librarian at Columbia College, and the college, through President Barnard, offered hearty support for the creation of a School of Library Economy.[4] The Board of Trustees of the college approved unanimously the establishment of the "school for the instruction of persons desiring to qualify themselves to take charge of libraries, or for cataloging, or other library or bibliographical work."[5] The opening date for the school was October 1, 1886. The chief librarian of the College (Dewey) was to have responsibility for the general direction of the school and of the course of instruction as established, with the style and title of Professor of Library Economy.[6]

The School opened officially on January 5, 1887 with an enrollment of three men and seventeen women. The presence of women in the first class was a portent of the ensuing difficulty between Dewey and the college trustees who did not want women students. College graduation was not a prerequisite for entry, although it was considered desirable; this allowance was in deference to the ALA Committee on the School which did not want to see such a requirement in effect.[7]

The school lasted approximately two years at Columbia College; it was moved to the New York State Library at Albany, New York, in 1889 to continue its program. For the next several years it was the only fulltime educational program in the United States, until the emergence of Pratt Institute in 1890[8], the Los Angeles Public Library Training Class, 1891[9]; Drexel Institute, Philadelphia, 1892[10], and Armour Institute, Chicago, 1893.[11] Armour transferred to the University of Illinois in 1897, where the university integrated it into the full undergraduate offering, conferring the Bachelor of Science (B.L. S) degree upon graduates of this program. Thus the Illinois activity more closely approximated the New York State Library School in its overall operation.

Library education in a formal sense developed slowly but surely between the 1890's and into the twentieth century. The Committee on Library Training of the American Library Association, appointed in 1900[12], did not act with either dispatch or vigor in pursuing recommendations about changes in the curricula of the schools which were in operation (Drexel, Pratt, Illinois, New York State)[12]. Indeed, for the next twenty-plus years, constant concerns were voiced and recorded about the direction, depth, effectiveness, and success of these and other training or education activities.

By 1903, ten library schools were operating, plus four summer schools not located at these ten institutions, and three training classes (Brooklyn, Cincinnati, and New York Public Libraries)[13]. In 1906, standards were formulated for "winter" and summer schools by the Committee on Library Training: of eleven schools then active, five met all these standards, and six failed them in part.[14]

A Section on Professional Training, ALA, had been approved in 1909, in spite of considerable opposition from many members of the Association. Library school instructors met regularly between 1911-1915 as a separate group from the section; these meetings led to the establishment of the Association of American Library Schools in 1911.[14] This Association was concerned with standards for the operation of the early schools; but from its inception as a body until the Williamson report of 1923, little action occurred on either standards for education or standards of admission to the association. Faculty, graduates, programs — all were the butt of criticisms from the profession as to effectiveness, focus, and development during these years.

Charles Clarence Williamson, librarian of the Municipal Reference Library (New York), was asked to study library training in 1918.[15] He was a statistician, and president at that time of the Special Libraries Association (SLA). [16]

The report by Dr. Williamson, *Training for Library Service*(1923), was considered a landmark in the development of the formal structure for the education of librarians. "One of the most important conclusions of this study is that the professional library school should be organized as a department of a university, along with other professional schools rather than in public libraries ....Schools now conducted by public should either take the definite status of training classes or be transferred to university auspices in fact as well as in name."[17]

Other aspects of the report dealt with the definition of "professional work, the curriculum, entrance requirements, faculty and methods of instruction, finances and salaries, specialized study, training in service, and certification of librarians and standardization of library schools."[18]

This brief historical background of the early twentieth century must mention a number of additional important actions which followed the Williamson report. Almost immediately after the issuance of his study, ALA appointed the Board of Education for Librarianship (BEL). This body became the accrediting unit of that Association for library education activities, developing and applying standards, sponsoring curriculum studies, and acting as the evaluative arm for education of the profession.[19]

The matter of formal training *versus* apprenticeship learning was a concern which remained unresolved for sometime; this concern held back the wholehearted support of ALA for formal education. The indecision was a reflection of the larger turmoil affecting American society in the last quarter of the nineteenth century. The rapid development of industrial organizations, the completion of a transportation link between the east and the west coasts of the country, the adoption of the German model for graduate education by American institutions of higher learning – these factors and others helped focus on the growingly important role of the library in its social setting, and on the role of the library as a unique facility for the preservation, organization, and utilization of man's recorded knowledge. These roles were increasingly reflected in the growth of the national organization (ALA), and especially in the demand for formally-trained librarians as an immediate future need.

The rapid rise of science and the application of technological developments across the industrial scene, including the suddenly-emergent needs of World War I, gave rise to rapidly-expanded library services in industry and government, to say nothing of performing a major service for the reading needs, serious and recreational alike, of military personnel. Coupled with the changing picture within higher education between 1890-1920 and the stimulus for growth of public libraries through Carnegie gifts, the need for library schools to provide modern, uniform educational programs was apparent.

By 1926, the Carnegie Corporation agreed to support library education through a large grant of more than $4,000,000, known as the Ten-Year Program in Library Service.[20] This grant included an amount of $1,385,000 for "the establishment of a library school of the highest type, which might be counted on doing for the library profession what the Johns Hopkins Medical School and the Harvard Law School have accomplished in their respective fields."[21] This school was established at the University of Chicago, and it became the first educational program to offer the Ph.D. in library science. The total grant provided support for a number of existing schools; it made possible, also, the combination of the New York Public Library Training Class and the New York State School (Albany) which became the new School of Library Service at Columbia University in 1926.

It is noteworthy that the Carnegie interest during the early decades of this century in building libraries was shifted to the support of education for librarians to operate those and other buildings. Charles Churchwell rightly noted that this "redirection of interests and financial resources was greatly encouraged by the reports of Alvin S. Johnson, Charles C. Williamson, William S. Learned, plus the results of several conferences on librarianship."[22]

However, a problem of jurisdiction and authority grew when the ALA's Board of Education for Librarianship was established as the Association of American Library Schools (AALS). Between 1924-1939, AALS was concerned with and defensive over the shift in authority to accredit schools from its body to the Board; this Association lost considerable professional presitige as this shift became known.   AALS did not pursue reforms in education during these years; rather, it committed itself strongly to defense of traditional concepts and curricula in library education.   The Board, on the other hand, felt responsible for attempting to change existing library education programs to provide personnel for all types of libraries.   That is, AALS helped maintain the older concept of education for specific positions in specific types of libraries, while the Board, in view of much heated discussion pro and con the proper focus of library education, attempted to push the schools in the direction of a general educational experience which would prepare graduates for service in several types of libraries.   Additionally, the shortage of school librarians, greatly aggravated by rapid changes in elementary and secondary school educational practices, was not of great concern to AALS which did not modify its requirements for the training of school librarians.[23]

Up to the onset of World War II, then, American library education was focused on a general provision of curricula which trained general librarians (those presumably capable of working anywhere in a library) rather than training for specific type-of-library jobs.   Thus, while the BEL *accredited* schools in respect of standards, AALS maintained a philosophical and orientative control over them vis-a-vis curricula.   The gulf between these positions was accentuated in the eyes of the BEL which saw clearly the need for diversity in the first year programs (the fifth-year B.S.L.S.)

POSTWAR DEVELOPMENTS

Little change took place from 1939-1949, reflecting the involvement of American resources in the war effort and then in the huge task of postwar reconstruction and redirection.   Considerable attention was spent in conferences and through writing on the proper or necessary changes to be made in the curricula and on the emphases of the immediate and future postwar graduate education.

In 1946, J. Periam Danton's essay, *Education for Librarianship, Criticisms, Dilemmas, and Proposals*, focused on just such matters.[24]   Among his criticisms were these points: 1) Library school curricula, in spite of much change since Williamson's report, were still too practical and too emphatic on techniques; faculties lacked members who were capable of enlarging and supplementing any new programs; too much was attempted for a one-year program; too little integration of library school programs with other university offerings was evident; schools did not educate for leadership; too little differentiation remained between professional and nonprofessional concerns in both the curricula and in the work world, even after Williamson.[25]

His proposals/remedies/solutions to these problems were: 1) to provide education for different levels of library activity and responsibility; to eliminate the Type III school (those without graduate courses and rearrange Type I (more than one year of graduate study) and Type II (one year of graduate programs) so as to encompass most of the needs for graduate study; 2) to obtain another study *a la* Williamson to determine where, what, and how to redirect library education; and 3) to obtain funds to endow four of five chairs of library education.[26]

In 1948, a conference was held at the Graduate Library School, University of Chicago. Its topic was *"Education for Librarianship"*, marking the twenty-fifth anniversary of the program at that institution. Recall that the Graduate Library School (GLS) was established mainly to offer the Ph.D. in library science; it added the M.S. within a few years of its opening. The editor of this conference report, Dean Bernard Berelson of Chicago, noted in the introduction, "Historians of American librarianship will undoubtedly note the years 1946-1950 as a period of major revision in the system of library education in this country, perhaps of equal importance of the period of the 1920's which was characterized by the Williamson Report."[27]

This conference was held at the time when Denver University's Library School announced that it would award the M.S.L.S. degree upon completion of a year of graduate study. Seven other schools announced their intentions to follow Denver in 1949 in offering the M.S. upon completion of a fifth year: Chicago, Columbia, Emory, Illinois, Pittsburgh, Southern California, and Western Reserve.[28]

What curricular changes and/or other concerns were emphasized in these years? One major concern dealt with the attempt to consolidate the "core of knowledge" for librarianship into commonly accepted areas, found in most of the accredited schools. This core – reference, book selection, cataloging, and administration – represented a compromise between the old concern over a practical approach and newer concerns over the incorporation of a basic thread of content for all students.

The Core of Education for Librarianship was the title of a conference held at the Graduate Library School (Chicago) in August 1953, as evidence of concern for this topic.[29] This conference and its resultant publication defined core differently – seven (7) content areas were listed (and agreed upon by the participants) as those which should be the common knowledge base of all students, and thus presented in the programs of all accredited schools. These areas were:[30]

Library in Society
Professionalism
Materials
Services

Administration
Communication
Research

How to implement these topics to represent "one-fifth of a minimum five-year program at the college level and beyond"[31] was a matter for each school to decide.   Not the least of the discussions at this conference attended to the implication for the profession generally of the inculcation of these concepts as future basic attitudes, etc.[32]

At the time of this development – the new fifth-year degree – the audiovisual area had developed greatly. The impetus of military training requirements and the technology derived from wartime use of audiovisual materials had begun to permeate the public schools widely; the U.S. library world was beginning to note this growth.   Yet no changes in teaching methods, or changes in offerings (including the core) reflected such developments during the 1950's in any measure.   It was not until 1963, well after the frenzied rush to change educatiomal practices following the appearance of Sputnik, that the first conference was held on the use of audiovisual matterials in library education.[33]   Successive conferences on this subject, or on other approaches to newer methodologies, were not held; it is fair to say that until the advent of the *Journal of Education for Librarianship* (1960), published by AALS (now ALISE : Association for Library and Information Science Education), little continuing attention was given to educational practices in library schools.

By the end of the postwar period (1948/49) which marked major step in the changed direction of library education, some forty-one library schools were operating in the United States.[34]   Of these schools, as noted, eight had adopted a fifth-year master's degree by 1949.   This group presaged the compilation and adoption of the 1951 *Standards for Accreditiation* (ALA), and these standards led to a wholesale reaccreditation of the schools operating in the decade of the 1950's.

During the next twenty years, American library education at the M.S. level developed in several major directions.   One such development was the provision in most curricula of a large number of courses from which students could select both required and elective courses.   All but one of the current sixty accredited schools offer electives for student selection.   All of the schools but one require the equivalent of the core course areas described earlier in this paper; while course titles and course scopes may vary, the intent of the curricula in all schools is to provide a common denominator of basic content upon which the student builds a program to satisfy degree requirements (which vary somewhat among these schools).

A second major difference (or new direction) was the slow but sure adoption of information science course content as both a focus for the curriculum and as elective courses.   By "information science" is meant attention to the processing of information in accordance with its characteristics, with detailed examination of how information is stored, manipulated, and made available.   Paramount to this area was concern for the role of computer applications in libraries and information centers; but this aspect is only one phase of information science education.

Much attention also was devoted to expanded reference and bibliography instruction, including government publications as a separate and widely available course.   The rapid growth of all fields of knowledge, coupled with a rapid growth in the number of new titles published in the United States, necessitated far greater consideration of new information-finding tools, which were being produced at an equally rapid rate.   Library schools quickly developed and offered new bibliography and subject literature courses, such as genealogy, audiovisual materials, Afro-American sources, etc.[35]

THE CURRENT SCENE

By the 1970's a number of library schools had provided joint degree programs, whereby students could complete studies in a specialty along with the library science component.   By planning carefully these joint programs, students reduced the number of hours required for each separate degree (music, art history, etc.) yet fulfilled requirements adequately in both disciplines. These programs required the completion of core content, usually to meet each discipline's demands.

Besides joint degrees, other specialties became available in many schools, dependent on the availability of offerings in other university departments and on the competencies of library science faculty.

A growing concern in the 1970's was that of recruitment of minority students, and the impact of this movement on the curriculum of the accredited schools.   Most universities undertook quickly, either through official pressure or through voluntary direction, such recruitment efforts; the resultant enrollment of a minimum number of black and other minority students brought about some changes in the programs of some schools.   Greater attention was given to the addition of such courses as *The Library and Social Problems*, *Special Populations*, etc.   Increased pressure from the field, especially in public and school libraries, for improved services to disabled and disadvantaged groups led to a greater availability of internships and practice work in programs serving such clienteles.[36]

The problem of adequate internship or practicum opportunity has been of concern for a long time. A number of schools provided such opportunities, required or elective, in the 1960's; the number has declined in the 1970's/1980's. Yet at the same time, an increased demand for the practicum was noted by many schools which undertook analyses of student reactions to programs.

Another noticeable enlargment of the programs of many schools is their increased attention to the sponsorship of a variety of continuing education programs. Such offerings range from off-campus degree programs to short-term conferences, workships, and institutes. Most schools have announced publicly their commitments to such activities through statements of objectives for their programs; while the commitment is not particularly new, the large number of such activities points to continuing education as concern of considerable priority.

The 1951 *Standards for Accreditation* served for nearly twenty years as guidelines for the development of the corpus of graduate library schools. By 1969, considerable headway had been made toward a revision of these standards, to the point that they were presented to the Council of the American Library Association in 1971. They were then adopted by the ALA Council in June, 1972. These standards became effective in January, 1973 as replacements for the 1951 version.

In an article summarizing the concerns voiced at hearings called to discuss the new standards, four major points were given:

1) The problem of quantitative/qualitative standards was resolved by rejecting quantitative ones. The major reasons for this rejection were: a) quantitative standards allow rigidity in their application; b) they tend to stifle creativity and innovation in that the quantities themselves become the minima of performance;
2) Delineation of special interests in the programs of schools would be met through the broad definitions in the *Standards* of librarianship and information science which allow such interests to be implemented;
3) Attention to social concerns in the education of future librarians would be met by the flexibility provided in the *Standards* which each school could interpret as needed;
4) Implementation of the *Standards* and uniform procedures would be applied by the issuance of updated revisions from the COA to supplement the *Standards*.[37]

The new *Standards*, now in effect for twelve years, have enabled the American/Canadian educational structure in graduate library education to function in a more cohesive, uniform, and developed way, while at the same time these *Standards* have encouraged individuality of specialties, innovations in teaching and student relationships, and faculty experimentation with curricular change.

One appraisal of the development of the MLS program in American schools thus might postulate that such development was a response to the total process of accreditation. That is, as the Board of Education for Leadership became the Committee on Accreditation (1956), the routines and responsibilities of maintaining uniform, but not precisely duplicated, standards of operation helped smooth out disparities in both philosophy and practice. For example, in the later *Standards* (1972) described below, schools are required to state clearly their goals and objectives, and demonstrate with evidence the derivation as well as the implementation of such statements.

This unifying influence has served well as a means of adding substance and quality to library education programs. There has been due allowance for local (institutional) differences in the review of each graduate facility, while at the same time, the COA accreditation/reaccreditation process requires minimum (and higher) conformance to the *Standards*.

Lester Asheim seconded the comments of Summers and Bidlack, referred to above, in an article on library education trends in the United States published in 1975. He pointed out that the *Standards* required clearly defined, publicly stated goals and specific objectives against which the school's program could be measured; such statements provided for individual differences and flexibility in evaluation of programs, as well as giving protection against exaggerated claims for programs. The *Standards*, further, demanded greater recognition of students as a "responsible segment of the academic community"[38] and attached more importance to their role in evaluation.

Innovation is encouraged through emphasis in the *Standards* as a motivation for schools to be as "inventive and as experimental as they can be", thus meeting "once and for all a traditional criticism of standards – that they impose uniformity and stifle innovation".[39]

Finally, Asheim noted out that the 1972 *Standards* have moved farther in the direction of qualitative, rather than quantitative standards. This direction is more challenging to the schools and "fosters imaginative, individual, flexible programming rather than prescribed and restricted conformity. It is the logical way to keep library education dynamic, responsive, and responsible."[40]

What can and should be said about current library and information science curricula in North American schools, using the *Standards* as a benchmark? *Standard II, Curriculum,* details the following matters:

1) The programs of the school should provide for the study of principles and procedures common to all types of libraries and library services.
2) A study of specialized service in either general or special libraries may occupy a place in the basic program.
3) Specialization should be built upon a foundation of general academic and professional education and should include interdisciplinary work pertinent to the program of the individual student.
4) The curriculum comprising the students' total learning experience should be based upon the school's statement of goals and should provide both adequate means and sufficient time for meeting the specific objectives of the programs.
5) The curriculum should be a unified whole rather than an aggregate of courses. It should (a) stress understanding rather than rote learning of facts; principles and skills rather than routines; (b) emphasize the significance and functions of the subjects taught; (c) reflect the findings of basic and applied research in librarianship and related disciplines; (d) respond to current trends in library development and professional education; (e) promote continuous professional growth.
6) A curriculum may be composed of a variety of educational experiences derived from the program objectives of the library school. Any such experience should take place within a learning environment in which (a) students have the benefit of guidance by a qualified member of the faculty; (b) adequate supportive materials and facilities are readily available; (c) provision is made for discussion or evaluation of the student's experience.
7) The curriculum should be continually under review and revision, and should be receptive to innovation.[41]

One set of answers to the question was given by Ralph Conant. He undertook a major study of the role and effectiveness of graduate library education. It was completed in 1977, and the report was published in 1980. It was and it is a controversial document which satisfied neither the original sponsor (ALA) nor the subjects of the study (library educators). It was heralded as the second Williamson report which was received also in its time with considerable distaste by many in the profession. Conant provided some valuable insights into the practices of schools (sixteen were visited and reviewed) specifically, and of the professional educational scene generally. He made some recommendations for the reform of education as he saw it in the 1970's, which included these points *re* curriculum:

1) Theory versus practice in instruction – more practice may be nesessary, but it is not possible to incorporate a valid practical experience in a one-year program without sacrificing valuable content;
2) Specialization was impossible in a one-year program beyond basic knowledge

of a type-of-library or type-of-service.   Specialization beyond such a basic
orientation should be confined to additional study;

3) Separation of professional/paraprofessional training must be clearly defined.
   Without such a separation no comprehensive general curriculum could be
   designed.   The intellectual level as well as kind of instruction must be differ-
   entiated, with the professional program covering all aspects of librarianship.[42]

The professional program's subject matter should encompass: foundations, administration, technical services, types of libraries, reference and
bibliography, and client group services.   Ideally, two years would be required
to accomplish this program.[43]

About two years after the distribution of this report and after considerable reaction had been published, Dr. Conant replied to critics and com-
mentators by summarizing these changes he had recommended in the present structure of graduate library education:

1) Separate clearly professional and nonprofessional education content;
2) Reduce the number of MLS programs so that the total number of graduates
   approximately equals the number of available jobs;
3) Improve the balance in educational offerings by:
   a) including a substantial internship in MLS programs;
   b) expanding the MLS degree requirements to four or five semesters or ad-
      ditional training as specialists, with increased research competencies and
      with enlarged administrative abilities;
   c) promote interdisciplinary work and planned distribution of specialist pro-
      grams among the accredited schools;
   d) move introductory courses to the undergraduate level of instruction;
   e) maintain continuing education as a high priority in library education;
   f) add professional evaluators from outside librarianship to accreditation
      teams to lend objectivity and to reduce the influence of local political con-
      siderations.[44]

Some of these recommendations had been partly implemented by the time the
report was distributed and discussed.   For example, the University of California/
Los Angeles had instituted a two-year MLS degree in 1972; in 1982, the University
of Washington followed suit, and the University of North Carolina/Chapel Hill
began an "extended program" in 1981.   The University of Illinois had considered
a two year plan which the Graduate School of Library Science had approved;
but the Graduate College of the university rejected the proposal.

Presumably the low status of the information profession in today's society has brought about, in the last few years, a large reduction in the num-

ber of new students entering almost all the schools, to the point where now, for the first time in a decade, a "graduate's market" is seen. For some time it has been known that the rapid expansion of library services which resulted from educational development in the 1960's-1970's had been reduced; the current major need for new personnel has resulted from attrition (retirements, changes in profession, deaths). While active recruitment is still evident in many quarters for traditional positions, a newly emergent demand is materializing for an education program which will effect both curriculum and practice, and which will enable graduates to undertake new information service roles.

If the predictions of F. W. Lancaster and others about the future of the printed page, hence the books which stock our libraries, were to be realized fully as they see it, a whole new approach to preparation to deal with radically different practices would be dictated. If most information transactions in the future were to revolve around electronic database utilization, and if most libraries were to shift purchases and operation from book collections/management to database services, obviously graduate study programs would require far greater attention to such competencies and techniques than they now do. Almost all of the American/Canadian schools provide either required or optional preparation in basic online database management (searching, compilation projects, etc.); but only a few schools would claim to graduate professional database managers capable of the responsibility of designing and managing a major electronic information service.

How fast such changes will occur cannot be predicted with any degree of accuracy. The rapid switch to the basic instruction in database operations is interesting in itself, in view of the even more rapid changes in hardware and software associated with computer applications. Within a single decade, at least two if not three, "generations" of computers have lived and died; the current great-grandchildren of the first computers in libraries bear only little resemblance to the original machines.

Consider briefly the relatively rapid rise of instruction in information science in relation to the rapid injection of computer activities in libraries. It is a scant thirty – thirty-five years since Taube, Shaw, Perry and other innovators wrote about changing modes of bibliographic organization, punched card utilization and application, coordinate indexing, etc. Garfield, Luhn, Summit, and Rogers in the late 1950's and early 1960's brought to fruition search systems, such as Medlars/Medline, KWIC (Keyword in Context), *Science Citation Index*, and other now familiar tools and routines.[45]

Concerns over the need for the preparation of persons capable of dealing with such new information concepts and realities brought forth a new "being" – the information scientist. Information science was defined as that science which investigates the properties and behavior of information, the forces governing the flow of information, and the means of processing information for optimum accessibility and usability.[46]

Between 1960-1965, several conferences dealt with education for information science; however, little incorporation of this new area into the curriculum was noted in most schools which were more traditionally focused. On the other hand, specialist programs were set up quickly enough at Georgia Institute of Technology, Lehigh University and elsewhere, where undergraduate and graduate curricula in computer and information science became common, concentrating on the design, operation, and development of computers.

By the 1970's many library schools had established full programs for students which provided strong information science emphases – Pittsburgh, Case Western Reserve (the first library school to offer such instruction), Rutgers, Drexel, Indiana, Illinois joined the Universities of Chicago and California/Los Angeles.

Within two decades, then, a relatively effective and close mating was established between the increasingly widespread use of computers and education for such use and adaptation. Yet it is evident that a big gulf exists between the projected "electronic library" of the early twenty-first century and the paper/ book library of the late twentieth century. The gulf, whether being narrowed or widened, will exist for a long time to come because of the major problem of financing those services which need and expect more rapid automation. Large libraries of whatever persuasion will arrive more quickly at the point of major change; but the thousands of small libraries which cannot afford full conversion must still be served through automated facilities which will charge them fees they cannot afford even today. The graduates of most of today's MLS programs have had the opportunity to become familiar with the basic knowledge and skills (competencies) capable of assisting and directing the conversions or changes which lie ahead; whether or not these graduates can undertake major redirection of automated operations in the majority of libraries in the U. S. which are small remains to be seen.

Perhaps more important than the change for the individual agency is the need for reorientation of the single unit toward multiunit operations: networks and systems of multitype libraries, pooling their provenance as well as their problems to accomplish the best possible information service in the years ahead. The basic change affecting all of these developments may well stem from the policies and decisions made by the producers of knowledge and information as the information age ponders more closely its directions and its profits.

An assessment, then, of current first professional degree programs is that they have directed only some of their energy toward preparation for a newer form of librarianship, whether or not that form is dependent on automated devices. There is no question that increased automation is a *sine qua non* for the growth of the present, as well as new, information utilities.

The information utilities of today may or may not be the utilities of tomorrow; one certainty, however, is that they will deal with even larger numbers of information bits (and pieces) than do such present services as Online Computer Library Center (OCLC); Research Libraries Information Network (RLIN); etc.

More effective utilization of and subscription to their services will depend on how adequately future (and self-advancing current) graduates will be able to obtain funds to maintain these utilities, and how well library agencies will pass on the benefits of utility services to their clienteles. This passing on, as it were, will be a function of the reality of the educational preparations for such responsibilities.

In summary, the first step in the professional direction, or onto the professional ladder, has been analyzed within the context of the traditional and hereditary development of the educational program, from an apprentice-like focus to full status as a graduate program in good standing in academic institutions. The growth has been difficult, if one views the current library educational corpus as a compromise between practioner and teacher. However, it might be better to view the current educational status and mass as a result of hard-won direction by a body of educators who saw clearly their goals: to challenge young people (or second-career persons, for that matter) to undertake a responsibility for relating information sources to human needs, and to discharge that responsibility effectively. The responsibility will remain, undoubtedly, no matter what happens to the agency – or the sources of knowledge and information – in the years ahead.

In 1926, Melvil Dewey presented remarks at the jubilee meeting of ALA, then fifty years old. His closing remarks were:

> "There is a tremendous work in this broader education to be done. To do it is the birthright of the American Library Association.... It is great work and it will require persistent patience.... The A. L. A. has this wonderful opportunity. If you look at the library problem of the next fifty years, serene, clear-eyed, and unafraid, you will see it.
>
> Men and women of the American Library Association, what will you do with this stupendous fifty years ahead?"[47]

Is his point still apropos the problems of tomorrow as seen today?

FOOTNOTES

1. Sarah K. Vann, *Training for Librarianship Before 1923* (Chicago: ALA, 1961), p. 12.
2. Ibid., p. 23
3. Ibid., p. 16
4. Ibid., p. 24
5. Ibid., p. 28
6. Ibid.
7. Ibid., p. 32
8. Ibid., p. 64
9. Ibid., p. 65
10. Ibid., p. 68
11. Ibid.
12. Ibid., p. 100
13. Ibid., p. 132
14. Ibid., p. 162
15. Ibid., p. 171
16. Ibid.
17. Charles C. Williamson, *Training for Library Service....* (New York, 1923), p. 142.
18. Ibid., pp. 136–145.
19. Charles Churchwell, *The Shaping of American Library Education* (Chicago: ALA, 1975), p. 27.
20. Ibid., p. 42.
21. Ibid., p. 62.
22. Ibid., p. 65.
23. Ibid., p. 86.
24. J. Periam Danton, *Education for Librarianships, Criticisms, Dilemmas and Proposals,* (New York: Columbia University, 1946).
25. Ibid., pp. 6-8.
26. Ibid., pp. 23-34.
27. Bernard Berelson, ed., *Education for Librarianship* (Chicago: ALA, 1949), p. 3.
28. Ibid., pp. 254-55.
29. Lester Asheim, ed.,*The Core of Education for Librarianship* (Chicago: ALA, 1954).
30. Ibid., p. 14.
31. Ibid., p. 52.
32. Ibid., p. 53.
33. Harold Goldstein, ed., *National Conference on the Implications of the*

New Media for the Teaching of Library Science (Urbana, Ill.: University of Illinois Graduate School of Library Science, 1963), 233 pp.
34. *American Library Directory* (New York: R. R. Bowker, 1948), p. 7.
35. Sarah R. Reed, "The Curriculum of Library Schools Today...", *Education for Librarianship: The Design of the Curriculum of Library Schools,* ed. Herbert Goldhor (Urbana, Ill.: University of Illinois Graduate School of Library Science, 1971), pp. 33-37.
36. Lester Asheim, "New Trends in the Curriculum of Library Schools", ibid, p.66.
37. F. William Summers and Russell Bidlack, "New Standards for Accreditation,"*American Libraries* (June 1972) : 658-660.
38. Lester Asheim, "Trends in Library Education — United States," *Advances in Leadership (5),* ed. Melvin J. Voigt (New York: Academic Press, 1975), p. 156.
39. Ibid.
40. Ibid.
41. *Standards for Accreditation, 1972* (Chicago: American Library Association),p.5.
42. Ralph W. Conant, *The Conant Report* (Cambridge: MIT Press, 1980), p. 177.
43. Ibid., p. 178.
44. Ralph W. Conant, "Conant Report — Reply to the Critics," *American Libraries* (January 1982): 35.
45. Saul Herner, "Brief History of Information Science," *Journal of the American Society for Information Science* 35 (May 1984): 157-63.
46. Robert S. Taylor, "Professional Aspects of Information Science and Technology," *Annual Review of Information Science and Technology (ARIST) 1,* ed. Carlos A. Cuadra (New York: Interscience, 1966), p. 19.
47. Melvil Dewey, "Our Next Half-Century," *Bulletin of the American Library Association* 20 (May 1926): 309-312.

BIBLIOGRAPHY

Advances in Librarianship, 5, edited by Melvin J. Voigt. New York: Academic Press, 1975.
American Libraries, (June 1972).
American Library Directory. New York: Bowker, 1948.
Annual Review of Information Science and Technology, 1, New York: Interscience, 1966.
Asheim, Lester, ed. *The Core of Education for Librarianship.* Chicago:

American Library Association, 1954.

Berelson, Bernard, ed.   *Education for Librarianship.*   Chicago: American Library Association, 1949.

Churchwell, Charles.   *The Shaping of American Library Education.*   Chicago: American Library Association, 1975.

Conant, Ralph W.   *The Conant Report.*   Cambridge: MIT Press, 1980.

"Conant Report − Reply to the Critics."   *American Libraries* 13 (January 1982).

Danton, J. Periam.   *Education for Librarianship; Criticisms, Dilemmas and Proposals.*   New York: Columbia University, 1946.

Dewey, Melvil.   "Our Next Half-Century."   *Bulletin of the American Library Association,* 20 (May 1926).

Goldhor, Herbert, ed.   *Education for Librarianship: The Design of the Curriculum of Library Schools.*   Urbana, Ill.: University of Illinois Graduate School of Library Science , 1971.

Goldstein, Harold, ed.   *National Conference on the Implications of the New Media for the Teaching of Library Science.*   Urbana, Ill.: University of Illinois Graduate School of Library Science, 1963.

Journal of the American Society for Information Science, (May 1984).

Vann. Sarah K.   *Training for Librarianship Before 1923.*   Chicago: American Library Association, 1961.

Stability and Change: Library and Information Science Education in the United States, 1985

Edward G. Holley
Professor and Former Dean
School of Library Science
The University of North Carolina
Chapel Hill, North Carolina, U.S.A.

INTRODUCTION

If one looks at the history of higher education in the United States in the last 100 years, he will find both remarkable stability and considerable change. Our rhetoric often leads our friends abroad to believe that cataclysmic change is an American way of life. We have done strange things to postsecondary education as it was known by our European ancestors. Since the mid-nineteenth century, we have embarked on programs of graduate education, technological education, and industrial education which are the envy of the world. In accordance with President Thomas Jefferson's declaration that no democracy could be ignorant and free, we have expanded formal education from kindergarten to post-doctoral study with the intention that no youth should be denied an equal opportunity to achieve the maximum of his or her intellectual potential.

With the advent of the GI Bill in the late nineteen-forties, and with the stimulus of President Lyndon Johnson's Great Society programs in the sixties, higher education has been particularly favored as an object of massive state and federal grants as well as private philanthropy. Currently more than twelve million persons are enrolled in some form of postsecondary education, either in community colleges, liberal arts colleges, or universities. Thanks to the Civil Rights movement in the sixties, more opportunities for the non-White population have been provided. This expansion of higher education in the post World War II period led many persons to believe that a new golden age was in store for the United States. In fact, the prosperity of the country during three of the four decades after World War II has lifted the level of material comfort for the average household in ways our ancestors could scarcely have imagined. Now we are promised new forms of technology, led by the computer, which will not only sustain our growth but lead to an "Information Age" of intellectual excitement and continued prosperity. Those who point out the problems we have *not* solved are derided for their lack of faith in the future. Prophets of gloom and doom have rarely held the upper hand in the U. S. body politic.

You will, I trust, forgive my relating this story of American "boosterism." However, only by understanding our basic framework can we grasp the position occupied by professional education in the United States. In many ways it is unique, and in no way more unique than in the confidence we have in education to solve all the problems of the world. That confidence is best seen in Clark Kerr's Godkin Lectures at Harvard, published in 1963 under the title *The Uses of the University*. Kerr postulated that education would do for the latter part of the twentieth century what the railroads had done in the late nineteenth century and the automobile had done in the early twentieth century. Despite some erosion in recent years, Kerr's view is still maintained by many persons, especially with the advent of high technology. "High tech" is clearly related to education – education at a very sophisticated level and with a need for employees to be upgraded continually to meet the development of even more advanced technology.

So the way ahead continues to look highly favorable for American higher education and especially for professional education which addresses technological concerns.

Yet despite our expansion of educational opportunity and our changes to keep in tune with society, the structure of higher education in the United States has changed little in the past 100 years. The American university remains basically an English undergraduate college onto which have been grafted Germanic graduate colleges and numerous professional schools. Most professional study in the United States comes *after* two years of under-graduate study. A few professional programs e. g. law, medicine, library science, follow four years liberal arts education. Some disciplines e. g. business, education, journalism, nursing, social work, still have undergraduate components, but the more sophisticated professional schools even in these disciplines have gradually abandoned work at the undergraduate level in favor of emphasis upon *graduate* professional education. (Winkler, 1985) A prestigious Association of American Colleges commission has castigated universities for the poor quality of undergraduate education and for permitting "vocational education" to take away from a first-rate undergraduate program. (Scully, 1985) There is considerable ferment in higher education as we grapple with the problem of making all persons "computer literate," as well as providing them with analytical skills in their own language, literature, history, and mathematics.

These higher education developments have profound implications for library and information science education. Do our professional programs need to look again at undergraduate work as a possible foundation for their graduate work or should they continue to insist that the MLS degree must remain the foundation for professional practice? Is there a role for library and information science schools in undergraduate education? Five years ago few library educators would have even entertained that suggestion. As a result of the program at the annual conference of the Association for Library and Information Science Education in January, 1985, that question is now receiving serious attention. The answer, however, may depend more on how university administrators view library education than what any association or group of associations may do. There are contradictory trends in higher education – one toward preserving integrity of liberal arts education and another toward providing computer literacy and information skills as necessary for an information based society.

EMERGENCE OF THE MLS DEGREE

As was true of most professional education, library science education began first as apprentice training. However, with Mevil Dewey's introduction of a library training program at Columbia University on January 5, 1887, the education of librarians became more formalized. Library schools were established in technical institutes, public libraries, and universities. Despite the technical emphasis, there was more to the training than mere techniques, as an examination of the courses and lectures clearly indicates. A certificate was awarded upon completing the course of study.

By the nineteen-twenties a fifth-year degree, the B.S. in L.S. or BLS degree, had become standard. The degree assumed some basic work in the liberal arts before library science courses were taken. After the famous C. C. Williamson report, library education moved into universities. By the thirties the American Library Association (ALA) had assumed responsibility for accreditation of library education programs. Several levels were recognized: advanced graduate library school, graduate library school, senior-undergraduate library school, junior-undergraduate library school, and "accredited for school-library work only" (16 hour curriculum). (White, 1976)

After World War II curriculum change came with incredible swiftness.

The basic degree changed from a fifth-year B. S. in L. S. to the master's degree.   By the late in the year 1949, twenty-seven of the then thirty-two accredited schools had either changed their basic degree from the B. S. in L. S. to the MLS or were in the process of doing so.   Two years later the ALA adopted a new set of standards which mandated the MLS as a basic professional degree.   There was some recognition in the profession that undergraduate programs were still needed for teacher-librarians, and concern was expressed for articulating the undergraduate programs with the new MLS degree programs.   However, within two decades the MLS degree had become the unquestioned standard entry level qualification for U. S. librarians.

THE MLS DEGREE TODAY

A recent ALA recruitment brochure, "Library and Information Careers in the 80s" asks the question "What education do you need?   The answer seems appropriate in the context of library and information science education in the United States in 1985:

> The more the better.   The basic education for professional positions is the master's degree in library science that builds on a broad foundation of undergraduate liberal arts study.
>
> Many employers require a master's degree from a graduate program accredited by the American Library Association.   There are a number of non-ALA accredited programs that also are sound for the preparation of librarianship but they may not lead to as great mobility or career flexibility.
>
> Most MLS degree programs can be completed in a calendar year if you are in school full-time.   Some may take 18 months or two years.   While there is a core of required courses, curricula can vary considerably in terms of electives and in-depth treatment of topics.   (ALA, OLPR, 1983)

These paragraphs summarize well the current position of librarianship as it is practiced today in the United States.   The beginning credential is the MLS degree from an ALA-accredited program.   The majority of persons who hold positions labelled "librarian" possess the MLS degree, and, often, additional graduate degrees, either in subject fields or in librarianship itself. Over 90 per cent of college and university librarians hold this degree, and most large public libraries and special libraries also select from a pool which contains such qualified persons. (Holley, 1985; Estabrook and Heim, 1980) The single exception is the school library group which still recognizes the teacher-librarian with 16-20 semester credit hours at the B. S. degree level.   Even that is changing as states like North Carolina revise their certification standards to require the MLS degree.

Despite this standardization of entry level qualifications, there are a number of well known librarians who do not hold MLS degrees; they are the exception not the rule. In recent years a debate has commenced on the necessity for the MLS degree. The attack on librarians in the federal service by the U. S. Office of Personnel Management, an ill-conceived effort to downgrade the position of librarians and thus reduce their salaries, is currently stalled, thanks to efforts in the U. S. Congress. (Robinson, 1983) Moreover, court attacks on the MLS degree as a requirement for professional positions, e. g. the Merwine Case in Mississippi, (Holley, 1984; 1985) have raised again the question of what the appropriate professional credential should be. There is thus the paradox of attacks on a credential which has upgraded the profession and an ambivalence among some librarians about defending their professional degree. Since my own stand on this matter is a matter of public record, I will not pursue that issue. Let me reiterate for the sake of this conference that the MLS degree, completed after four years of undergraduate liberal arts education, is currently *the* major credential held by American librarians, including those north of the border in Canada.

WHAT DOES THE MLS DEGREE PROGRAM CONTAIN?
LENGTH OF PROGRAM

Except for the seven Canadian Schools and five of the United States Schools, most ALA accredited master's degree programs represent thirty to thirty-six semester hours work beyond the bachelor's degree. Canadian programs have long required two academic years for completion. In the U. S., three schools, the University of California – Los Angeles, the University of Washington (Seattle), and the University of North Carolina at Chapel Hill require two academic years of work for the MLS, while the University of Chicago requires five quarters and the Louisiana State University requires 43 semester credit hours. (Holley, 1981) At the University of Illinois a master's degree is awarded after 30 units of work, but some students remain for the Certificate of Advanced Studies, essentially another year beyond the MLS degree. While it is possible that recent movements toward reintroduction of an undergraduate program could extend the length of some programs, the movement in the sixties toward four academic semesters instead of three seems to have ceased. (Bidlack, 1980, 1982; Holley, 1981).

CONTENT OF THE MLS PROGRAM

The content of library education programs (either one or two years in length) is scarcely standardized. Such programs range all the way from the highly structured (many requirements) to the highly unstructured. However, most master's degree programs have some kind of basic course requirements which reflect the traditional emphasis on the functions of acquiring, cataloging, classifying, and preparing materials for use, and then making these materials accessible to people through user services (reference, bibliographic instruction, database searching). A few schools have a full year of courses to be taken by all students. Others give students a maximum amount of freedom in selection of courses with very few courses required. This common body of material is usually designated "the core," and may be taught either as an integrated component of the program or as a series of independent courses with little apparent relationship to each other.

Nonetheless even within the frame work of the most structured program, some provision is made for specialization. Increasingly our colleagues in research librarianship, medical librarianship and special librarianship call for even more specialization to accommodate their needs. A partial response to their criticism has been the two-year programs, the sixth-year certificate programs, the doctoral programs and continuing education programs. Even those most committed to a one-year program recognize that very little specialization is possible in thirty semester credit hours. Unless one has had an unusually strong undergraduate program to introduce him or her to basic theory and practice in our increasingly fragmented field, or substantial experience in a library or other information agency, a one-year program now seems modest indeed.

In addition to the core and recommended courses for specialization, some programs include requirements for a comprehensive examination and a master's paper or thesis to be completed at the end of the course work.

A review of current catalogs indicates that the main features of traditional librarianship continue to be taught in most schools. That their content has changed to reflect the current trends and the development of new technologies, especially the computer, seems clear. As indicated above, the basics still emphasize how one acquires, organizes, and makes material available to users. In the January, 1985, *Library Quarterly,* Dean Herbert White of Indiana and his doctoral student, Marion Paris, reported on a survey of directors of academic, public, and special libraries to determine what they think constitutes a basic curriculum for a beginning librarian. The responses vary widely, as one might expect. (White and Paris, 1985)

Yet there are some common elements.   Here are the commonalities for academic and public librarians:

Academic Libraries	*Public Libraries*
Basic reference	Basic reference
Collection development	Collection development
Academic libraries	Public libraries
Personnel and human relations	Introduction to information science
Introduction to information science	
Organization of materials – Dewey	

Under various descriptions these commonalities are present in most U. S. library schools.   Incidentally, there was no evidence of consensus on a core among special librarians.

New to most programs within the past decade are courses in bibliographic data bases, information management, information storage and retrieval, online searching of data bases, measurement and evaluation of library and information services, indexing and thesaurus construction, and interpersonal relations.   The behavior of users has also become a topic for study and research.   Occasionally one can add to these courses topics in networking and consortia, records management, telecommunications, and systems analysis.   Thus far most library schools have attempted to integrate the newer elements with the old.   In other words, many library educators see library and information science education as two parts of a unified structure. Exceptions to this approach can be seen at Pittsburgh and, possibly, Drexel. Both offer undergraduate degree programs in information science and Pittsburgh also offers two master's degrees: one in library science and one in information science.   I would now like to turn your attention to the information science part of the MLS program.

THE INFORMATION SCIENCE COMPONENT
OF THE MLS CURRICULUM

The major concern among library educators is the information science component of the curriculum.   How should information science be taught? Where should it be taught?   What facets of it should be taught?   There is little agreement on these questions but most schools are wrestling with the questions in a serious way.

Initially, library schools introduced a course called "library automation." This course was designed to familiarize students with the emerging technology (chiefly OCLC), circulation machines, and other approaches to solving specific library problems. The early library automation courses were simply an "add-on" which bore little relationship to the other courses. Critics of these courses noted that the integration of computers into the total program was both urgent and necessary. These courses contained some basic information about the then-state of automation and a good deal of enthusiasm about future possibilities. Remembrance of that kind of course has been aptly described (if in sometimes exaggerated terms) as a movement away from the boredom and drudgery of three by five cards to a more challenging future in which machines did the routine work and the rest of us sat around cerebrating about the values of books, libraries and information.

In the last decade all library schools, however benighted, have added to that lonely course many other courses in the information area. Some schools have changed their curricula completely to reflect a behaviorist, technological, or managerial approach. Many schools now require program language skills and competence in database searching. Most accept their responsibility to give students "hands-on" experience with OCLC, RLG, UTLAS and bibliographic utilities generally.

With the advent of these courses has come a recognition of the need to broaden the scope of the library school and to change direction. Many library schools have recognized this change of direction or emphasis by adding to their titles some additional phrase "Library and Information Studies," "Library and Information Management," "Library and Information Service," etc. Skepticism about these name changes, such as that expressed by Richard De Gennaro, has had little effect on the bandwagon approach that has resulted in thirty-eight schools adding "information" to their titles. (De Gennaro, 1982)

Whether these title changes do indeed reflect a fundamental change in the curriculum is not always clear. Some schools with fairly traditional-sounding course titles are very much involved in the new approaches. Other schools with impressive course titles seem to be teaching the same old material under new rubrics. Yet, I would assert that no library school has been unaffected by the computer revolution of the last decade. OCLC terminals and microcomputers are now standard equipment in most library schools. No longer can any library school boast of its single terminal connected to OCLC, or its single course in library automation, as indications of its belonging to the modern world of librarianship. All of us are struggling to find the right combination of courses and experiences which will meet the needs of today's and tomorrow's student.

Two approaches to curricular development seem to be emerging: (1) a sharp delineation between the new discipline, information science, and the traditional discipline, library science, through the setting up of two distinct programs within a school; and (2) a concerted attempt to make information science an integrated part of the traditional library science program. At this point we have too little experience with either to make a judgement about which is best or whether the two should be permitted to go their separate ways.

If there is to be an integrated approach, without an undergraduate component, then a program longer than one year is probably inevitable. As Asheim has noted, a longer program will be necessary "because of the cumulative effect of new knowledge that does not displace old knowledge, and because of the higher degree of intellectual command of our subject matter that will be expected when support staff takes over many of the functions that once used to be in the job description of the librarian." (Asheim, 1982)

MLS INTERNSHIPS

Another major problem has been a sorting out of the perennial arguments about theory versus practice. There has been a revival of interest in internships. Many students have reacted negatively to the theoretical and research approaches to course content. So have many librarian-employers. Thus sixty schools now offer opportunities for paractical experience as a part of the formal curriculum. Six require such experience whether it is designated "field experience," "internship," or "work-study," the latter somewhat similar to cooperative engineering school programs. Others make internships optional. What appears to distinguish the new approach from the old "practice work" is a strong involvement of faculty with library supervisors and sudents in a planned program of professional development. (Holley, 1981)

Of course one might note that most library school students work in libraries during some portion of their degree program. However, this experience is normally seen as a means of supporting oneself through graduate school and not necessarily a valid professional training experience. No one has ever claimed that shagging books from the stacks, however necessary a task, is a "professional experience." Schools are now working more closely with librarians to introduce an element of professionalism into these activities.

Post-master's internships have been developed and operated in a number of places for a long time with the best example being the Library of Congress. The Iowa State and University of New Mexico programs have been described in the literature and the University of Michigan has developed its research library residency program. (Carter, 1980; Lemke, 1980; Trumpeter and Gherman, 1980) Other university research libraries are likely to follow Michigan's leadership with assistance from a new program of grants for residency programs developed by the Council on Library Resources.

That the issue of internships is a concern to the profession became apparent in a variety of forums in the last few years. Both library educators and their practicing colleagues want internships, so one can predict, given reasonable support, that the number of such programs will expand during this decade.

UNDERGRADUATE PROGRAMS IN LIBRARY AND INFORMATION SCIENCE

Although the master's degree has become the standard entry level qualification, undergraduate programs in library science continue to exist in many places. These programs, though, no longer serve as basic preparation for librarian-type jobs. Indeed, most graduate library schools prefer that their new students not bring with them any library science undergraduate courses when they enroll. Undergraduate courses are certainly not seen as the foundation for the master's degree, as was assumed to be the case after the introduction of the MLS degree as the basic entry level requirement by the 1951 ALA Standards. (Rufsvold, 1962)

Nonetheless, many library schools still offer some courses for under-graduates. Most of these fall into two categories: (1) preparation of school librarians, because many school systems still try to get by with teacher-librarians who have minimal preparation and therefore do not cost as much as the degreed librarian; and (2) bibliographic instruction courses to teach the thousands of undergraduates how to find their way amid the complexities of the modern university library system. In the latter case they also add to a school's FTE enrollment and thereby help justify a larger number of faculty. Some of my colleagues disagree with this cynical assessment, but evidence shows that there is little connection between most undergraduate library education programs and basic preparation for professional work in libraries today, the United States Office of Personnel Management, and the recent Merwine case in Mississippi State University, to the contrary notwithstanding.

Now emerging among the members of the Association for Library and Information Science Education is the possibility of reintroducing an under-graduate program in library/information science. The best expression of this point of view has been expressed by Evelyn Daniel, former dean at

Syracuse and current dean at North Carolina.   In a response to my paper at the Whistler Conference Dean Daniel noted:

> The study of information and how it is processed is a liberal art in an information society.   Our needs for basic knowledge of technical, conceptual and communication skills before entry into a graduate school are as strong as our needs for a broader understanding of the various more traditional disciplinary fields.   I suggest we need to consider a more closely articulated development of a strong liberal arts undergraduate program in information studies.   (Daniel, 1985)

If I understand Dean Daniel's position, she believes that the faculty of library/information science schools are in an excellent position to contribute to an undergraduate liberal arts program.   Certainly in an information age we cannot continue to produce undergraduates who cannot deal with the computer and with a wide variety of information sources.

This concept of assisting the university in achieving computer literacy for its undergraduates as well as providing a foundation for professional graduate work seems to me to have considerable merit.   That, however, is not the position of Pittsburgh and Drexel, both of which have developed undergraduate majors in information science for those students who wish to pursue careers as information specialists in various environments of business and industry.   There is a heavy emphasis upon computer skills, e. g. learning programming, file management, statistics, and user behavior skills.   Some of the courses are similar to those in library science, e. g. database management and online retrieval; others are quite different.

At the 1985 ALISE Conference on undergraduate degree programs there was a broad discussion of the opportunities as well as the problems in moving into an undergraduate program.   That the issue has resurfaced after 30 years is not surprising.   There is unquestionably a demand for computer literate persons but this demand comes from persons not necessarily interested in the traditional library.   Many of the B. S. degree graduates will find rewarding jobs in business and industry.   What is not yet clear is how much the new computer/information science degree programs will compete with information segments of programs in business administration, journalism, public health, and computer science itself.   As Richard De Gennaro has reminded us, "the library world will provide only one access point in the information age, albeit a very important one."   (De Gennaro, 1982).

In my opinion, based on the arguments in teacher education, it is naive to suggest that the tasks most employers expect to be performed by beginning librarians can be obtained from the simple technical skills that may be taught in modest courses at the undergraduate level. That basic information handling skills are needed by every college student I do not doubt. That library schools can provide those courses I also do not doubt. But that such courses provide anything more than a basic familiarity with the library and/ or information worlds, I doubt very seriously. Professional education at the level of a major probably cannot be incorporated into the undergraduate curriculum without doing harm to those basics the American Association of Colleges Commission says should be possessed by the well educated woman or man and which most of our citizens believe a BA or BS graduate should possess. (Scully, 1985) The current concern over the professionalization of the sciences, the weak courses in teacher training, and the emphasis in major universities on advanced graduate study in business, etc., plus the hue and cry over neglect of the humanities, seem unlikely to me to change radically the undergraduate English college concept of most colleges of Arts and Sciences in most universities.

JOINT-DEGREE AND THE SIXTH YEAR CERTIFICATE PROGRAMS

Also emerging in a number of schools are joint-degree programs and/ or relationships with other departments on campus. In essence, joint-degree programs enable an individual to secure two professional degrees in less time than the two degrees could normally be acquired separately. Included among the joint degree programs offered by twenty-six schools are business administration, history, pharmacy, social work, journalism, public health, and law. Such programs benefit not only library science students but also disciplines like history whose graduate enrollments have declined sharply over the past decade. Among the critics of such programs is Guy Garrison who has stated, "I am particularly alarmed at the hasty marriages evident in the proliferation of joint-degree programs...the library science content is sacrificed and the programs seem more directed at finding jobs for surplus humanities and social science graduates than toward preparing in-formation specialists." (Garrison, 1978) One has the impression that joint-degree programs have not attracted large numbers of students. They have undoubtedly been important for that small number who are involved, yet no one has worked out what the costs are in terms of faculty time, a library school's most expensive budget item.

Enrollments in sixth-year certificate programs are also modest. According to the ALISE *Library and Information Science Education*

Statistical Report, 1984, only five schools had as many as ten FTE post-master's students enrolled in sixth-year programs in the fall 1983. Although their educational value has been generally acknowledged, the sixth-year programs often take a disproportionate amount of faculty time and their economic viability appears questionable in the absence of outside funding.

In connection with joint-degree programs some mention should be made of archivists. The Society of American Archivists has long struggled with the problem of what is the appropriate preparation for archivists. (Berner, 1981; Helmuth, 1981) Some believe library education is the best preparation; others believe history departments can manage better. No one, however, has surveyed the field to examine the numbers and assess the potential. Meanwhile, a number of library schools offer courses in archives and have informal arrangements with history departments where individuals can build their own programs in the light of their objectives. There are also a few master's degree programs in archival management in history departments at various universities.

THE DOCTORAL PROGRAMS

The doctorate in library science has now been in existence for sixty years. Prior to World War II only the University of chicago offered such a program. There are now approximately two dozen schools with doctoral programs and they produce about sixty to seventy doctorates a year – not a large number by anyone's standards.

In the fall term, 1983, there were 498 doctoral students enrolled, 183 full-time and 315 part-time. The largest numbers (head count) were at Rutgers (62), Columbia (56), Pittsburgh (53) and Indiana (41). These figures probably include those who have completed course requirements, taken their qualifying exams, and then taken jobs while working on their dissertations, but who are required to be registered continually until they finish their degrees. (Some universities do not require continual registration).

Doctoral study is expensive, time-consuming, and important in meeting the research needs of the profession. Up to this point, possession of the doctorate has been lucrative for most who receive the degree. Many graduates become administrators or library educators where their research skills are presumably most needed. The degree titles range from the traditional PhD to the DLS (a professional degree, but the distinction is not very clear) to the DA (Doctor of Arts). Although the Carnegie Commission on Higher Education placed great hope on the DA as a teaching degree (in library science it is an administrative degree), universities and colleges have been as reluctant to accept this departure from the traditional doctorate as they were earlier to accept the EdD. Yet one would have to agree with William Summers that the most important improvement in the quality of library schools in the last thirty years has been the strengthening of the faculty through the requirement of the earned doctorate for most tenure-track appointments. (Summer, 1972)

QUALITY ASSURANCE

As discussions continue about the role of the MLS, undergraduate programs, sixth-year certificates, doctoral programs, and continuing education, many persons have raised the question of the quality of the current programs. The key question has become "How does one ensure quality and does accreditation serve that function well?" Many librarians believe it does not. They are joined by a number of citizens who have voiced unhappiness with regional accreditation as well as accreditation in other professional schools like business, medicine and law.

One of the most articulate critics of accreditation is Dean Herbert White who asked if there were not minimal levels of enrollment, faculty, and expenditures necessary for a library school to maintain in order to function effectively in today's complex world. (White, 1979) Others, including the present author, have echoed White's concerns. From the ALA Committee on Accreditation's open meetings have come a number of sharp criticisms of both the current standards and their implementation. This author, at the ALA Denver meeting in 1982, suggested that no library school could provide a program of adequate quality if its faculty number fewer than ten, if its student body comprises fewer than one hundred students, and if its total budget is less than $400,000.

Though many have agreed that there need to be some minimal numbers, few have rushed to embrace the so-called "Holley Criteria." The reasons are not difficult to find. According to Bidlack, if the Holley criteria were put into effect, sixteen United States schools would fail to satisfy all three criteria. (Bidlack, 1982) Only twenty-two of the sixty-three accredited United States schools fully meet the Holley criteria, though not surprisingly, only five of these twenty-two schools failed to appear on any of the lists of the fifteen best schools in Herbert White's study of the perception of quality by library educators and ARL administrators. (White 1981)

The White study has been a topic of frequent discussion among library educators since White first revealed his findings at the AALS meeting in Washington two years ago. Those in the top ten have not been bashful about publicizing their ranking – on and off campus.   As Bidlack has remarked, the White rankings are likely to have more influence on administrators making decisions about the future of their library schools than recent decisions of the ALA Committee on Accreditation.   (Bidlack, 1982)

Yet it is important to remember one important caveat White made: his research was a study of the perceptions of quality and not a study of quality itself.   Still, he also noted that there was remarkable similarity in the perceptions of the top ten by both library educators and ARL directors. One has to deal with perceptions, valid or not, and one also has to be concerned that fourteen of the seventy schools were not mentioned once by any of the 318 persons completing the questionnaire.

Since accreditation in the United States is voluntary and there are no government imposed standards, the process of accreditation is largely left to professional associations or groups of associations.   ALA has long been designated the accrediting agency for master's degree programs in library science.   Currently accredited library schools in the U. S. and Canada operate under the ALA Standards approved in 1972.   In view of the changes which have occurred in the past decade, ALISE requested a grant from the H. W. Wilson Company to convene a conference of interested associations for the purpose of discussing the current status of accreditation and how more associations could be involved.   (ALISE, 1985) At the same time the ALA Committee on Accreditation was discussing with the U. S. Department of Education (USDE) the possibility of funding a study of the accreditation process.   The ALISE Accreditation Conference occurred on September 16-18, 1984, and provided a "springboard" for the ALA Accreditation Project which began in January, 1985, under the direction of Robert M. Hayes, Dean of the Graduate School of Library and Information Science at UCLA, and current chairperson of the ALA Committee on Accreditation.   Six study groups are now working on the project under the direction of a steering committee from 11 library and information science associations.   Appropriately, the Committee should complete its work on a future direction for accreditation by the time of the Library Education Centennial Symposium scheduled for the summer of 1986.

SUMMARY AND CONCLUSION

What can one say about stability and change in library and information science education in the United States in 1985?

The basic pattern for educating librarians and the newer information specialists who work in libraries bears a strong resemblance to programs introduced a century ago. Professional education programs which purport to train persons to work in library and information agencies still have to introduce students to the processes of acquiring, organizing, storing, and disseminating information in a variety of forms. The way in which they do this has changed, for instance, as the typewriter and then the computer have replaced library handwriting as a technical skill. But the intellectual process of organizing material for efficient and effective use remains. The inclusion of more sophisticated techniques such as systems analysis or artificial intelligence or bibliometrics will change the content of programs but we are left with the problems of how to bring under control the world's massive output of records in a way that insures efficient use.

Library and information science schools will certainly give increased attention to information science (however defined), nonprint media, computer and satellite technology, video disks, economics, and user behavior. They will doubtless find that this must be done within the framework of the educational institutions of which they are a part. Relating to the information professions and the academic environment in which the schools are located will still be a fundamental problem for them. Both the profession and the university are important for the schools, but their goals are not the same. Library education must change as the profession itself must change but those changes should be the result of careful interaction among the diverse constituencies the schools try to serve. Certainly the dialogue now going on among the various Accreditation Project task forces can lead to significant improvements. One also hopes that the recent conferences sponsored by the Council on Library Resources and the Association of Research Libraries, and a number of individual meetings between deans and library directors will result in improvement of the MLS degree within the constraints placed on all of us. However, as White and Paris have noted, the issues before us are complex and defy simple solutions.

Will the academic structure remain the same? Will other degree patterns emerge and will we again incorporate undergraduate education into a formal education program for preparing librarians and information specialists? That is not at all clear at this moment. Some schools are moving in that direction but the results are not yet in.

Given the history and tradition of library education in the U. S., I would predict that the MLS will remain the basic entry level credential for those positions labelled "librarian." That the MLS will not remain the sole credential, especially for academic librarians, I have also predicted. If the ALA brochure is right, i. e. "the more [education] the better," then many librarians will add master's and doctoral degrees to their credentials, as well as continuing education through research institutes, technical institutes, and other non-traditional programs now being developed by the private sector.

So the current status of library/information science education in the U. S. is in a state of ferment. We believe this is healthy. Behind all our rhetoric and all our enthusiasm for change, though, there are likely to be some common elements that remain. Agreement on the *right element to keep* as well as the *new elements to adopt* is our major challenge. With my typical American optimism, I believe our profession will meet that challenge.

REFERENCE

American Library Association. Office for Library Personnel Resources. "Library and Information Careers in the 80s" Brochure. Chicago: ALA, 1983.

Asheim, Lester E. "Education for Librarianship: Present and Future," *The Bookmark* (University of North Carolina). 51-52 (1982): 149-162.

Association for Library and Information Science Education. "The ALISE/ H. W. Wilson Foundation Accreditation Conference," ed. Charles A. Seavey. *Journal of Education for Library and Information Science* 25 (Fall 1984): 63-162. The entire issue is devoted to the conference papers and related documents.

Association for Library and Information Science Education. *Library and Information Science Education Statistical Report*, 1984.

Berner, Richard C. "Archival Education and Training in the United States, 1937 to Present," *Journal of Education for Librarianship* 22 (Summer-Fall 1981): 3-19.

Berry, John. "New Threats to the MLS?," *Library Journal* 110 (Mar. 15, 1985): 23-26.

Bidlack, Russell E. "Fiscal and Economic Implications of the Two Year Programs in Library Education," in Richard L. Darling and Terry Belanger, eds. *Extended Library Education Programs; Proceedings of a Conference Held at the School of Library Service, 13-14 March, 1980.* New York: Columbia University School of Library Service, 1980.

————. "Some Economic and Demographic Realities Facing Library Education – An Expression of Personal Concern," Association of Research Libraries *Minutes*, 101st meeting, Arlington, Va., October 13-14, 1982. Also in *Public Library Quarterly* 4 (Spring 1983): 5-15.

Carter, Jane R. "Library Education, Curriculum," in *ALA World*

Encyclopedia of Library and Information Services. Chicago: American Library Association, 1980.

Daniel, Evelyn. "Commentary," in Basil Stuart-Stubbs, ed. *Changing Technology and Education for Librarianship and Information Science* (Greenwich, Ct.: JAI Press, 1985), pp. 77-82.

De Gennaro, Richard. "Libraries, Technology, and the Information Marketplace," *Library Journal* 107 (June 1, 1982): 1045-1054.

Estabrook, Leigh S., and Heim, Kathleen M. "A Profile of ALA Personal Members," *American Libraries* 10 (December 1980): 654-659.

Garrison, Guy. "Needed: A Core Curriculum for a Diversifying Profession," *Journal of Education for Librarianship* 19 (Fall 1978): 179-183.

Helmuth, Ruth W. "Education for American Archivists: A View from the Trenches," *The American Archivist* 44 (Fall 1981): 295-303.

Holley, Edward G. "Current Developments in Education for Librarianship and Information Science," in Basil Stuart-Stubbs, ed. *Changing Technology and Education for Library and Information Science* (Greenwich, Ct.: JAI Press, 1985), pp. 55-75.

________. "Defining the Academic Librarian," *College and Research Libraries* 46 (November 1985): 462-468.

________. "Extended Library Education Programs in the United States," *Advances in Librarianship* 11 (1981): 51-76.

________. "The MLS Degree as a Foundation for Professional Practice: Where Are We Headed?" *Journal of Educational Media and Library Sciences* 22 (Summer 1985): 329-342.

________. "The Merwine Case and the MLS: Where Was ALA?," *American Libraries* 15 (May 1984): 327-330.

Jacobson, Robert L. "University Education Deans Seek Elite Corps of School-teachers," *Chronicle of Higher Education* 30 (June 12, 1985):1, 16-17.

Kerr, Clark. *The Uses of the University.* Cambridge, Mass.: Harvard University Press, 1963.

Lemke, Antje B. "Library Education, Specialization in," in *ALA World Encyclopedia of Library and Information Services.* Chicago: American Library Association, 1980.

Robinson, Barbara M. "Librarianship under Attack," *Library Journal* 108 (Feb. 15, 1983): 347-348.

Rufsvold, Margaret I. "Undergraduate Library Education Standards – Problems of Implementation and Articulation," *Southeastern Librarian* 12 (Spring 1962): 10-24.

Scully, Malcolm G. "Panel Calls Bachelor's Degree Meaningless, Asks

Professors to Take Lead in Restoration," *Chronicle of Higher Education* 29 (Feb. 13, 1985): 1, 13.

Summers, F. William.   "The Emergence of Library Education," *American Libraries* 3 (July 1972): 791-794.

Trumpeter, Margo C., and Gherman, Paul.   "A Post-Master's Degree Internship," *Library Journal* 105 (June 15, 1980): 1360-1369.

Van House, Nancy A. *et al.*   "Librarians: A Study of Supply and Demand," *American Libraries* 13 (June 1983): 361-370.

White, Carl Milton.   *A Historical Introduction to Library Education Problems and Progress to 1951.*   Metuchen, N.J.: Scarecrow Press, 1976.

White, Herbert S.   "Accreditation and the Pursuit of Excellence," *Journal of Education for Librarianship* 23 (Spring 1983): 253-263.

————.   "Critical Mass."   Unpublished Speech, COA Open Meeting, ALA Conference, Philadelphia, July 11, 1982.

————.   "Critical Mass for Library Education," *American Libraries* 10 (September 1979): 468-70; 479-81.

————.   "Perceptions by Educators and Administrators of the Ranking of Library School Programs," *College and Research libraries* 42 (May 1981): 191-202.

White, Herbert S., and Paris, Marion.   "Employer Preferences and the Library Education Curriculum," *Library Quarterly* 55 (January 1985): 1-33.

Winkler, Karen J.   "Rigor Is Urged in Preparation of New Teachers," *Chronicle of Higher Education* 30 (March 6, 1985): 1, 13.   Complete text of the National Commission for Excellence in Teacher Education's report, "A Call for Change in Teacher Education," is included on pp. 13-21.

The Management of Libraries: An Assessment of Library and Information Science Curricula

Robert M. Hayes
Professor and Dean
Graduate School of Library and Information Science
University of California at Los Angeles
California, U.S.A.

INTRODUCTION

I've been asked to present an assessment concerning curricula for library and information science. That's a tall order, since there is such a diversity of contexts and views with respect to what should and does constitute a proper education in this broad field. Beyond that, there are changes occurring in the profession which make curricular assessment especially risky at this time. Automation is only one of them, although it is the one to which most attention has been paid. More fundamental is the general recognition, certainly in the United States but more generally throughout the industrialized world, that we are undergoing fundamental societal changes as "the information economy" becomes increasingly important. The field of library and information science must respond to those societal changes if it is to survive and prosper. There are persons far more qualified than I to comment, but there are things I do want to say, and that's why I'm grateful for the opportunity to do so.

My specific focus is going to be on an assessment of curricula for teaching management in libraries and information activities, since I regard that as a vital part of education in our field but one to which scant attention has been paid. However, I want to set the frame of reference for that specific discussion by discussing the more general context.

THE GENERAL CONTEXT

The fundamental question is, what constitutes a professional education?

It was the question uppermost in importance when Abraham Flexner, perhaps the key figure in identifying the elements of professionalism as well as of professional education, was examining education for medicine and social work. He asked whether social work was a profession and, in answer, compared it with the following six criteria:

1) Intellectual operations coupled with a high level of individual responsibilities
2) Raw material drawn from science and learning with a basis in systematic theory
3) Practical application
4) Educationally communicable techniques (a horrid way of stating it, but that was his language)
5) Tendency toward self-identification and organization as a group
6) Altruistic motivation − a code of ethics.

Since he first stated those criteria, he and others have repeatedly examined specific "professions" to determine whether they in fact were professions in that sense. Most recently, Amitai Etzioni did so, in a book called "The Semi-professions", and specifically included librarianship in his discussion. I am not here going to review those discussions, nor am I going even to ask the question implied by them. However, there are three points I would like to make with respect to the criteria and their applicability to library and information science.

The first point relates to the relative importance of the criteria. While I accept them as useful means of characterizing a profession, I think Flexner really missed the point or, at the least, failed to emphasize what I regard as the crucial criterion. It's buried in the first of his criteria, when he refers to "intellectual operations", coupled with large individual responisbilities. It's the individual responsibililty that to me really characterizes a profession, and I think that every other aspect is simply a component in fulfilling that primary criterion.

The second point relates to the responsibilities of library and information science and why they are important. In a sense, these may be self-evident, even truisms, but I think they need to be said. The responsibility of the librarian is three-fold:

1) to preserve the record,
2) to provide access to the information in the record,

3) to maintain the tradition that information is intrinsically important.

In a sense, these are parallel to comparable responsibilities of the physician, except that it is information rather than life itself that is responsibility of the librarian.   One might argue that life is infinitely more significant than information, and it would be hard to say otherwise, but I must record that historically people have identified "things of the mind" and the "preservation of the record of the past" as second in importance only to the maintenance of life. The responsibility of the librarian is by no means a trivial one.   The tradition that information is important is itself a central responsibility of the librarian. There is an intellectual element in it, which says that works of the mind are important; there is a social element involved, which says that information is essential to maintenance of society; there is a pragmatic element involved, which says that information is useful, in decision-making and in carrying out the day to day work of society.   Above all, there is the tradition, in our society at least, that open access to information is a right of every citizen, and the librarian has a responsibility to maintain that tradition.

The third point relates to the role of education for library and information science.   Given what I have just been saying, I think that it should be clear that I regard the primary function of eduction as that of providing the student with the sense of responsibility that goes with being a professional. That isn't to say that technical competence isn't important.   Obviously it is, but its role is in support of those responsibilities, not as an end in itself.   Beyond that, though, I want to comment on the responsibilities of the school in providing the educational experience.   Some have claimed that the school should serve as a "gate-keeper", as a means for controlling entry to the "profession" (that term taken in the narrow sense).   Such a view places primary emphasis on the evaluative aspects of an educational program, including evaluation of personal characteristics as well as of technical competence.   I personally reject that view.   I think the responsibility of the school is to the student, not to the profession.   It is to provide the student with the technical skills and the orientation that will characterize the information professional in the broadest sense of that term, in the sense that I've tried to imply in my characterization of the responsibilities of the professional.

THE DEVELOPMENT OF LIBRARY EDUCATION

With that as the general context, I do want to review briefly some of the stages in development of library education.   In doing so, I don't want to duplicate what others have said better than I will, but there are several key points that I want to highlight.

It's important to recognize that formal education for librarianship (or now, library and information science) is relatively recent. The first program was created (by Melvil Dewey) at Columbia University in 1887. Prior to then, education was essentially based on apprenticeship, but even after he started his program, it maintained a strong emphasis on "practical training" and in fact was moved from Columbia to the New York State Library in 1889. During the subsequent 30 years, other programs were established, but they too were highly practice-oriented and were located in technical institutes or in libraries (one of them, in the Los Angeles Public Library). The turning point occurred in 1923 when the Williamson Report recommended that library schools should be placed in universities and that their programs should put much greater emphasis on theoretical content (rather that on practice) and on development of research. Funded by Carnegie and Federick Keppel, it showed the need for truly academic education that would conform with the criteria that had been spelled out by Flexner.

Williamson proposed that "not more schools but better schools were needed", that the curricula should "provide for the first year a general program in basic library subjects followed by a second year devoted to specialization".

I think it is important to note that from the beginning, the basis for librarianship was essentially humanistic. It grew up in that kind of environment; the librarians tended to be drawn from such backgrounds. But the effort to integrate the library school into academy carries its own imperatives, and one of them is the need for "research". That was recognized at the Chicago Graduate Library School, and led to the work by Louis Round Wilson to incorporate the social sciences and integrate them with the humanistic traditions. Shera describes the Chicago school as it was under Louis Round Wilson. Of particular interest is the fact, as Shera pointed out, that the students continued to be "humanists".

In making these comments, I am not making pejorative comparison between the humanities and the sciences. Each of them is equally important in its own frame of reference. The problem, though, is that our field is an applied discipline, much though we may be trying to establish a theoretical foundation of our own. That means that the tools that are used, the methods of research, even the kinds of problems identified as suitable for research are usually based upon the traditional academic disciplines. They may be the tools, methods, and problems typical of the social sciences – sociology, history, psychology – of the humanities – bibiliography, textual analysis – or of mathematics – statistics, models. But increasingly, they are also drawn from the other applied disciplines – computer science and management, especially. Despite that derivative character of the research, however, there is a discipline for the field itself, and the fact that the methods may be drawn from other disciplines doesn't detract from the value and importance of that discipline or from its separate identity. The discipline is in the focus on a particular set of problems in the context of a particular kind of institution. The problems are those in the formalization of the processes in the handling of recorded information; the institution is the library (or one of its current reincarnations). And that discipline makes for proper research and stimulates creative minds in a way that would not be possible without it. Furthermore, the discipline relates directly to the primary instructional role of the school in the sense that the problems relevant to our discipline are precisely those about which the faculty need to be creative in order to teach the up-coming generation of professionals.

Because of this emphasis on practice, the crucial problems for research grow out of and are identified in present or historical professional practice or are those that the most creative minds can identify as likely to be significant to future practice. The point is that the research cannot be separated from the context without losing the most crucial aspects of it. That means that the faculty must maintain continuing contact with the profession, must be aware of the most current issues and trends in the field, must be leaders in the identification of problems and methods for solution of them. This puts the faculty in an uncertain, ambiguous, ill-defined position between academic research and applied research. And it is this that makes it so difficult to base research in library and information science solely on the humanistic disciplines.

The problems in developing a research discipline, though, have been nearly insurmountable. Danton's criticism it seems to me is especially relevant:

> "...library schools are not training for leadership... they are attempting to turn out librarians who will be 'all things to all people' – at the very least to all libraries of one or another broad type...."

He goes on further to state criticisms about "...the lack of adequate connection with a theoretical discipline to serve as its foundation...", the inability to meet the demands for librarians "...with strong subject specialization and scholarship...", that library schools had been content to follow rather than to lead.

But the groundwork was there so that when the intellectual ferment of the 50s began there was a context in which research in library and information science could develop.   Suddenly, the need for "information" was recognized in areas where it had previously been only subliminal.   Demands for improved "information for science" combined with the efforts to utilize computers for information handling and resulted in adding new dimensions to the field, both as a profession and as a research focus.

The reason that the effort to utilize computers has forced increased interest in research is really quite simple.   To program a computer, we must have formalized the processes it's to carry out.   There is no other way to do it.   But that means that what may have been "understood" by the practitioner must now be analyzed.   Furthermore, the decision as to whether or not to use the computer is a complex combination of objectives (always difficult to identify and more difficult to measure), benefits, and costs.   For us to make that decision effectively has required a much clearer understanding of all three of those — objectives, benefits, and costs.

The result over the past twenty to thirty years has been a steady increase in the amount and I think in the quality of the research carried out in the field of library and information science.   And I want to make it very clear that I am not equating either amount or quality with the "information science" component.   What I'm trying to do is identify the climate that has led to this third stage — the research stage.

I think it is important to note, though, that the MLS degree is still the focus of every library school in the United States.   At UCLA, it represents over 85 % our enrollment (130 out of 150 students).   And unlike some academic disciplines the master's degree is the expected terminal degree rather than being an interim degree or a consolation prize.   This places a specific burden upon library school faculty to assure that that primary focus is adequately served, that the graduates of it are able to move rapidly into professional practice, and that the curriculum and education are completely current with professional practice.   But that also means that the natural focus of attention is on the professional curriculum and educational program, which creates a natural tension between that concern and the imperatives of research and academic respectability.   In some schools, that tension is the source of conflict and divisiveness, with the professional curriculum taught by staff not oriented toward or qualified for research (frequently by part-time staff, in fact) and the research, PhD oriented curriculum taught by the "real faculty".

SPECIALIZATION

So we have seen library education move from a first stage of apprentice training to a second stage of academic education to a third stage, in which the research basis has been developing. Now I think we are moving into a fourth stage, in which there will be increasing emphasis on specialization. The beginning of it may lie in the efforts of the Medical Library Association to increase the qualifications of its members; that started some 20 years ago. The climate for it today though is much richer. The major evidence is the increasing demand for "management competence". Since I regard this development as one of immense importance, I'd like to focus directly on it.

As it presently is, each school professes to cover virtually every specialty encompassed by our field and to do so at every desired level of competence. School librarianship ? We each cover it. Medical or law librarianship ? We each cover them. Academic or public or special librarianship ? We each cover them. Name a specialty, and each school will claim to cover it.

The problem is compounded by the requirement for accreditation by the ALA that the graduates of an accredited program must be able to function at an entry level position in any kind of library.

And I'm sure that each school accomplishes exactly that. In some respects, it's essential that they do so, in view of the fact that few graduates can determine exactly what specialty they will find as their first job. Even fewer entering students are even aware what the possible specialties are or which ones will be of interest to them. Furthermore, each school serves a geographic area, providing the source — sometimes the only source — for personnel for the full range of libraries in that region. So I'm not questioning the value or validity of trying to serve the full range of specialties. But I am questioning the level at which we can serve them.

To be specific, it seems to me that one can distinguish perhaps five levels of competence applicable to every specialty:

Vocational Competence. The ability to perform identified tasks effectively.

Entry-level Competence. The ability to begin work as a professional, meaning that there is not only vocational competence but the sense of responsibility that is essential to the professional.

Fully Professional Competence. The competence to be expected of the professional after perhaps a year of experience, gained either on the job or through appropriate, supervised field experience.

Managerial Competence. The competence required to manage an information activity, either as an entity (if large enough to require management) or as part of a larger entity.

Problem-solving Competence. The ability to identify problems that need to be solved and that can be solved, to acquire and analyze the data needed to solve them, and to effect the solutions.

Although I have identified a range of competencies, I should make it clear that I'm not suggesting that immediate graduates of a library school program will be hired initially at other than entry-level professional positions. Some may even be hired at vocational level (paraprofessional) positions. The issue isn't what the first job will be; it's what the individual knows and is, in principle, capable of doing.

If a school professes to provide its graduates with more than entry level professional competence in a specialty, there should be clear evidence that its program meets some standards appropriate for measuring how well it does so. It seems to me that this is an issue that the current Standards for Accreditation do not address. As a result, some of the specialties — medical and law librarianship, in particular — have established criteria for certification of individuals, though not of the programs that may have professed to prepare them.

Thus, I agree with Conant that the lever may be the Standards for Accreditation. A national planning effort could identify the additional requirements by which to measure the extent to which an academic program met its professed aims. The accreditation process might then require each school to identify exactly what specialties it covers and, for each, the level of competency that it professes to provide. The requirements in a given specialty, for a given level of competence, may well be different from those of other specialties, for the same level of competence.

The objective in this suggestion is to provide an incentive for each school to develop faculty, programs, and resources that would be consistent with high levels of competence in chosen specialties, while preserving the essential requirement of providing at least entry-level competence in virtually every specialty. The result would be to create "centers of excellence" in specific specialties.

"Management" and "problem solving" competencies represent the level that I think the best schools aspire to provide. Doing so involves a complex combination of objectives. We must provide the person being educated with motivation, with understanding of context and objectives, with personal attributes that make for a good manager, with technical skills that will assure competence in performance, and with research skills that are the basis for effective problem solving.

That there are needs is evident. If nothing else, the focus of the Council on Library Resources on this area, with respect to academic research library management, represents the allocation of what are, for library education, major resources.   The number of management "seminars", "workshops", and other tailored course work further substantiates the fact of interest.   In a recent paper, Rutherford D. Rogers discussed the particular circumstances of the moment that seem to be relevant in the academic library context:

1. Sheer size of collections and budgets
2. Increased rate of acquisitions
3. Increased demand for services
4. Staff growth and increased specialization
5. Increasing numbers of rare book and special collections
6. Usage of computers
7. Usage of microforms
8. Usage of networks and other forms of cooperation
9. Concern with copyright
10. Preservation problems
11. Effects of international standards
12. Range of sources of financial support
13. Organizational complexity

There are obviously important issues that make the management of libraries of all kinds a matter of significance.   But I think the concern is much more fundamental, reflecting not so much specific problems as something else.   Why are we concerned about library management?   In fact, my own view is that libraries are relatively well managed, that they operate as "frugal systems" that perform their work with optimum balance of needs and resources, that they have a role in society of unheralded importance and that they fill that role with minimal resources allocated to them.   And they have done this without recognition and praise for the quality of their management.

When I review the range of problems that I think library management has handled better than the management of other institutions, I really begin to wonder why the issue of management is of such concern.   There is an element of self-flagellation involved, I suppose.   There is certainly the general perception of the library as a "passive, archival" organization, which therefore really couldn't be managed very well.   There is the perception of "information transfer" functions that the library could, or should, assume but that the library's management doesn't seem to be able to handle.

But the facts are that libraries have handled those functions and done so very well.   The facts are that libraries have handled automation better than most organizations.   In many respects, they have been in the van of innovation (thinking particularly of the National Library of Medicine and its pioneering work in development of on-line access to data).   The facts are that libraries have handled issues of social importance better than most organizations.   They again have been in the van of providing service to various groups of the population — decades in advance of most other agencies.   The facts are that libraries have dealt with the "information revolution" more effectively and more immediately than most organizations.   They have been in the van of developing new information services, new methods of information handling, new structures for information distribution.

Someday, it would be worthwhile to identify a number of developments, such as I have just listed, and evaluate the extent to which various kinds of organizations — industrial, commercial, academic, governmental — have been both innovative and successful in handling them.   I conjecture that the library will show up as among the best, not the worst.

And that all reflects good management, good balancing of resources with requirements, good determination of priorities, good motivation of staff. Why then does the library profession then go repeatedly through this process of self-flagellation?   Why does it strive to solve problems that it really is solving very well?   Of course, part of the answer is that by being continually self-critical, by continually trying to do a better job, the professional does indeed assure that there will be good results, not bad.

But that doesn't answer the underlying question of why the profession goes through this process.   I have my own picture, relating to the motivation that leads people to this profession, and I'd like to present that picture because it embodies many of the fundamental problems that we face in the educational process.

Consider the typical student choosing to enter a library school.   The odds are three to one in the United States that the student is a woman (although I understand the ratio of men and women in Canada is much more even); the odds are four to one that the student is from the humanities or social sciences.   The odds are overwhelming that there is a positive aversion to "management", not an attraction to it, the student far preferring to work with people as colleagues and friends rather than to "manage" them.   The student almost certainly is of high intelligence, with excellent abilities in written and oral communication and with a deep respect for intellectual pursuits.   The student has a deep sense of responsibility both to self and to society, but there is a rejection of the values and priorities that characterize "business".   (In fact, it was probably the combination of intellectual interests and social concern that led the student to choose academic work in the humanities and social sciences.) Beyond that, though, there is a real fear of anything smacking of mathematics, so any coursework involving numbers was assiduously avoided. The student is what I have called "abysmally innumerate".

Now consider that student during the MLS education. The student loves the courses on service to various population groups (such as children, especially); loves the courses on literature; tolerates the courses on reference; dislikes the courses on cataloging; loathes the course on "management"; fears the course on library automation (though discovering that really it's not all that bad and in fact does superbly, once past the fears). If given the chance, the student concentrates all of the time and energies on the courses that are loved, begrudging every minute spent on those required in "management" or "the computer".

And now that student graduates, goes to work, and given the inherent abilities, within one to two years becomes a manager — a department head, a branch head, a unit head. Indeed, with the increasing use of library technical assistants, even the recent graduate of a professional program will almost certainly have major supervisorial responsibililties. And if the library is small enough, the new graduate may be thrust into the position of responsibility for everything in the operation. The new manager suddenly needs a host of practical skills — not the interpersonal skills, although there are problems there that anyone has, but the technical skills — that simply are missing. The librarian accuses the school of having been too "theoretical" and of not providing the practical knowledge needed actually to manage a library operation. But the new manager also discovers that he or she can function well as a manager, that the professional knowledge really is good, that the inter-personal skills are adequate, that the technical skills can be learned "on-the-job" or are handled by others and therefore don't depend upon one's own knowledge.

And as the career advances, experience grows, skills become as good as anyone's, inherent abilities to manage bring the responsibility that can be well handled. But the librarian carries along a residue of the initial gestalt of values, of views of what library schools failed to provide, of what are seen as personal gaps and deficiencies. So the librarian says, "We need to have better education for library management."

HOW DO CURRICULA MEASURE UP?

What are the means by which we can meet the needs of that person and of the profession as a whole?

Through pre-requisites for admission to library school
Through coursework in the library school which provides a general introduction to management concepts and techniques

Through courses in the local, friendly school of management

Through specialization in the library school, with coursework and independent study that develops technical knowledge

Through requirements that force the student to gain "problem-solving" competence

Through internships or other "practica" that give supervised professional and managerial experience, either during the lilbrary school program or subsequently

Through tailored programs, especially post-MLS

Through other forms of "continuing education"

In the following comments, I'm going to examine each of these in turn, identifying what I see as the advantages and problems associated with each. In doing so, I will draw heavily upon my own personal knowledge, based on our experience at UCLA, since the published literature, which I have reviewed as thoroughly as I could, simply provides little guidance concerning other programs.

PRE-REQUISITES

Almost universally in the United States, the pre-requisites for admission to programs of library and information science are minimal, limited simply to graduation from an undergraduate curriculum with acceptable grades and, in some cases, an acceptable performance on a standardized test (typically, the Graduate Record Examination). The stated objective is to assure that the student has a "broad liberal arts background".

If I had my own wishes satisfied, library school students would come to our program prepared with a range of skills — in mathematics, in computer programming, in accounting. But alas such is not the case. As I've pointed out, the candidates for library school have assiduously avoided any numerical or even analytical demands.

However, the faculty at UCLA did decide that we should specify two requirements for admission in addition to the then existing foreign language requirement: 1) a college level course in statistics and 2) competence in a standard computer programming language. Of course, if we strictly enforced those two, we would have virtually no students, so I, as dean, can admit students under the proviso that they must complete all of the admission requirements before the beginning of their second year. The crucial point is that, since these are admission requirements, the student gets no credit for coursework taken to complete them, so there is no degradation in the quality of the professional program.

The rationale for these admission requirements has been well spelled out and I think is quite valid. To summarize, all three requirements are considered to be essential to the instructional process. We want to deal with material in a variety of languages, so we want the student to have the discipline of learning at least one foreign language; we want to utilize quantitative methods in a number of courses, but especially in the management and information science courses, so we want evidence that the student can handle numerical processes; we utilize computer-based methods throughout the program, in cataloging , reference, and management, so we want the student to understand the nature of computer processing. In each case, the competence must be solid and technical rather than simply descriptive. A course in the literature of a foreign country, however valuable it may be culturally, doesn't give facility with the language itself; a description of statistical methods doesn't provide the ability actually to perform statistical analyses; a survey course on computer systems doesn't provide the ability actually to control what the computer does.

The relationship of the additional two requirements to management skills is multiple. First, they are powerful management tools and our graduates should feel more comfortable with them than otherwise. Second, by requiring them for admission, we take a giant step toward crossing the psychological barrier that numerical concepts represent. Third, in principle, it permits *us to move* further and faster into the technical skills of management themselves. Fourth, it provides a powerful screening tool on applicants, eliminating those of faint heart, unwilling to risk the challenges of our program and its emphasis on preparation for management responsibility.

Does increasing the requirements for admission accomplish these purposes? That's difficult to answer, although I think the answer is yes. I do know that the numerical competence of our students, at least as measured by the quantitative and analytical scores on the GRE, has greatly increased. While the number of applicants remained constant, the average quality increased and admissions are to the same number as they ever were. We have been able to demand increasingly more of our students in the program, although with periodic complaints about the workload.

Do I recommend this same approach for other schools? Frankly, yes. I think we need the kind of increased demand in these areas that doing so would present. As it is, an increasing number of schools are requiring statistics and/or computer programming within their MLS programs, so the problem isn't one of the ability of the students. My question is, why water down the professional program itself by devoting time to what are really underlying skills ?

In any event, one means for increasing the level of management preparation is the use of admission requirements.

MANAGEMENT COURSES IN THE LIBRARY SCHOOL

Now, let's examine how management is taught in the library school itself. I have recently had occasion to review the required or "core" courses of the several accredited programs in library and information science. About half of the programs require a single course that covers general library management. The titles vary ("The library as an organization", "Library organization and management", "Management of libraries", "Library administration", "Principles of library management and automation", "Information facility management", "Management of libraries and information centers", "Management environment of the library", "Current issues and library management", "Theory of library administration", etc.), but the overall purpose of these courses appears to be clear. They are concerned with general management principles, in a library context, to be sure, but not for specific types of libraries. An additional ten percent of the programs require a course concerned with a type of library or information activity (public, school, academic, etc.), which presumably include coverage of management issues relevant to that specific context. Another 15% or so of the schools require a general introduction to librarianship or "core course", which usually covers management principles as a module. The remaining 25% of the schools apparently do not require any coverage at all of management.

It seems clear that general introductions and "core courses" are unlikely to provide much substantive detail about management; there simply are too many things specific to the profession that need to be covered. Even courses devoted to specific types of libraries are likely to devote only minimal time to management issues, even in the specific context; there are just too many aspects of a professional character that need to be covered. And many of the courses specifically devoted to management must cover many more issues than management as such (judging from titles and course descriptions, anyway). Overall, it would seem that fewer than 25% of the programs require as much as a quarter or semester course in management (say 40 to 45 class contact hours); about 50% of the programs probably require no more than 20 class contact hours in management; the remaining 25% apparently do not require any course work at all. It's debatable how many concrete management skills can be learned in 20 class contact hours (plus the associated time for preparation and personal study), but I'm convinced that there isn't enough time to provide more than what I'll call "descriptive instruction".

How about those courses that do devote a considerable time to management — say a full quarter or semester?   What do they provide ?   In preparation for this talk, I've reviewed the literature and textbooks concerned with instruction in library management.   It is all, every bit, "descriptive instruction" — "case studies", theoretical constructs, descriptions of "organizational structures", illustrations.   The work required of the student is of the same kind.   In other words, there is nothing, in any of the material I've seen that is identifiably used in instruction, that requires the student to learn budgeting, accounting, personnel procedures, ordering forms and procedures, management use of information, costing, performance measurement.   It's comparable to teaching reference without requiring the student actually to examine and to use specific reference materials, to teaching cataloging without requiring the student actually to use LC subject headings and to catalog specific books, to teach bibliography without requiring the student to prepare an actual bibliography.

In these general management courses, heavy emphasis is placed on the problems in inter-personal relation, in motivation of people, in setting objectives; problems are identified in working with governing boards, in setting goals for various levels of supervision.   But there is nothing that requires the student to create job descriptions or to produce procedure manuals. Wheeler and Goldhor, certainly one of the classic texts of the field, devote one fifth of the structure of the book — one out of five parts — to these "administrative" aspects, but the actual text is only about one-twentieth of the book (31 pages out of 560).   But that's where the action is; that's where the librarian must exercise the technical skills of management.   And that's where our library education has failed.

What's missing ?   Why is it missing?   And is it important that it's missing?   I think I've made clear what is missing, but let me say it again.   It's the solid technical skills, the ones that give the librarian the ability to deal with financial people, to negotiate with funding agencies, to handle personnel matters, to deal with the substance of management rather than the form.   Why is it missing ?   That's a much more complex question.

First, there simply isn't the time, even in a full course involving 40 to 45 hours of class contact, to provide both the descriptive orientation and the solid technical substance.   Second, in the traditional one-year MLS program, there isn't the time overall to give the student the opportunity to gain these skills.   Third, most library school faculty reflect the same orientation that I have described for the student.   Even those that teach management prefer to deal with the descriptive components rather than the technical ones;

it's just easier not to fight the battle of forcing students to learn something they are averse to learning.

Is it important that these solid technical skills are missing from the traditional MLS curriculum?   I think it is, despite what I've said and believe about libraries really being superbly managed.   I hear my colleagues say that the technical skills can be provided by support staff and that the librarian should concentrate on the "professional" aspects of the management.   But I know how necessary it is to effective management to have the technical understanding.

And there are some kinds of library specialties for which the technilcal skills of management are absolutely essential.   My own professional focus has been on information system analysis and design, both generally and in library contexts.   My experience is that in that area it is vital to know managerial accounting, systems and procedures, and scientific management.   From the list I've presented from the Rudy Rogers paper, I conclude that academic research library management is another context in which those same skills are equally essential.   Frankly, I suspect that other contexts of library management are no different.

It was recognition of these needs that led me to establish a degree program, the Master of Science in Information Science (Documentation), within the UCLA program fifteen years ago as a two year program.   There simply needed to be time enough for the student to gain these technical skills. Furthermore, the library school courses then, and even now, didn't provide those skills, even in the UCLA program, which demands about as much in this respect as any program in the United States or Canada.   So at that time, and still, I turned to the Graduate School of Management at UCLA for the answer.

COURSEWORK IN SCHOOLS OF MANAGEMENT

The typical professional MBA program requires courses in accounting, personnel management, and marketing that provide exactly the kinds of technical skills to which I have been referring.   Of course, it would be irrational and even impossible to require our student to take that set of core management courses, valuable though the skills would be.   But at least some of those courses would give the fundamental orientation that I wanted the students to have, and I identified "managerial accounting" as the one that was central in importance.   It was therefore a required course for the MSIS degree and then, when our MLS program became a two year program, it became a requirement for the information science specialty in the

MLS.

Of course, once the two-year MLS program had been launched, it became possible to expand the offerings within the School in the area of management so as to provide students with other specializations the opportunity to gain management skills within the courses presented by the School — personnel administration and space planning were two specific courses added. I must confess to the feeling, however, that management courses are probably best handled by the school of management and that our students ought to take them there.

There are problems, though, of which I am painfully aware. They can be roughly grouped in three categories:

1) administrative, 2) students, 3) substance.
While the first two are important, it is the substantive one that is most generally significant. First, at an intellectually trivial but practically important level, the examples used in teaching management to management students are predominantly drawn from the world of business. Focus rightly is on issues of profitability and associated practices in accounting and in management. Even when examples may be drawn from the "not-for-profit" sector, they are likely to be remote from libraries. We desperately need suitable instructional material that will be meaningful to the library school student and the future library manager. Fortunately, we are beginning to have a core of such materials from the ARL Office of Management Studies (their SPEC Kits), but they haven't become an integral part of the instruction in schools of management. But second, and far more important, is the fact that management philosophy and accounting principles have not yet even begun to recognize the significance of "information" as an economic resource. As a result, the traditional accounting practices almost totally fail to provide the tools needed for effective management of information resources. The studies of the "information economy" (by Machlup, by Marshack, by Porat) are beginning to identify the magnitude of the phenomenon, but the accounting profession hasn't even begun to deal with it. As a result, library school students must struggle to reconcile issues that even the researchers haven't resolved.

SPECIALIZATION IN THE LIBRARY SCHOOL

I now turn to perhaps the most important means for management education in the context of the formal MLS program. It's specialization, and it really is meaningful possible only in the framework of a two-year program.

As I pointed out, the introduction of the two-year program at UCLA permitted us to add coursework specific to management — personnel, space planning, and systems analysis in particular — but that's only the starting point. There is now time for students to take the coursework in the school of management or elsewhere. There is the requirement for a "specialization paper" in which the student specializing in management can develop a topic in depth and in the process learn more about management than could be given by any number of courses.

To me, the most important aspect of specialization is the requirement of a "specialization paper", in which the student must identify a "solvable problem". The crucial thing isn't what that problem may be or how deep it may be, but that the student must identify it and solve it. That embodies all the essential elements of problem-solving competence, perhaps the most important qualification for professional success.

I don't think I need to spell out details of specialization in management or related areas, such as information system analysis and design. Let me simply say that we have become increasingly specific about the courses required for them, and we include courses in the management school (managerial accounting in particular) as well as in other schools and departments.

INTERNSHIP

Internships have value both within the MLS program, as exemplified by those we provide, and after completion of the first professional degree, as exemplified by the Library of Congress internships and the one sponsored by the Council on Library Resources — their "management interns". The value is self-evident I think in the opportunity to work under supervision and to observe library managers "in operation", as they carry out their day-to-day work. In the case of the LC interns, of course, much more is involved than "management", but the program is designed to provide the interns with the kind of experience across-the-board that would otherwise be impossible and that will give the best candidates for management responsibility the opportunity to demonstrate it.

The internships within the UCLA program also cover much more than management, and most of them in fact are focussed on professional issues, not managerial ones. But there are sufficient opportunities for management experience to make this a most significant means for management training.

TAILORED PROGRAMS & OTHER FORMS OF
CONTINUING EDUCATION

With the relative paucity of coverage of management issues in the typical curriculum on library and information science, there should be little wonder at the repeated requests from librarians for the schools to fill the gap with special programs, tailored to the needs of the practicing librarian as parts of programs of continuing education.

The problem, though, is that the school of library and information science is poorly equipped to provide such programs except in very specific, highly tailored contexts.   For one thing, while the rhetoric may imply a real demand, actual enrollments in continuing education courses rarely are sufficient to cover the costs.   For another thing, all of the factors that limit the coverage of the field of management within the standard MLS curriculum apply with even greater force to the continuing education context.

There have been some notable successes however.   I think especially of the ARL management training institutes and of the Senior Fellows program conducted at UCLA under sponsorship of the Council on Library resources.   In the latter program, which has been now given three times over the past four years, there is specific emphasis on managerial concerns.   There is a formal course on "managerial accounting"; there is a research seminar for group discussion of topics of general management concerning preservation, economics, and the future developments of automated systems.   The time involved − now at four weeks in residence during the summer − is adequate to provide full in-depth experience.

SUMMARY

In this talk, I've tried to give a picture of the following issues:

What are the elements involved in professional education ?
How have those elements developed in our field ?
What is the role of specialization ?
What are the levels of competence ?
How can managerial and problem solving levels of competence be achieved ?
How does all of that relate to curricular assessment, with special emphasis on education for management ?

In the presentation, I have placed my emphasis on education for management because I feel it is the single greatest gap in current curricula in library and information science professional education.

REFERENCES

Conant, Ralph W. *The Conant Report: A Study of the Education of Librarians.* Cambridge, Mass.: MIT Press, 1980.

Danton, J. Periam. *Education for Librarianshilp.* Paris: Unesco, 1949.

Davis, Donald G., Jr. "Education for Librarianship". *Library Trends* 25 (July 1976): 113-134.

Dewey, Melvil. "Apprenticeship of Librarians". *Library Journal* 4 (May 1879): 148.

Etzioni, Amatei. *The Semi-professions and Their Organization.* New York: The Free Press, 1969.

Flexner, Abraham. "Is Social Work a Profession?". *School and Society* 1 (26 June 1915).

Hayes, Robert M. "Managerial Accounting in Library and Information Science Education". *Library Quarterly* 53 (July 1983): 340-358.

Shera,Jesse H. *The Foundations of Education for Librarianship.* New York: John Wiley, 1972.

Wheeler, Joseph L. and Goldhor, Herbert. *Practical Administration of Public Libraries.* New York: Harper & Row, 1962.

Williamson, Charles C. *Training for Library Service: A Report Prepared for the Carnegie Corporation of New York.* Boston: D.B. Updike, 1923.

The Role of Practical Work in Library and Information Science Curricula

Rupert Hacker
Professor and Director
Department of Librarianship
Bavarian Civil Servants' College
Munich, Federal Republic of Germany

INTRODUCTION

The question of how theory and practice should be combined in library education is a permanent issue which has, almost since the beginning of the present century, generated controversial discussions by library educators and library practitioners.   It is true that there is general agreement nowadays, that a professional education must be based both on theory and practice, because every profession "rests on mastery of a body of knowledge on the one hand and mastery of professional skills on the other".[1]   This dual foundation of education for librarianship is valid, irrespective of whether this education is established on a university level or not.   There is dispute, however, about how and to which extent practical training should be included in the study program for future librarians.   Two aspects seem to be of primary interest:

1—How can elements of practical experience be integrated into the teaching-learning processes going on in library school instruction?

2—Should shorter or longer periods of practical work in one or more libraries, called fieldwork, practicum, internship, or in-service training, be included in the library school curriculum?

I want to deal briefly with the first aspect and then discuss in more detail the second one.

PRACTICE-RELATED METHODS OF INSTRUCTION

Most library educators seem to agree on the value of such methods of instruction which allow the student to acquire practical skills and to gain experience by being confronted with practical problems and procedures. All these methods have in common that learning by practical experience is closely coordinated with classroom instruction and is planned and supervised by the teacher. The most important of these methods are visits, case studies, role plays, projects and laboratory work.[2] *Visits* to libraries and *observation* of library work, if carefully prepared, and analyzed afterwards, give the student a direct insight into library functions and techniques. *The case study method* (or simulation method) trains students in applying theory to a complex situation; it has proved to be useful especially in library administration and reference work.[3] The case method may include a *role play* when interaction between two or more people is involved. *Projects*, where individuals or groups are assigned to investigate and report on some topic of library practice, are expected to promote the students' abilities in problem solving, independent study, and cooperation. Above all, *laboratory work* is a widely recognized training method, suitable for subjects dealing with the handling and processing of books and other library materials, for instance: cataloguing, classification, reference work, and bibliography; it is indispensable, of course, for all kinds of computer application.

The importance of these practice-related methods in library instruction has been emphasized in many publications by competent library educators.[4] All these methods try to bridge the gap between the classroom and the field of professional practice. All of them have their advantages and their limitations, one of which is that most of these methods require careful and time-consuming preparation on the part of the teacher. If applied in the right proportions, such methods serve as the necessary supplement to theory-centered instruction and study.

PRACTICAL EXPERIENCE BY FIELDWORK

The second aspect of the theory-practice-problem in library education relates to fieldwork (practicum, internship), i.e. the placement of students in libraries for a period or several periods of practical experience. The question whether fieldwork should be a formal part of library education has been answered differently at different times. Besides, educational traditions in different geographical and cultural areas have led to different solutions.

In many countries of continental Europe, fieldwork traditionally constitutes an important element in library education at all levels, often amounting to a length of 12 or 18 months, i.e. one third or even one half of the total duration of the library school program. In Great Britain, library schools usually have a fieldwork component in their courses, which is, however, limited to a few weeks in duration. As a compensation, pre-library-school experience may be required by students, whereas on the other hand a post-library-school period of practical work is necessary in order to obtain recognition as a qualified librarian.[5] In the United States, opinion prevailed for a long time that fieldwork or internship could not contribute effectively to the objectives of library education, at least at the postgraduate level, and therefore should not be an essential part of the core of library school programs.[6] In recent years, a moderate "renaissance" of fieldwork can be perceived in North America, so that more library schools now tend to integrate fieldwork periods into their curricula.[7] The Conant Report of 1980 criticized the lack of adequate practical instruction in American library schools and recommended a period of supervised practical experience (internship) as an essential aspect of professional training.[8]

CRITICISM OF FIELDWORK

Critics of fieldwork as a part of library education often justly emphasize the defects and shortcomings that may occur during fieldwork periods. There may be a misunderstanding on the side of the host library about the status of the student and the purpose of fieldwork. Consequently, sometimes only routine tasks of a low level are assigned to students who then feel that they are used merely as cheap labour. In other cases the student may be treated as a guest who should not be expected to work at all. Library staff may lack teaching abilities, and explanations given to the student may therefore be unsatisfactory. Library staff may be overworked or not interested in the success of fieldwork, so that supervision of the student's work may often be inadequate. The time-lag between course work and fieldwork raises the problem of deferred instead of concurrent experience. It is inevitable that sometimes discrepancies arise between what the student has been taught in classroom and what he observes in the library. There is always the risk of haphazard or fortuitous or one-sided experience, and it is unfortunately true when Jesse Shera states that "experience can be the source of error as well as of wisdom".[9] All these reasons may lead to the verdict that fieldwork is inconsistent with pedagogical objectives and therefore should not be a formal part of library education. [10]

ADVANTAGES OF FIELDWORK

Such criticism perhaps ignores the fact that most of the defects and failures of fieldwork only occur if fieldwork is not sufficiently structured and organized, and if there is no close cooperation between library school and host library.   It is my conviction that most of the troubles and difficulties of fieldwork can be avoided or can be reduced to a tolerable measure if fieldwork is systematically planned and managed by the library school and is carefully executed under the guidance of the outside training library.   If these prerequisites are given, fieldwork appears to be an indispensable part of library education.   Librarianship or library work itself is not a science.   Librarianship (like engineering or teaching) is an applied discipline for which library and information science provides the theoretical basis.   It seems evident that a sound preparation for the library profession should incorporate an equal emphasis on both theory and application.   The existence of library schools does not eliminate the need of training in a library.   Only active participation in library and information work can give the student a proper idea of professional reality with its complex functions, procedures and techniques. Only when working for some time under every-day library conditions, especially in the field of users' services, the student can acquire professional skills and competence to match newly arising problems.

OBJECTIVES OF FIELDWORK

The objectives of fieldwork may be divided into cognitive and affective levels.[11]   Cognitive learning here means the intellectual appreciation and understanding of the various activities in the library; affective learning consists of the emotional assimilation of the atmosphere, policies and values of the profession.   Both types of objectives should be achieved if fieldwork is to be successful.   The experiences of the fieldwork student should include the actual practice of library routines, the relating of theory to practice and the opportunity to apply ideas presented in library school instruction.   The results would be an improved and deepened understanding of library activities and the ability to analyze and solve typical problems arising in professional work.   On the other hand, fieldwork can initiate the complex process of the student's socialization and identification with his future profession, and may, ideally, strengthen his motivation, enthusiasm and self-confidence.

DURATION OF FIELDWORK

It is important to realize that the duration of fieldwork should be relatively long in order to be successful.   In an investigation recently carried out in a British school of librarianship,[12]   a four-week fieldwork period was evaluated and assessed by the participating students, the staff of the host libraries and the library school tutors.   The results showed that most of the affective objectives had been achieved, whereas in the cognitive domain only few of the objectives were satisfactorily met.   Obviously this was due to the very short time of four weeks which did not allow the students to gain a full understanding of and a comprehensive insight into the complicated machinery of a large library.

According to German experiences, fieldwork in public libraries should amount to at least four months, whereas fieldwork in academic or research libraries should have a total duration of nine to twelve months (in a three- or two-years-course of librarianship).   If a practical period is too short, the student cannot get fully acquainted with all aspects of library service. Besides, short spells of fieldwork sometimes assume the character of extended visits : the student is learning by being shown and being talked to.   However, there is a limit to the amount of demonstration and lecturing which is possible for the instructor or which can be absorbed by the student.[13]   The periods of fieldwork must be long enough so that the student really becomes involved in the everyday work of the library (learning by doing) and can get acquainted with all major activities and problems of a library.

To avoid social hardships during a long fieldwork period, financial support should be granted to students who need it.   This can mostly be done within the system of library education in West Germany, because those students preparing for service in academic and research libraries and documentation centers usually have the status of "Anwärter" (candidates), that is, they are unestablished civil servants and therefore receive a (modest) salary during the time of their library education .   Other students, who do not have this status, for example those preparing for public library service, can receive a grant in case of need.[14]

FIELDWORK IN LIBRARY EDUCATION IN WEST GERMANY

In the Federal Republic of Germany, the theory-practice problem in library education had to be reconsidered during the last years.[15]   Within the framework of a general reform of professional education, study programs for "Diplom-Bibliothekare" (Diploma Librarians or Certified Librarians) were re-organized on the level of "Fachhochschulen", i.e. institutes of higher education on the tertiary level which correspond to the British polytechnics or to similar advanced technical colleges.   The final diploma examination is equivalent with or slightly below a master's degree.   Duration of the program normally is three years.

In West Germany, library school instruction and fieldwork are considered to be two complementary parts of a unity.   The amount of fieldwork varies depending on whether the program prepares for public library service or for service in academic or research libraries.   Programs preparing for public library service include four months of practical work.   (There is a tendency, however, to extend fieldwork up to six months.) In education for the service in academic and research libraries or documentation centers, a period of long-term fieldwork has been considered as necessary; it normally lasts 12 months, that is one third of the total three-years-program; in some library schools it amounts to 9 or to 18 months.[16]

THE EXAMPLE OF THE FACHHOCHSCHULE (POLYTECHNIC)

OF HANOVER

To give an example, I would like to report on the Department of Librarianship, Information and Documentation of the Fachhochschule Hanover.[17]   During a pilot project aiming at the "Development of integrated programs of study in the fields of Librarianship, Information and Documentation", which was conducted from 1978 to 1985 , new educational concepts for Diploma Librarians and Diploma Documentalists were established.   One of the basic premises of the pilot study was that all programs of study should be oriented to practical competence and train students for professional work. The length of the study program being set at seven semesters (3 1/2 years), it was determined that two periods of a "practicum" or fieldwork in libraries or documentation centers, lasting six and three months respectively, should be integrated into the study program.

The sequence of theoretical and practical periods in this program, which may well be called a "sandwich course", is as follows:
– instruction at library school (1year)
– "long" practicum (6 months)
– instruction at library school (3 months)
– "short" practicum (3 months)
– instruction at library school (1 1/2 year)

It was considered an essential point that both periods of fieldwork were placed neither at the beginning nor at the end of the study program, but in the middle, so that every period of fieldwork is preceded and followed by a period of library school instruction.   Only in this case students can acquire a thorough knowledge of librarianship and information science before starting fieldwork so that they have a better understanding of practical work and can fulfil the tasks assigned to them more effectively.   On the other hand, as every period of fieldwork is followed by a period of study, the students' practical experiences can be analyzed and assessed in classroom.   The long and the short practicum are done in different libraries, for example in a university library and a special library, or in a state library and a documentation center, so that th student gets acquainted with at least two types of libraries.

REGULATIONS FOR FIELDWORK

In Hanover, exact regulations for fieldwork have been laid down in a "practicum order" (Praktikumsordnung).[18]   These rules stipulate in which fields of library and information work the student has to be trained, how long he should deal with the various professional activities and which skills he is expected to acquire.

The regulations lay down that the student, by means of observation of and participating in library work, should acquire proficiency in the basic activities of a library on the level of "Diploma-Librarians", namely book selection, accessioning; cataloguing and classification, maintenance of catalogues and catalogue systems; lending routines, procedures of interlibrary loan; bibliographic work; management of open access areas, reading rooms and closed stacks; handling of technical equipment; reference work and information retrieval.

To achieve this, the student has to work for several days or weeks in every department and section of the host library or documentation center, ranging from the acquisitions department to the rare book division and to the information center utilizing external databases.   At the end of fieldwork, the student is expected to be able to explain, analyze and assess the functions of the libraries concerned, their legal status, financial funding, acquisition policy, the organisation of book-processing and readers' services, manpower planning and staff development, the libraries' buildings and equipment, and their history.[19]

A steering committee of the Hanover Polytechnic selects libraries and documentation centers suitable for fieldwork, and assigns students to them. In every library or documentation center, a "fieldwork supervisor" or training officer (Ausbildungsleiter) is appointed who organizes and controls the practicum according to the regulations.   It is considered important that the staff in the host libraries are well informed about the objectives of fieldwork. Every staff member concerned with fieldwork is obliged to observe the regulations.   The steering committee and the instructors keep close contact in all matters regarding fieldwork and meet in regular intervals to discuss relevant questions.

During the practicum, lessons are taught once a week by the fieldwork supervisor or other librarians regarding problems and peculiarities of the library concerned.[20]   Every student doing fieldwork chooses a particular library or information problem developed from one of the working situations in which the student has been placed.   This problem serves as a topic for a field-oriented project which is continued at the library school and which often is taken as the basis for the examination paper or thesis necessary for the attainment of the diploma.[21]

FIELDWORK ABROAD

A special feature of the fieldwork concept in Hanover is that students can do the short practicum in a foreign country.   Thanks to cooperation between the Polytechnic of Hanover and the College of Librarianship Wales at Aberystwyth, about 30 German students could spend a fieldwork period in British libraries in the past years.[22]   It is obvious that a period of fieldwork abroad is for any student, both personally and professionally, a most rewarding experience.   A similar cooperation with libraries and documentation centers in France is about to begin.

A systematic evaluation of the Hanover fieldwork concept, carried out by questioning students, instructors and library school teachers, resulted in a general approval of the main features of the program.[23]

I want to mention only in passing that in Hanover classroom tuition is accompanied by a good deal of practical training for which a system of laboratories has been conceived.   These consist of a Computer Laboratory, an Online Training Center, the Department Library which is used as practice area for library tasks and as a model library, a Documentation Training Center, and a Reprography, Bookbinding and Book Preservation Workshop.[24]

FIELDWORK IN PROGRAMS OF
OTHER GERMAN LIBRARY SCHOOLS

In other German library shools preparing for the degree of Diploma Librarians, fieldwork and practical training play a similar role as in Hanover. In the Department of Librarianship of the Bavarian Civil Servants' College in Munich, for example, fieldwork lasts one year and is preceded and followed by one year of library school study.[25]   The fieldwork period is structured and supervised in a similar way as in Hanover.   In the near future, the sequence of study and fieldwork periods will be as follows : instruction at library school (6 months), fieldwork (6 months), library school (12 months), fieldwork (6 months), library school (6 months).   It is expected that this will ensure a better integration of fieldwork experience and study program.

Finally it should be mentioned that, in West Germany, education programs for "academic" or "scientific librarians"[26] (höherer Bibliotheksdienst, "administrative grade") also include a period of organized fieldwork. Education of academic librarians is established at a post-university level and qualifies for subject specialist work as well as for administrative and supervisory activities. Duration of these programs is two years, one of which is dedicated to fieldwork, normally in different types of libraries. Here, as in library education at other levels, care is taken that fieldwork periods are systematically planned, organized and supervised by means of a close cooperation between library school and host libraries.[27]

REFERENCES

1. Joe Morehead, *Theory and Practice in Library Education: The Teaching-Learning Process* (Littleton, Colo.: Libraries Unlimited, 1980), p. 14.
2. Ibid., pp. 54-74. Josefa E. Sabor, *Methods of Teaching Librarianship*, Unesco Manuals for Libraries, no. 16 (Paris: Unesco, 1969), pp. 93-103. Peter G. New, *Education for Librarianship* (London: Clive Bingley, 1978), pp. 91-94.
3. Thomas J. Galvin, "The Case Method in Library Education Reconsidered," *Reference Services and Library Education: Essays in Honor of Frances Neel Cheney* (Lexington, Mass.: Heath, 1983), pp. 225-236.
4. Morehead, op.cit., pp. 125-134.
5. Ronald J. Edwards, *In-Service Training in British Libraries: Its Development and Present Practice* (London: Library Association, 1977). Library Association Working Party on Training, ed., *Guidelines for Training in Libraries*, 3rd rev. ed. (London, 1983). Frank Gibbons, "From Librarianship to Library Science: The Professional Education of Librarians in the United Kingdom, the United States, and Australia," *Reference Services and Library Education*, op. cit., pp. 247-263.
6. *Encyclopedia of Library and Information Science*, s.v. "Internship," by Patrick B. Penland. S. D. Neill, "The Place of Practice in a Graduate Library School," *Libri* 25 (1975): 81-97. R. J. Prytherch, "Towards an Understanding and Evaluation of Student Fieldwork in Libraries," *Journal of Education for Librarianship* 22 (1982): 173-186. K. Subramanyam, "Current Concerns in American Library Education," *International Library Review* 15 (1983): 299-305.
7. Edward G. Holley, "Extended Library Education Programs in the United States," *Advances in Librarianship* 11 (1981): 51-76. Prytherch, op. cit.,

p. 175.

8. Ralph W. Conant, *The Conant Report: A Study of the Education of Librarians* (Cambridge, Mass. and London: MIT Press, 1980), pp. 168-169, 179, 181.

9. Jesse H. Shera, *The Foundations of Education for Librarianship* (New York: Becker and Hayes, 1972), p. 436.

10. Morehead, op. cit., pp. 48-49.

11. Prytherch, op. cit., pp. 176-178.

12. Prytherch, op. cit., pp. 179-184.

13. New, op. cit., p. 96.

14. Gisela von Busse, Horst Ernestus, and Engelbert Plassmann, *Libraries in the Federal Republic of Germany* (Wiesbaden: Harrassowitz, 1983), pp. 208-211.

15. Ibid., pp. 206-214.   Paul Kaegbein and Diann D. Rusch, "Library and Information Science Education in West Germany," *Journal of Education for Librarianship* 22 (1982): 154-172.   Wilhelm Gaus, *Berufe im Archiv–, Bibliotheks–, Informations– und Dokumentationswesen: Ein Wegweiser zur Ausbildung* (Berlin: Springer, 1986).

16. "Bibliothek, Dokumentation, Archiv: Ausbildungs-und Studiengaenge nach Ausbildungsstaetten," *Nachrichten fuer Dokumentation* 35 (1984): 111-116.

17. Gunter Bock, "Integrated Curricula for Education in the Fields of Librarianship, Information and Documentation: A Pilot Study," *The Infrastructure of an Information Society*, ed. E. El-Hadidy and E. E. Horne (Amsterdam: North Holland, 1984), pp. 201-223.   Gunter Bock, Rolf Hueper: *Informationstransfer als Beruf: Abschlußbericht des Modellversuchs* (Hannover, 1986).

18. Gunter Bock et al., "Entwurf einer Gemeinsamen Praktikumsordnung fuer die Studiengaenge Bibliothekswesen, Allgemeine Dokumentation und Biowissenschaftliche Dokumentation an der Fachhochschule Hannover", *Materialien zum Modellversuch* 6 (Hannover: Fachhochschule, 1980).

19. Ibid., pp. 10-11

20. "Praxisbegleitender Unterricht: Vorschlaege zu Inhalt und Methode des praxisbegleitenden Unterrichts in der Ausbildung des gehobenen Dienstes an wissenschaftlichen Bibliotheken." (Bochum, Stuttgart: Verein der Diplombibliothekare an wissenschaftlichen Bibliotheken, 1982.)

21. "BID-Workshop '82, Hannover, 9. - 10. Maerz 1982. Praesentation und Diskussion erster Ergebnisse des Modellversuchs BID," *Materialien zum Modellversuch* 12 (Hannover: Fachhochschule, 1983), pp. 122-152.

22. Michael J. Wells, "BID-Studenten in britischen Praktikumsstellen: ein Bericht," *Internationaler BID-Abschlussworkshop '85* (cf. Reference No. 23), pp. 57-74.

23. "Internationaler BID-Abschlussworkshop '85 am 13. und 14. Maerz 1985 in Hannover. Praesentation und Diskussion der Ergebnisse des Modellversuchs BID," *Materialien zum Modellversuch* 25 (Hannover: Fachhochschule, 1985), pp. 45-55. Joachim Kutz, "Integrierte Fachhochschulpraktika und ihre Evaluation," *Fachhochschule im Wandel.* Hrsg. von Rolf Hueper und Manfred Gahrens. (Hannover: Postskriptum Verlag, 1985), pp. 57-66.

24. Bock, op. cit.,, pp. 204-205.

25. Rupert Hacker, "Zehn Jahre Fachstudium fuer den gehobenen Bibliotheksdienst am Fachbereich Archiv-und Bibliothekswesen der Bayerischen Beamtenfachhochschule (1975 - 1985)," *Bibliotheksforum Bayern* 13 (1985): 239–244.

26. Busse, Ernestus, Plassmann, op. cit., p. 210.
Diann D. Rusch, "Comparative Trends in Library and Information Science Curricula in the USA, Canada and the Federal Republic of Germany. (Paper No. 133-Train-4-E presented at the IFLA General Conference, Munich, 1983), p. 3. *International Guide to Library and Information Science Education,* ed. Josephine R. Fang and Paul Nauta, IFLA Publications 32 (Muenchen: Saur, 1985), pp. 162, 164, 169.

27. For a recent example of regulations for the education of "academic librarians", see "Verordnung ueber die Ausbildung und Pruefung fuer die Laufbahn des hoeheren Bibliotheksdienstes im Lande Nordrhein-Westfalen vom 21. April 1985," *Mitteilungsblatt des Verbandes der Bibliotheken des Landes Nordrhein-Westfalen,* N. F. 35, (1985), pp. 339-349.

Design of the Curriculum for a 2-year Library Technical Assistant Program in the Recruitment Plan of the Republic of China

Chien-chang Lan
Professor and Chairman
Department of Library Science
Fu Jen Catholic University
Taipei, Taiwan, R.O.C.

I. HISTORICAL BACKGROUND

China had her first library school in 1920 when Miss Mary Elizabeth Wood (1861-1931) founded Boone Library School in Wuchang, Hupeh Province.   Miss Wood, a 1919 Simmons College graduate, came to China to see her priest brother Robert then preaching at an Episcopalean Church in Wuchang.   It was a time of chaos in modern China where warlords tyrannically ruled over their occupied lands and social order was at its worst.   The Woods decided to stay in China in order to help the Chinese people fight for freedom of faith and freedom of learning.   At first, Boone Library School was only a department of Boone University (named after the Episcopalean Bishop Boone of the Central China parish, who initiated the founding of the University in the 1890s); students enrolled in this depatment spent four academic years at the undergraduate level, and were conferred a Bachelor's degree in Arts, majoring in library science.

After the unification of China in 1928, Boone University was suspended for a final merging of a number of Episcopalean colleges scattered throughout Central China and reorganized as a new university named Central China University; but its Department of Library Science was independently established as a professional school with formal accreditation of the Ministry of Education of the Chinese Government a year earlier.

In fact, Boone Library School was a 2-year professional school.   It admitted students who had finished the first two years in various fields of studies in the university, and they were awarded scholarships from the Sino-American Cultural and Educational Funds which was the outcome of Miss Wood's mission to the U.S. Congress where she succeeded in getting back the Boxer Indemnity to the Chinese government for promoting cultural and educational affairs.   The erection of the National Peiping Library and the recruitment plan exercised in Boone Library School were the two great achievements Wood had accomplished.

The curriculum of Boone Library School was eventually designed as career courses for the selected students.   It consisted of :

> Introduction to Library Science
> Library Administration
> Selection and Acquisitions of Graphic Materials
> Cataloging and Classification of Chinese Books
> Cataloging and Classification of Western Books
> Chinese Reference Sources
> Western Reference Sources
> Chinese Bibliography
> Writing of Book Reviews
> Public Libraries
> Library Service to Children
> Story Telling
> Library Publicity

Besides, there were some elective courses such as

> Chinese Epigraphy
> Bookkeeping
> Archival Management

Comparing the above pattern with those practiced by Melvil Dewey in the 1920s, we can clearly see that these two types resembled each other to a certain extent — both were centered on technical services.   This training program lasted for twenty years through the twenties and the thirties.   Most of the graduates of this period were employed by university and college libraries – and of course the only national library which was the National Peiping Library (National Central Library was formally established in 1940 in Chungking during the Chinese-Japanese War, 1937-1945).   Quite a few were employed as catalogers.   Since Bibliography has been considered in China as a discipline of Historical Science for centuries, and it has been also regarded by scholars as well as the general public as the gateway to learning, naturally librarians are publicly acknowledged as the most reliable persons and professional interpreters to readers of the contextual value of books.   Moreover, they were trained in compiling bibliographies and catalogs for use in libraries. One more excuse was that students of that period were prone to seek opportunities for catalogers because catalogers are compatible with bibliographers to whom the Chinese customarily pay great respect.   To our regret, seldom could they be promoted to chief librarians unless they went abroad to further their education in the library science field and got advanced degrees which were, and still are, requested by authorities.   The explanation, in my personal opinion, is that these students, before they entered library schools, though they have had two years devoted to each of their relevant studies, had only taken the fundamental courses of the pertinent field (except a few had earned B.A. degrees in various fields), and later in the library school, the courses offered were not leadership-oriented, hence the executive of the institution would not feel safe to appoint his employee the head of the library. On the other hand, if the institution appointed a non-professional official to head the library, or, if the status of the library in the organization remained at a lower level, the function of the library would certainly be limited and very much subdued, or even altered.

During the Chinese-Japanese War years of 1937-45, Boone Library School was transformed into its third stage.   It changed to a 3-year technical college with two integrated divisions, namely, Library Science, and Archival Management respectively.   The admittance requirement for students was lowered to senior high graduates instead of undergraduates in universities as previously did.   Although the duration of schooling was shortened from 4 years to 3 years, the core courses remained the same as aforesaid.   Up to this present day, after almost forty years, I feel abashed to point out the defects in the design of the curriculum.   Obviously, the former curriculum practiced in Boone Library School was formulated on university and college education basis, but the transformed school was aimed at training of library technicians, therefore, the new school should alter its curriculum toward the fulfillment of its present goal.

II. THE PRESENT CONDITION OF THE LIBRARY TECHNICAL ASSISTANT PROGRAM PRACTICED IN THE WEST AND THE EAST

1. American scene

According to a survey made for institutions offering or developing courses in Library Technology*,

> 62 institutions offer 2-year post high school programs, in junior or community colleges
> 2 offer 3-year programs

    2 offer 2-year programs, but in the framework of a 4-year college
or university
    1 offers a 1-year program

Since this paper emphasizes Curriculum, I would like to mention the curriculum at Ohio University–Lancaster ** in the seventies as the model for my proposed curriculum for possible adoption in the Republic of China.

The Program was designed on a 2-year (6 quarters) basis as listed below:

LIBRARY TECHNICAL ASSISTANT CURRICULUM

First Year

First Quarter	Credit Hours
Introduction to Libraries and Library Technology	4
General Psychology	5
Fundamentals of Speech	3
Elective Social Science or Natural Science	3-5
	15-17

Second Quarter	
Support Operation for Public Services I	4
Literary Themes	5
Elective Social Science or Natural Science	3-5
	15-17

Third Quarter	
Support Operation for Technical Services I	3
Support Operations for Public Services II	4
Introduction to Sociology	5
Elective Social Science or Natural Science	3-5
	15-17

---

* Summary of Information Resulting from a Survey of Institutions Offering Training for Library Technical Assistants in the United States and Canada. For the Survey, conducted between April 1,1970 and May 10, 1970, 122 questionnaires were sent to institutions listed in the Directory of Institutions in the United States and Canada Offering or Developing Courses in Library Technology (2nd ed.) 73 questionnaires were returned, representing 59.9% of those appealed to for information.

** McCauley Hannah, "We Are Trained to Work in Libraries." *Protean* 1(Sept. 1971): 59-63.

Second Year

First Quarter

Library Services for Specific Groups I	4
Support Operation for Technical Services II	5
Audio Visual Methods and Materials	4
Comparative Arts	3
	16

Second Quarter

Library Technician Internship I	3
Library Service for Specific Groups II	4
Preparation of Audio Visual Materials	3
Business and Industrial Communications	3
Elective	3
	16

Third Quarter

Library Technician Internship II	8
Interpretation of Fiction/Poetry	5
Management	4
	17

Total number of minimum credit hours   94

LIBRARY TECHNICAL ASSISTANTS CAREER COURSES

Introduction to Libraries and Library Technology
Support Operation for Public Services I & II
Technical Services in the Library I & II
Library Services for Specific Groups I & II
Library Technician Internship I & II
Audio Visual Methods and Materials
Preparation of Audio Visual Materials

On observing the courses listed above, we can clearly see that the philosophy of this type of training is to provide supporting personnel by offering courses in general education (50%) and courses in library technology (50%). It's clear that in such a training program, the library activities could be satisfactorily performed and its functions adequately achieved through a teamwork of professionals and technical assistants.

If we group these courses by contents, they will give us a breakdown as follows:

The humanities	Credit hours
Fundamentals of Speech	3
Literary Themes	5
Comparative Arts	3
Interpretation of Fiction/Poetry	5
Subtotal	16

Social Sciences	
General Psychology	5
Social Science or Natural Science (Elective)	9-15
	(3 quarters)
Introduction to Sociology	5
Business and Industrial Communications	3
Management	4
Subtotal	26-32

Career Courses

Introduction to Libraries & Library Technology	4
Support Operations for Public Libraries I & II	8
Technical Services in the Library I & II	8
Library Services for Specific Groups I & II	8
Library Technician Internship I & II	11
Audio Visual Methods and Materials	3
Preparation of Audio Visual Materals	3
Subtotal	45

The Fifty-Fifty pattern:	Credit hours
General education	42-48
Library technology	45
Grand total	87-93 C/H

2. Chinese scene

Plainly speaking, the design of the curriculum specifically laid out for the 3-year library technical training program was primarily based on the curriculum which had been devised in the forties.   It is not only out of date but also inadequate in the present "information age."   Its core courses like the courses now practiced in the Department of Library Science in universities, also consists of*

> Selection and Acquisitions of Library Materials
> Cataloging and Classification of Chinese Books
> Cataloging and Classification of Western Books
> Chinese Reference Sources
> Western Reference Sources
> Library Administration
> Chinese Bibliography
> Nonbook Materials
> Applied Computer Science
> Second Foreign Language

We must admit that the essence of supporting function of the library assistants has not been thus far recognized by the authorities concerned. Thence the courses which have been developed for library technicians in the United States are entirely excluded or overlooked in China.   Furthermore, it is obvious that much repetition would occur if the same curriculum were carried out at two different levels — a 4-year undergraduate program and a 3-year technical college program, yet the latter would suffer from cutting of credit hours.

According to the revised standard for courses offered in technical colleges effective in June 1981, the Division of Technical and Vocational Education of the Ministry of Education of the Chinese government has determinedly prescribed a number of civic training courses as common requisites to any field of studies.   I am not opposing this presription, but the credit hours needed for these courses, totalling at 26, would certainly affect the full attainment of the designed curriculum and the fulfillment of its goals in particular.

As I mentioned above, the new curriculum for the Library Assistant Program consists of some 10 core courses.   Besides, there are a number of relevant courses such as, Journalism, Library and Mass Communication, Introduction to Chinese Studies, Applied Microphotography, Speed Reading, which together with the 10 core courses, made a total of 54 credit hours.

The third category in the new curriculum are those in Library Practicum, i.e., laboratory hours.   In this group, 28 credit hours are required.

---

* Republic of China.   Ministry of Education.   Technical and Vocational Education Division.   A List of Required Courses for the 3-Year Technical Colleges as Amended in June 1981. 三年制專科學校必修科目表，教育部技術及職業教育司編印. 70年 6 月

Among the electives, courses on Introduction to Literature, Introduction to Philosophy, Introduction to Social Science, Introduction to Science, Political Science, Economics, Psychology, Sociology, Chinese Politics and Government, Comparative Politics and Government, History of Thought, Second Foreign Language, are offered to students for 12 credit hours on elective basis.   All in all, the minimum credit hours for the 3-year program is 120.

III. EVALUATION

1. Common topics as requisites: 26 credit hours

Chinese (8 C/H) — Chinese students have had 6 years in elementary schools and another 6 years in high schools devoted to the study of their mother tongue, and, for the third time, they have to spend still 8 more credit hours at 4 credit hours each semester for one year, I suspect this repetitious process in learning would cause students boredom, consequently, the result would not be satisfactory.   If a complete deletion could not be done, a reduction to 4-6 credit hours would be more acceptable.

English (8 C/H) – English was taught from the first year in junior high schools in China and continued through the third year in senior high schools, thus the course in English has been taught throughout the 6 years on the level of secondary education.   This additional year in English learning would be more beneficial if Special English for librarians is stressed and if possible, Sophomore English offered to students would be much more appreciated.

History of Contemporary China and History of Modern China (2 courses at 2 credit hours each for the first year) — Since these two courses are designed to be given consecutively, it would be better to combine them in one course as History of Modern China at 3 credit hours for each semester in the first year.

International Relations (2 C/H) – This course is now discontinued in universities.   The topics discussed could be covered in History of Modern China.

Out of the 26 credit hours originally designed, a deduction of 2 credit hours for Chinese, 1 credit hour for History of Modern China, 2 credit hours, thus the total credit hours for Common Topics has been reduced to 21.

2. Career courses : 54 credit hours

Journaliam (4 C/H) – The reason for the inclusion of this topic is, until the present day, the Library Technical Assistants Program is now offered only in the World College of Journalism in Taiwan; thus Journalism is a common requisite for all departments in the College.   It is also true in the case of the course of Library and Mass Communication. Generally speaking, these two courses would not be essential to the training of Library Assistants.

Library Administration (2 C/H) – Since this course is specifically designed for decision making on library operations, it is primarily offered to graduate library school students who tend to be library administrators in their careers. However, though library assistants are supporting in nature, it would be definitely helpful to the professionals if some clerical and technical operations were offered in the Practicum.

History of Printing (2 C/H) – This topic is specifically designed for graduate studies. It is too rigid for library assistants. I suggest that it be deleted.

Introduction to Chinese Studies (4 C/H) - This is another rigid course inappropriate for library assistants. The deletion would be appropriate and acceptable.

Chinese Bibliography. Although only two credit hours are assigned to this course, which means this is but a brief course, I suggest to combine it with the course on Cataloging and Classification of Chinese Books - or rather Cataloging and Classification of Books. Such an alteration would render it more applicable to library assistants.

Cataloging and Classification of Chinese (also Western) Books (4 C/H each for Chinese and Western) - In cataloging and classification of graphic materials, language problems should not be considered as an element grave enough to split into vernacular and foreign systems. I regret to mention that such a device is, up to the present, still being practiced in the 4-year program in China. I would be only too glad to see the merging of these two courses into one. And, as a result of such alteration, a special course on "Cataloging of Chinese Rare Books" would be most helpful if we offer it to be included in graduate schools.

Chinese Reference Sources and also Western Reference Sources (2 C/H each) – To my knowledge, reference service, as a rule, usually requires intensive training in bibliography and some field specialities, thus, reference work is performed by professionals; library technical assistants could only operate on supportive basis.

Nonbook Materials (4 C/H) – This is the topic which needs intensive training, that is to say, students are not only being taught principles and methods, but also trained with manufacturing skills. Therefore, I suggest this course should be split into two respective courses as I have explained above.

Microphotography and Speed-Reading are the two other courses whose inclusion in the curriculum I do not agree with, because the themes of these two subjects are not closely related to librarianship and would be too technical for library technical assistants.

3. Practicum courses: 28 credit hours

Courses offered in this category are essential to this type of recruitment plan.   I quite agree with the design of the topics except Microphotography, Speed-Reading and Reference Services.

4. Electives: 12 credit hours

As listed in the curriculum, there are some 11 courses offered for choice. The breakdown would run like this:

Humanities	Subtotal 10
	(Credit hours)
Introduction to Literature	4
Introduction to Philosophy	4
History of Thought	2
Social Sciences	Subtotal 26
Introduction to Social Science	4
Political Science	4
Economics	4
Psychology	4
Sociology	4
Chinese Politics and Government	2
Comparative Politics and Government	4
Science	Subtotal 4
Introduction to Science	4

The course on Psychology would be adequately allocated in the Common Courses for it is almost the trend to require Psychology in the curriculum for students in the humanities and the social sciences.

IV. THE PROPOSED NEW CURRICULUM FOR THE 2-YEAR LIBRARY TECHNICAL ASSISTANT TRAINING PROGRAM

First year	
First semester	24 C/H
Chinese	4
English	4
Dr. Sun Yat-sen's Thought	3

History of Modern China	2
Introduction to Libraries and Library Technology	3
History of Chinese Literature	3
General Psychology	3
Typing	2
Second semester	**24 C/H**
Chinese	2
English	4
History of Modern China	2
Introduction to Libraries & Library Technology	3
History of Chinese Literature	3
General Psychology	3
Book Selection & Acquisitions	4
Introduction to Computers	3

Second year
First semester	**24 C/H**
Cataloging and Classification	3
Reference Sources	3
Chinese Bibliography	2
Audio Visual Methods & Materials	3
Library Service for Specific Groups	3
Business English	2
Filing and Indexing	2
Electives	6
Second semester	**24 C/H**
Cataloging and Classification	3
Reference Sources	3
Audio Visual Methods and Materials	3
Support Operations for Public Services	5
Chinese Bibliography	2
Library Management	2
Electives	6
Grand total:	96 C/H

Education and Training for Online Use of
Databases in the Republic of China

Lucy Te-Chu Lee
Professor
Department and Graduate Institute of Library Science
National Taiwan University
Taipei, Taiwan, R.O.C.

INTRODUCTION

We are living in the "information age".   Information is a vast, dynamic, and inexhaustible resource that affects all disciplines as well as the lives of all people.   In this information-rich and information-seeking era, information seekers are constantly striving to maximize the utility of graphic records. But unfortunately, we are facing a crisis — the rapidly growing cost of productions and processing of publications which many libraries neither have the budgets to purchase nor the place to house them.   Traditional techniques and technologies used by many libraries cannot cope, and changes must take place in order to keep pace with the increasing volume of information.

Fortunately the timing is right; with the assistance of modern technological innovations and capabilities, the control and the demand for accessibility, speed, efficiency and effectiveness of information can be more easily fulfilled with online database searching.   This refers to the use of computers to retrieve information online from databases.   A database is a collection of data in machine readable form for the purpose of information storage and retrieval. Online computerized bibliographic databases have been here with us since the early 1970s; the number of publicly available bibliographic and non-bibliographic databases has grown to more than 2,000 in 1984,[1,2] and they are increasing at a rate of 20-30% per year.[3] At the same time, the number of online database searches performed each year has rapidly grown from 700,000 in 1974 to an estimated 10 million in 1984.[4]

Kent said, during the 1977 Pittsburgh Conference on the Online Revolution in Libraries, that online bibliographic searching gives us "a new kind of power" which can be used as an enhanced basis for selection and exploitative control of world information.   He also cautioned us that as "with any kind of power, both evil as well as good can result."[5]   That is, one must posses the appropriate knowledge and skill in order to use this powerful tool efficiently and effectively.   Therefore, the education and training for use of online databases is of vital importance.

The purpose of this paper is to provide an overview of the present status of education and training for the use of online databases in Taiwan, the Republic of China: the background development; the types of organizations that provide education and training; the types of persons to be trained; the problems involved with education and training and possible solutions to them; and the future planning for education and training in the use of online databases.   In addition, a recent survey of online databases searchers / intermediaries in this country will also be reported here.

BACKGROUND DEVELOPMENT IN GENERAL

General Background

The beginning of database production was in the late 1960s.   In view of the literature, one can easily recognize that the online database searching service originated in the United States, the country that also produces the world's largest quantity of databases.

In 1977, Williams identified four phases in the history of database generation in U.S.: in the first phase, computer-readable databases were generated as a by-product of hard-copy production of A & I (Abstracting and Indexing) Services; in the second phase, computer-readable databases were generated as a direct product of A & I Services production activities; in the third phase, computer-readable databases were generated as distributable tapes but with no hard-copy counterparts being published; and in the fourth phase, computer-readable databases were generated as direct product but with no physically distributable tapes — only electronic distributions are available.[6]   Figure 1 shows the four phases of database generation and their characteristics.[7]

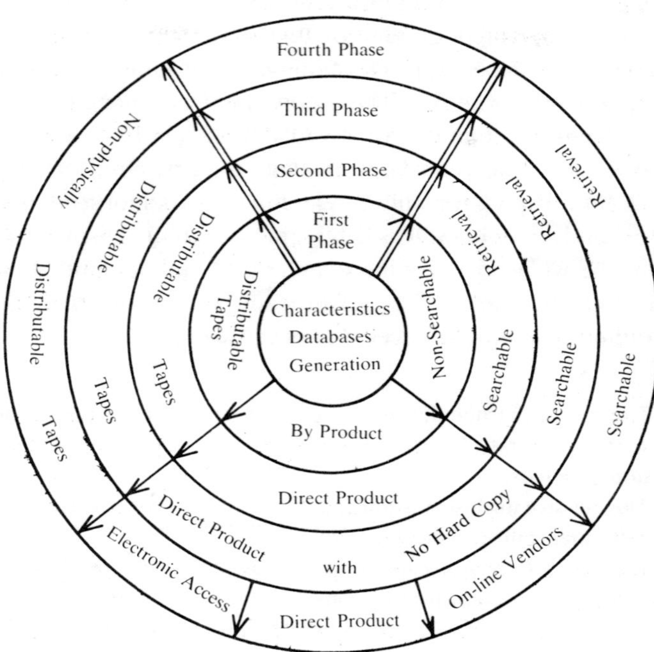

Figure 1.   Databases Generation Phases and their Characteristics

There are various types of databases existing today, and they have multifacet characteristics.   They are often called bibliographic, non-bibliographic, numeric, graphic, textual, or mixes type databases.   The commonly used databases can also be classified in three categories: 1) by type of parent organization, such as profit, non-profit organizations, or governmental agencies; 2) by subject, such as multidisciplinary, science and technology, social sciences and humanities, news, business and finance, law and legal, and medical/ biological sciences databases; and 3) by type of source materials, such as books, journals, patents, dissertations, current research, government reports and publications, newspapers, etc.

The Development of Online Database Searching Services

Online bibliographic searching was first investigated by Bagley in 1951, and it was several years before the first demonstration of bibliographic searching in 1954 in the form of batch searching, but the online bibliographic searching system was not shown until 1960.   The delay was due largely to the absence of appropriate technology, such as computer time-sharing, remote terminal equipments, and communications capability. The first public demonstration of online bibliographic or text searching was conducted in the U.S. in 1960 using the System Development Corporation's interactive system known as Protosynthex. The second public demonstration was made by Lockheed online system known as CONVERSE in 1964, using an in-house library database. Two years later, in 1966, the first public use of a cathode ray tube (CRT) display for online searching was demonstrated with Lockheed system and also with SDC's Bibliographic Online Display (BOLD) system.[8] But the widespread online searching of bibliographic databases was not begun until the early 1970s. Christain pointed out that the development of online searching services was because:

1). The increasing number and cost books and journals publications; library staff and operating costs of libraries are rising each year; and user information demands.

2). The massive unclassification and declassification of government documents with important technical information.

3). The switch to photocomposition and computer-aided production technology in the part of publishers of conventional A & I Services.

4). Technological progress in computer processing, storage, terminal and communication.

5). The dramatic decreases in the cost of necessary equipment.

6). The increased acceptance and recognition by librarians of the power of online databases searching services.

7). The availability of sophisticated commercial online services to provide efficient, nationwide access and worldwide access to various individual database.[9]

Database Producers and Online Service Vendors

According to the latest survey, there are more than 2,000 publicly available databases, 176 database producers, and nearly 400 online vendors. Among them, fifteen vendor services are the major distributors, they are

    BRS − Bibliographic Retrieval Services
    CAS − Chemical Abstracting Service, CAS Online
    DIS − DIALOG Information Services
    DJN − Dow Jones
    INF − INFORM (now called Vu Text)
    ISI − Institute for Scientific Information
    LEG − Legislate

MDC — Mead Data Central
NLM — National Library of Medicine
NYT — New York Times (now on MDC)
PER — Pergamon Inforline
QUE — QUESTEL
SDC — System Development Corporation
SRC — The Source
WST — Westlaw

Of the fifteen online vendors included in the survey, seven of them account for all of the most used database vendors in terms of usage connect hours and user expenditures.   The seven vendors are: BRS, DIALOG, Mead Data Central, National Library of Medicine, New York Times, SDC, and Westlaw.[10,11]

Education and Training Methods

Online searching of bibliographic databases has been an integral and continually growing facet of librarianship.   Education and training activities have been instrumental in the diffusion and adoption of online retrieval technology in order to maximize such a powerful searching mechanism.

It is not always easy to make a clear distinction between education and training; apparently they differ in functions, but educational objectives may sometimes well require training components and vise-versa.   To quote Fenichel and Hogan's statement on education and training definitions, "education encompasses the basic principles and theories of information science and information retrieval systems.   Its scope is much broader than training which focuses on the specific information and skills needed to operate the systems. In the context of these definitions almost all instruction for online searching has been 'training'.   So far only library schools have attempted to educate."[12]

1). Who Are the Trainees?
A spectrum of audience can be identified as the potential trainees for online searching training programs, they are:
  — Intermediaries/searcher/information broker
  — Working librarians and library staff
  — Library school students
  — End-user group: Researchers, faculty, graduate and undergraduate
                     students, the general public, etc.
2). Who Are the Sponsoring Body/Trainers for Education and Training?
Education and training for online searching have been conducted by various types of organizations and professionals in U.S. and in other coun-

tries, they usually are:
- Database Producers/ Search Services
- Database Processors/ Online Vendors
- Schools of Library and Information Science
- Online Training Centers
- Continuing Education Extension Programs
- Professional Societies and Associations
- Consulting Firms
- Internal/In-house Training Programs
- Online Users Groups

3). Methods of Instruction

The methods of instruction for education and training programs are of two types: the formal and the informal training programs.

3-1). The Informal Training : The methods are used usually for self-learning purposes.   Online searchers teach themselves the searching techniques by:
- studying systems workbooks and manuals.
- practicing on practice files which are usually provided by online vendors, e.g. Lockheed's ONTAP (Online Training and Practice).   Or using BRS/After Dark, DIALOG's Knowledge Index, the self-service method.
- Computer-assisted Instruction(CAI), such as "TRAINER" of the University of Pittsburgh, and "MEDLEARN" of the National Library of Medicine.

3-2). The Formal Training Programs : Keenan identifies three types of formal training programs:(1) Promotional activities for potential users; (2) educational training for library students, working librarians and information specialists; (3) operational training for searchers/intermediaries.   In many countries, formal training in online searching is offered by database producers, database processors, online vendors, schools of library and information science, continuing education extension programs, consulting firms, etc.[13]

3-2-1). Online Vendors/Database Processors Training Programs.

The contribution of online vendors and database processor to education and training of online users is extensive, especially in the U.S.   In fact, most of the training of online searchers in the U.S. has been done by the online vendors, such as NLM, BRS, DIALOG, and SDC.   The mode of instruction of BRS, SDC, and DIALOG is usually one to one and one half day training sessions aimed at either the beginners or advanced searchers, incorporating lectures, online demonstrations, and online student practice for a minimal fee.[14]

Wanger's "Survey of Users, 1974-75" indicated 55% of searchers are learning to use systems through formal workshops given by online vendors/database processors; 45% of searchers learned the system informally.[15]

3-2-2). Database Producers/Suppliers Training Programs.

Some of the database producers support active educational programs; others have none.   Some are free and some charge a fee.   Today, the active database producers in U.S. in this area are Chemical Abstracts Service (CAS), BioSciences Information Service of Biological Abstracts (BIOSIS), National Library of Medicine (NLM), and Educational Resources Information Center (ERIC).

3-2-3). School of Library and Information Science Education and Training Programs.

The emergence of online searching service as a powerful and useful tool has also been reflected in library school curriculums.   In a 1977 survey, Harter found that at least two-thirds (42 of the 64) of ALA-accredited library schools were providing some sort of instruction in the use of online systems.[16]   Again in 1981 Fenichel and Harter's *Survey of Online Searching Instruction in Schools of Library and Information Science*, 116 questionnaires were mailed; 72 returned.   Sixty-eight of 72 responding schools (94%) indicated that they are providing some types of instruction in online searching as part of their regular curriculum.[17]

The level of instruction provided by library schools varies widely.   Some give only introductory sessions and others devote an entire course to online searching, covering such topics as file organization and evaluation measures. Students who combine such a course with the courses of reference service, computer science, information science, and information analysis and retrieval systems offered by library schools should have a firm knowledge of both the principles and practice of online searching.   Most of the schools are using either in-house systems or the commercial search systems, such as Lockheed's DIALOG, SDC's ORBIT, or BRS systems for instruction as well as for hands-on student use, the amount of connect time provided varying widely from school to school.

Perhaps the most extensive program of this kind undertaken by a school is at the Online Training Center of the School of Library and Information Science (SLIS) of the University of Pittsburgh.   Software are developed to replicate the languages, formats and search capabilities of DIALOG, ORBIT AND BRS − emulators of these systems which are operating on a dedicated DEC VAX computer and using samples from sixty commercially available databases.   The students work at their own terminals, to gain a great deal of "hands-on" experience.   Two types of programs are given at the Online Training Center: 1). An Online Bibliographic Retrieval course for SLIS students, and 2). A four-day training program for people of outside communities.   Since April 1978, the Center has trained approximately 1,100 searchers, and over 800 of them are students.[18]

The financial support for this type of programs is always difficult to obtain.   Although vendors provide the service to the library schools for educational use at much reduced rate of US$15 per hour, the costs still mount up rapidly with many students using it.   Because of this problem, some schools have designed in-house systems or other teaching aids for training students, such as audio and digital recording devices, audio-visual aids – overhead transparencies, slides, tape-slide programs, videotapes, films, have been developed and used also for education and training for online searching.[19]

3-2-4). Professional Associations and Societies, Consulting Firms, National and Research Organizations.

Professional associations and societies, consulting firms, national and research organizations usually conduct a one-day workshop or pre-conference seminars on online training for their members, such as Cuadra Associates, Inc., National and International Online Conferences, and national libraries.

3-3). Online Training Materials.

Written materials are very important educational and training aids for online searching and for keeping up with the field.   The publications are online database directories, online searching system manuals, database manuals and workbooks, thesaurus, word lists, and newsletters.   Most of the online vendors are providing some training materials for their customers for a fee.

3-4). Evaluation and Assessment.

Little has been written on the evaluation analysis of education and training programs for online use of databases.   A recent article by Swanson was a study primarily on the application of various instruction methodologies to teach the use of online databases of nine U.S. programs, and he identified two "must" elements of instruction programs: "printed manuals" and "hands-on" practice.[20]   The criteria used for evaluation of this kind are often difficult to determine and formulate.

Survey of Online Professionals

The 1980 Online Users Survey reported that the average online searcher in the U.S. is a full-time person, spends 8.86 hours per week online, making $19,900 per year, is a female, and has a degree in chemistry and library science.[21]   And also, Marquis, after surveying online professionals in 46 countries, published its *Marquis Who's Who Directory of Online Professionals* in 1984, which contains 6,100 names.   The collected data indicated that a majority of online professionals work in the private sector and have between two and nine years of experience in the field; 32 per cent of them hold a master degree in library science; three-quarter (72 percent) of the online professionals are between the ages of 25 and 44, and fifty-eight per cent of them are women.   DIALOG is the most frequently used system, and 69 per cent of the respondents still searched using dumb terminals; but the online industry has predicted that there will be a major shift in 1984 and 1985 using the micro-computers with 1,200 baud modems to conduct searches.[22]

Problems and Trends

Cost will still be the important constraint related to the education and training for online use of databases in many library schools; promoting and marketing of online services are continuously needed; the good, inexpensive, and easy to use training packages will still be in great demand; and also the standardized procedures for training and education of skilled professionals as well as end users must be developed.   Now, it seems that the growth in number, size and diversity of databases is directly proportional to the increasing market demand for trained personnel in many organizations, and the training activities will definitely continue for some time to come.   Thus, the library schools, database producers, online vendors, professional associations, and consulting firms will be more and more involved in the education and training for online use of databases than ever in the future.

EDUCATION AND TRAINING FOR ONLINE USE OF

DATABASES IN TAIWAN, R.O.C.

Background Development

Taiwan, the Republic of China, is a small and beautiful island, 13,892 sq. miles in size with a population of over 19 million.   The economy of the Republic of China continues to grow in 1985 despite the slow recovery of the world economy.   The national economic growth in 1984 was 4.92 per cent. Per capita income at market price reached NT$87,270 in 1981, NT$121,467, or the equivalent of US$3,067 in 1984.[23]

It has been realized that in order to maintain the growing speed of the economy and the advancement of scientific and technological development of the country, information and information services are the vital factors. For years, the greatest emphasis in ROC was on scientific, technological, and industrial research and development, and overlooking the importance of information and information services that are related to it; unfortunately, these have caused the repetition of research works, and wasted time, and money.

Information is power; one must be in control and in an active position with the most up-to-date news and information on hand in order to compete with others and survive. Also, the best and fastest way to introduce new technology and foreign know-how is through information and information services. Consequently, in 1978, the Chinese government announced the Twelve New Construction Projects. The Twelfth Project is the Construction of Local Cultural Centers including libraries, museums, and music halls in each city and county at a cost of NT$1,500 million.[24]

In 1979, the National Science and Technology Development Program was initiated by the Chinese Government, and in the same year, the Information Industry Institute (III) was established in Taipei with the missions of assisting, up-grading, and developing the nation-wide information industries, such as computer hardware, software, micro/mini-computers, Chinese computers, Chinese character sets for information interchange, databases management systems (DBMS), manpower training, etc. In 1980, the government announced that the second week of December, a week after Library Week, will be the National Information Week. And at the same time, the Library Automation Planning Committee (LAPC) was established by the Library Association of China, in cooperation with the National Central Library of ROC with the purpose of improving information services and meeting the diverse needs of libraries in a local and international environment. The Committee has since draftedthe National Library Automation Project, which is to be implemented according to the following stages:

I.   Automation Project for Chinese Library Materials.
II.   Automation Project for Western Language Materials.
III.   Development of Library Operational Systems, and
IV.   Planning and Implementation of a National Information Network.[25]

For the past five years, with the strong support from the government, the concepts and the importance of information and information services have been widely publicized throughout the country. People have realized that information and information services are not only of vital importance to support decision making, research and development, but also for the production of goods and services that touch all parts of our lives.

Libraries, Library Schools and Their Programs

In 1943, there were 95 libraries in Taiwan as whole. Now, according to a 1982 survey of libraries in ROC there are 4,094 libraries. The various types of libraries are listed in Table 1.[26]

Table 1.   Types of Libraries in R.O.C.

Type of Library	Total Number
National	1
National Branch	1
Public	217
College & University	135
High School and Vocational School	1046
Elementary School	2474
Special	220
Total Libraries	4094

There are five colleges and universities in R.O.C. with library science departments; they are: National Taiwan University, National Taiwan Normal University, Catholic Fu-jen University, Tamkang University, and the World College of Journalism. In addition, the Chinese Culture University is offering a graduate program in Chinese bibliography. The only formal graduate institute of library science at present is at the National Taiwan University. The Institute was established in 1980. The following Table 2 will provide the latest information on library schools and their programs in R.O.C.[27]

Table 2.   Library Schools and Their Programs in R.O.C.

Institution Name	Date of Est.	Admission Requirements	Duration of Study	Degree Conferred
National Taiwan Univ.				
Graduate Institute of Libr. Science	1980	Bachelor Deg.	2 yr. +	MA
Dept. of Libr. Sci.	1961	High School Graduate	4 yr.	BA

National Taiwan Normal Univ.				
Dept. of Social Ed.,				
Section of Libr.		High School	4 yr. +	EDB
Science(Day)	1955	Graduate		
Night School	1980	Teachers of		
		All Levels	4 yr.	EDB
Chinese Culture Univ.				
Graduate Institute of				
History, Libr. and	1970	Bachelor Deg.	2 yr.+	MA
Archives Section				
Catholic Fu-jen Univ.				
Dept. of Libr. Sci.				
(Day)	1970	High School	4 yr.	BA
(Night)		Graduate	5 yr.	
Tamkang University				
Dept of Educational	1971	High School	4 yr.	BA
Media Sciences		Graduate		
World College of				
Journalism				
Section of Libr. Sci.	1964	High School		
(Day)		Graduate	3 yr.	— —
Section of Libr. Sci.	1965	High School		
(Night)		Graduate	4 yr.	— —

The Development of Online Databases Searching Services

On December 28, 1979, National Telecommunication Day, the International Telecommunication Administration (ITA) of the Ministry of Transportation of the Republic of China announced the opening of the Universal Databases Access Service (UDAS) to academic, research, commercial, industrial, and governmental organizations in the country. The purpose of UDAS is to provide domestic users via satellite with the accessibility to world coverage of online bibliographic and non-bibliographic information systems, such as Lockheed Information Systems (LIS), BRS (Bibliographic Retrieval Services), SDC's ORBIT system, Data Resources, Inc.(DRI), and public data network in other countries, to satisfy the needs of local information users and further help the social, economical, scientific, and technological improvement of the country.[28]

UDAS, How It Works?

The telephone and telecommunication systems in R.O.C. are owned by the government. Therefore, ITA provides the UDAS subscribers with all the international telecommunication connection facilities to foreign countries, such as international leased line, telex, telephone, terminal rentals, and the basic usage training of such facilities. The arrangement of UDAS service routing to other countries is shown in Figure 2.

Figure 2.   Arrangement of UDAS Service Routing to Other Countries

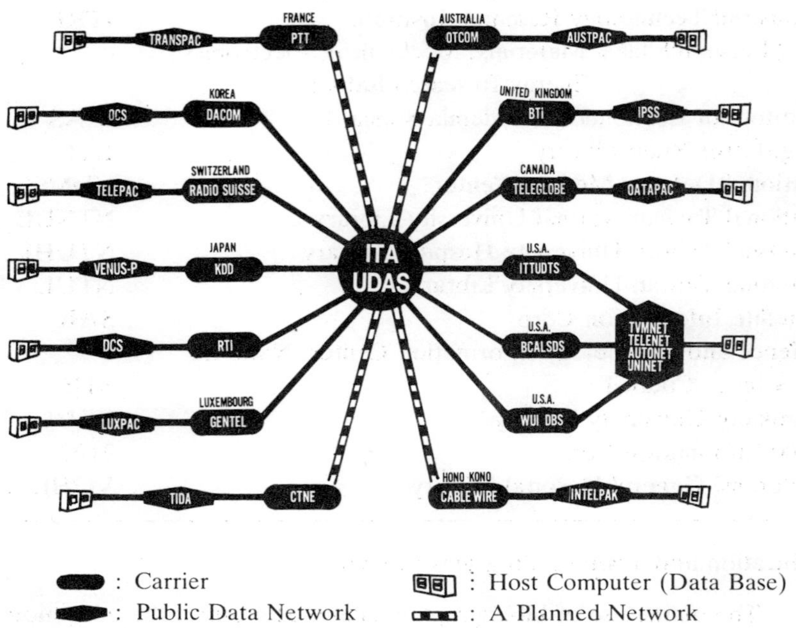

Present UDAS Subscribers, Who are They?

After ITA announced the opening of UDAS to the public in 1979, the first subscriber requested to use the service was the Bank of America in March, 1980. By September the same year, the total of subscribers was 12. Total usage time from March to September in 1980 was 79,638 minutes; 29,244,000 words were transmitted.[29] Now, November, 1985, five years later, the average monthly usage time is over forty thousand minutes, and monthly transmitted words are averaging over 50 million. The total subscribers are 63; 33 are private companies, 14 banking and financial oranizations, and 16 academic and research institutions. Among 63 UDAS subscribers 19 are using the service for information retrieval purposes.   They are:

Name of Oranization	Abbreviation
Agricultural Science Information Center	ASIC
Chemical Industrial Research Laboratories	CIRL
Industrial Technology Research Institute (ITRI)	
China Steel Corporation	CSC
Chung-hua Institution for Economics Research	CHIER
Chung Shan Institute of Science & Technology	CSIST
Directorate General of Budget, Accounting & Statistics	DGBAS
Industrial Technology Research Institute	ITRI
(4 research labs: Materials, Mechanical, Electronics, Energy Research Labs.)	
Institute of Economics, Academia Sinica	IEAS
Legislative Yuan Library	LYL
National Defense Medical Center	NDMC
National Taiwan Normal University Library	NTNUL
National Taiwan University Hospital Library	NTUHL
National Taiwan University Library	NTUL
Satellite Information Corp	SAIC
Science and Technology Information Center, National Science Council	STIC
Tamkang University Library	TKUL
2100 Information Corp.	21IC
Veterans' General Hospital Library	VGHL

Education and Training Programs in ROC

The online use of bibliographic databases requires the education and training of users of online services.   In ROC, the faculties of library schools have long been aware of the trends in online searching services.   They not only realized that online searching of databases is a powerful tool for reference service, but also they knew that in recent years it has become an increasingly important means of accessing information resources in libraries worldwide.   Thus, they have started to introduce the concepts of online databases and the search strategies in a number of related courses.   (Shown in Table 3) And at the same time, they made suggestions to ITA and urged the government to support ITA to establish connections with various online databases vendors in the U.S. and in other countries.   So the UDAS was inaugurated in 1979.[30]

Table 3.   Library Science Courses Related to Teaching and
Education of Online Databases Concepts

Institution Name	Course Name	Searching Facility/ Location/Systems
National Taiwan Univ. Graduate Institute & Dept. of Libr.Sci.	*Online Searching Library Automation Library Trends *Information Analysis & Retrieval S. & T. Literature *Abstracting and Indexing Intn. to Info. Sci. Info. Sci. Seminar	NTU Library and Hosp. Library Online Facility/DIALOG Online Demo for Students
National Taiwan Normal University Dept. of Social Edu., Section of Libr. Sci.	*Information Searching Library Automation Reference Services Intn. to Info. Sci.	NTNU Library Online Facility/DIALOG, BRS 10 min./student
Catholic Fu-jen Univ. Dept. of Libr. Sci.	*Information Ret'l Intn. to Info. Sci. S. & T. Literature	No Online Facility/ Demo 20 min./ DIALOG (STIC)
Tamkang University Dept. of Educational Media Science	*Information Centers & Services Library Automation Reference Services S. & T. Literature A & I Course Intn. to Info. Sci.	Tamkang Univ. Libr. Online Facility/ DIALOG Lab. Fee for On-line practice
World College of Journalism	*Chinese Cat. & Class. Documentation	No Facility/No Demo.

At present time, there are no established training centers or training
programs in the country.   In the beginning, the training sessions were conducted occasionaly by the vendor representatives who were in Taiwan marketing their products and services, or upon the requests of the customers in
Taiwan to solve certain problems.   At the same time, ITA and the vendor

would schedule a short (two-day) training session for local subscribers and potential users, usually free of charge.   Since then, the training sessions were handled by the subscribers themselves to train their searchers and users, and sometimes other libraries' personnel.   In addition, the Science and Technology Library Network (SATLINE), an inter-library loan organization, and a few experienced subscribing institutions are also conducting workshops and seminars on online databases.   Table 4 lists training sessions which were given from May, 1980 to the present.[31]

Table 4.   Training Sessions Given From May, 1980 — Present

Training Institution	Trainer	Training Period	No.Trainee	Fee
National Taiwan Univ.	DIALOG/ NTU Hosp. Searcher;	Regular Class	12	Free
	Libr. Auto. Workshop	Aug. 29, 1980	42	Fee
	Instructor & NTNU Searcher	Aug. 18, 1981	42	Fee
National Taiwan	SDC/ NTNU-	May 12-13, 1980	138	
Normal Univ.	Searcher	Nov.28-30, 1980	40	Free
Library		May 10-11, 1980	15	
		Regular class	6-8	Fee
Science & Technology	DIALOG/	Aug.26-27, 1980	12	NT$1000
Information Center		Aug.28-29, 1980	12	NT$1000
	STIC	Dec.15-19, 1982		
	Searcher	(half day)	37	Internal Training
ITA	DIALOG	May 16-17, 1982	40	Free
Tamkang University	DIALOG	Jan. 1982	Faculties	Free
Library	Searcher	July, 1982	& Students	
		(half day)	L.S. Graduates (30)	Fee
	Class Instructor	Regular Class once/semester	Whole Class	Lab. Fee

| 21 Cent. Info. Co. | DIALOG | Two Days | 50+ | ? |
| SATLINE | Intn of Major S.& T. Online DBs No online Training | Sept.16-17, 1985 | 130 | Fee |

The Graduate Institute and Department of Library Science of the National Taiwan University is now offering courses, such as "Online Searching" and "Information Storage and Retrieval" to train students in online searching concepts and techniques.   At the present time, both NTU Library and its Hospital Library have subscribed to DIALOG Service, which will be used for the university community, online demonstration, and library students online hands-on searching practice.   In the future, if there is any indication of great demand for training or education in online use of databases in the country, the National Taiwan University would consider expanding its program to establish a National Training Center for the entire country.

Survey of Online Users in R.O.C.

To understand the present status of online users, their problems and needs, a recent survey of online searchers was conducted.   Questionnaires are mailed to 18 online subscribing organizations and their searchers, and 16 (88.8%) subscribers returned the questionnaire.   The survey results indicated that there are approximately 40 online searchers in 16 subscribing organizations, among them, 12 (30%) full-time searchers, 29 (72.5%) of them library science graduates, and the majority of them learned to search by themselves.

Their problems and needs are: the lack of subject background; difficulty in negotiating with users; not enough searching tools and lack of familiarity with the existing ones; problems in getting the original articles; lack of adequate online education and training programs; no one to solve searching problems; and some databases, such as economics, commercial databases are not relevent to the practical needs of industrial organizations in the country.   All of them agreed that they needs continuing education and training especially in the areas of online database structure, design principles, new search strategies, and functions.   Major findings of online users, and frequently used databases are listed in Table 5.

Table 5.   Major Findings of Online Users in R.O.C.

Orgn. Name	Av. Month Searches	No. of Searchers (fulltime)	Degree	Search Learn. Methods	Cont. Ed. & Train. Needs	System Name
ASIC	40	4(1)	Marine & Agr. Sciences	Self-learn. In-house	yes	DIALOG BRS ORBIT
CIRI	26	2(1)	Chem. Econom.	Self In-house ITA	yes	DIALOG BRS ORBIT
CSC	20-30	1(0)	Lib.Sci.	LS Class	yes	DIALOG
CHIER	5	1(0)	Banking	In-house	yes	DRI
CSIST	38	2(1)	Lib.Sci.	LS Class Others	yes	DIALOG
DGBAS	2	1(0)	?	Self Vendor	yes	DRI
ITRI: ERL ERSO MRL MIRL	38	8(0)	Lib.Sci. German Ind. Engr.	Self In-house Others Vendor ITA	yes	DIALOG
IEAS	3-5	1(0)	Econom.	Self Vendor	yes	DRI
LYL	7	5(3)	Lib.Sci.	LS Class Self Others	yes	DIALOG
NDMC	30	3(1)	Lib.Sci.	Self Others Seminar	yes	DIALOG
NTNUL	30	1(1)	Lib.Sci.	Self Vendor	yes	DIALOG ORBIT
NTUL	?	6(1)	Lib.Sci.	Self ITA	yes	DIALOG

NTUHL	40	1(1)	Lib.Sci.	Self	yes	DIALOG
STIC	90	1(1)	Lib.Sci.	Self	yes	DIALOG
				Others		BRS
				Vendor		ORBIT
				ITA		
TKUL	?	1(1)	Lib.Sci.	LS Class	yes	DIALOG
				Self		
				Others		
				Vendor		
VACRS	80	2(1)	Lib.Sci.	Self	yes	BRS
				In-house		
				Others		
				Seminar		

Most Frequently Used Databases are:
1. CA Search
2. MEDLINE
3. BIOSIS
4. COMPENDEX
   INSPEC
   CLAIM
   PIS
5. WPI
6. NTIS
7. US Central
   DRI-CEI
   U.S. Patent
8. CAB
   IPAB
   ERIC
   LDC-ASIA
   LC
   CIS
   FSTA
   Geoarchive
   ISMEC
   Magzine Index

Present Problems and Future Prospects

Online databases searching services just began in the ROC, but there are many problems to be solved. Formal education and training programs for online use of databases must be established and formulated in the country to train skilled searchers. Fortunately, a number of seminars, workshops, and training sessions have been conducted for online searchers and potential users by various organizations in the country. On November 8th, 1985, at the SATLINE Annual Meeting, a proposal to establish an "Online Users Groups" has been formally approved by its members. The Group will consist of online users in this country who will have formal and informal meetings to discuss and exchange experiences among themselves.

Another important problem is marketing of online searching services. Many authors, such as Williams, Keenan, and Tedd[32] have suggested strongly that marketing is important! Williams identifies that "Marketing is concerned with making various target groups aware of services and of the content, characteristics, features, advantages, and benefits that accure to specific searching databases. Marketing is also concerned with motivating or contracting for products and/or services."[33] Online searching is indeed a dynamic tool, but it is the duty and responsibility of librarians, information specialists, and library schools in the country to promote online searching services and make them known.

Another major problem of online searching is the cost. Cost of using the online services, cost of setting up an in-house searching system, cost of subscribing to the commercial searching services, and a minimum cost just to maintain it. It seems that the cost problem is the same in ROC as in other countries.

It has been realized by researchers in the country, that besides using UDAS service for locating foreign materials, another important factor also should be taken into consideration; that is the development of online databases of Chinese language materials. For years building databases of resources in Chinese language materials has long been an emphasized research area of various academic and research organizations in the ROC. And now, with advanced Chinese computer technology, many bibliographic and non-bibliographic Chinese language databases exist in the country. To name a few: the Chinese Database for Educational Resources Information System (CERIS), five databases of Agricultural Science and Technology Information Management System (ASTIMS), the Freedom Council Information Abstracts (FICA) database, and the National Science Council database etc.[34] Now, with modern computer and communication capabilities, and joint cooperative efforts in research, the country is strongly urged to develop a national centralized online interactive bibliographic search service system in ROC.

CONCLUSIONS

In ROC, online service has just begun, and the tasks of developing the education and training programs for online use of databases will not be easy. Perhaps, with strong support of the government, the cooperative endeavor of local professionals and library schools, and also using other countries' experiences as a guide, the education and training for online use of databases in ROC will soon become a reality.

I would like to conclude this paper with some thought of Lancaster,[35] who has once identified the goals of online education and training, especially in library schools, as train information services librarians who specilize in provision of information service from machine-readable databases. Such a librarian must be knowledgeable about databases, search systems, evaluation methodology, indexing techniques, vocabulary control procedures, and search strategies, and he felt that education programs should do more than prepare individuals to work with the online systems. Moreover, he further said that many current technological applications are moving rapidly in a paperless direction, and eventually we will enter a paperless society. In this paperless environment, users will depend heavily on their online facilities, especially the terminals or their personal computers, and education and training in online searching will be more in demand than ever, not only to train the information professionals but also the end users a well. It seems to me that in the future society, paperless or not, one, any one must posses online searching skills in order to survive!

REFERENCES

1. Martha E. Williams, "Highlights of the Online Databases Filed — "Statistics, Pricing and New Delivery Mechanism." *National Online Meeting 1984: Proceedings of the Fifth National Online Meeting, New York, April 10-12, 1984.* (Medford, N.J.:Learned Information, 1984), p. 1.

2. Emil H. Levine, "The National Online Meeting 1984," *ASIS Bulletin* 19 (April 1984) :9.

3. Martha E.Williams, "Usage and Revenue Data for the Online Database Instry," *Online Review* 9 (September 1985): 205-210.

4. C.H.Fenichel and Thomas H. Hogan, *Online Searching: A Primer.* 2nd

ed.   (Malton, N.J.:Learned Information, 1984), p.3.

5. Allen Kent, "The Potential of Online Information Systems," *Online Revolution in Libraries* (New York: Marcell Dekker, 1978),pp. 28-29.

6. Martha E.Williams, "Education and Training for Online Use of Data-Bașes," *Journal of Library Automation* 10 (December 1977) : 326.

7. Lucy Te-Chu Lee, "Bibliographic Databases and Online Retrieval Services," *Journal of Library and Information Science* 5 (April 1979) : 79-103.

8. Charles P. Bourne, "Online Systems : History, Technology, and Economics," *Journal of ASIS* 31 (January 1980) : 155-160.

9. Roger Christain, "Bibliographic Data Bases," *The Professional Librarian; Reader in Library Automation and Technology* (White Plains, N.Y.: KIP, 1980), pp.22-35.

10. Williams (1985) , *op.cit.*, p. 1

11. Fenichel, *op.cit.*, p.3.

12. Ibid.

13. Stella Keenan, "Promote, Educate or Train?"   *Third International Online Information Meeting* (Malton, N.J.: Learned Information, 1979), pp.342-349.

14. Charles Bourne and Jo Robinson, "Education and Training for Computer based Reference Services: Review of Training Efforts Todate," *Journal of ASIS* 31 (January 1980): 25.

15. Judith Wanger, "Education and Training for Online System," *Annual Review of Information Science and Technology* vol.14 (White Plains,N.Y.: KIP, 1979), pp. 219-245.

16. S.P.Harter, "An Assessment of the Instruction Provided by Library Schools in Online Training," *Information Processing and Management* 15 (1979) : 71-75

17. Carol H.Fenichel and S.P.Harter , *Survey of Online Searching Instruction in Schools of Library and Information Science* (Dublin, OH: OCLC, 1981), p. 8.

18. Conversation with Dr. E. Duncan, Director of the Online Training Center of the University of Pittsburgh School of Library and Information Science, August, 1985.

19. Lucy A. Tedd, "Teaching Aids Developed and Used for Education and

Training for Online Searching," *Online Review* 4 (Spring 1981) : 205-216.

20. R.W.Swanson, "An Assessment of Online Instruction Methodologies," *Online* 6 (January 1982) : 38-55.

21. M.M.K.Hlava, "Online Users Survey 1980, " *Online Review* 4 (June 1981) : 294-299.

22. Carol Tenopir, "Online Professionals," *Library Journal* 110 (February 1985) : 122-123.

23. Information supplied by the Directorate General of Budget, Accounting and Statistics, R.O.C., March, 1985.

24. *Central Daily News*, R.O.C., Feb.15, 1985.

25. Library Association of China.   "Library Automation Planning Program." *Library Association of China Newsletter* 22 (1980): 9-10.

26. National Central Library, R.O.C., *A Survey of Libraries in Taiwan, R.O.C.*   (Taipei: NCL, 1982), p. 28.

27. Chen-Ku Wang.   "Libraries and Librarianship in Taiwan , R.O.C." *The 1980 Library Development Seminar Proceedings* (Taipei: NCL, 1980),pp. 293-298.

28. S.F.Cheng.   *Chao Tung Chieh Sheh.*   (December 1980), pp. 16-24.

29. Conversation with S.F.Cheng of ITA Office, March and November 1985.

30. Conversation with various organizations and library Schools in ROC, March and November, 1985.

31. A Survey on Online Searchers was conducted in November, 1985.

32. Lucy A. Tedd.   "Education, Training and Marketing for Online Information Retrieval Systems."   *Online Review* 3 (June 1979) : 205-212.

33. Williams (1977), *op.cit.*,p.321.

34. T.S.Fung , "Chinese Data Processing Systems." *The International Workshop on Chinese Library Automation Proceedings* (Taipei: NCL. 1981) , pp. I-XVIII.

35. F.W. Lancaster and L.C. Smith.   "Online Systems in the Communication Processing : Projections." *Journal of ASIS* 31 (September 1980) : 196-200.

Continuing Education and Staff Development
for Librarians in the Republic of China

Shih-hsion Huang
Director
Tamkang University Library
Tamsui, Taiwan, R.O.C.

INTRODUCTION

The systematic, planned development of the library profession in Taiwan, R.O.C. has only been relatively emphasized for the past ten years. Along with the miraculous economic growth of our society, the need for information and knowledge seems to be increasingly felt by the general public. Nevertheless, some major factors that keep the libraries in Taiwan on the right path and help them to flourish and bloom are: qualified librarians newly trained by library schools[1] ; and the Library Association of China's active, decisive leadership.

The directors at all levels of libraries found that they have to keep expanding library collections and equipment in order to satisfy their clientele's daily rising demands.   In addition, they have to pay immense attention to technologicial needs of the library professionals.   What they generally did to cope with these trends was, besides hiring more library school graduates, to encourage the librarians to participate in, or even sponsor themselves, continuing education programs.   At the same time, the rapidly changing new technologies, especially in telecommunications, have enormously altered the management models of libraries.   Library operations, whether for individual libraries or for library network cooperatives, become more and more specialized, from manual practice to computerized systems.   Library practitioners have already recognized the fact that their pre-professional education can no longer be applied to this transition, and that they need to learn and to keep abreast of the current events and skills; that is to say, they must keep themselves a step ahead of professional obsolescence.   By the same token, the library administrators have also recognized that only with competent staff can they strengthen their libraries to fulfill their missions more effectively and efficiently.

Continuing education can be provided by means of formal library school education, seminars, conferences, independent studies, and publications, to supplément the individual practitioner who has limited experience. Staff development, on the other hand, takes the form of short-duration workshops, lectures, site-visits to gain familiarity with the library's daily practices, established policies and procedures.[2] At the present time, there are five colleges and universities in Taiwan that offer undergraduate programs in library and information science: National Taiwan University, National Taiwan Normal University, Fu-Jen Catholic University, Tamkang University, and the World College of Journalism. University of Chinese Culture and National Taiwan University also offer programs at gradate level. Their curriculum are mostly in the nature of preprofssional pre-paration. However, some of these institutions also provide continuing education courses to librarians in the summer session.

For example, National Taiwan University Library School sponsors annually a seminar on Library Automation with the expectation that it will provide library professionals the knowledge, for coping with the library's future trends and demands. The Department of Educational Media & Library Sciences of Tamkang University holds each summer for its alumni and library staffs brief-duration courses stressing the development and impact of new technology, such as Artificial Intelligence, Expert Systems, Principles of Statistics and Analysis, Data Base Structure and Design, and Online Searching. These courses have received rather high praise. The Department of Library Science at Fu-Jen University sponsored in the summer of 1985 a similar seminar for the alumni. The Department of Social Education, National Taiwan Normal Unversity also offers continuing education to the elementary and secondary school librarians and administrators. All of these programs and academic activities have been extremely helpful to the library community in obtaining needed skills and knowledge. It is true that courses offered in graduate library schools are also considered as one of the approaches preparing students for their professional careers. In the West, an MLS degree is deemed a basic credential for securing a professional library position. However, for those graduate students who already have practical working experience in libraries before going to graduate library schools, advanced studies are basically for the pursuit of higher degrees or better job opportunities. Hence for them a graduate library school education fulfills the dual functions of preparatory and continuing education.

THE LIBRARY ASSOCIATION OF CHINA (LAC)

One of the major objectives of the Library Association of China (LAC), since its foundation in 1954, has been to educate and train library workers in this country.   It has been trained more than 3,000 people since its summer seminars first began in 1956.   As Professor Chien-Chang Lan, Dean of the Library Science Department, Fu-Jen University, said: "A seminar of this kind is especially for those library workers from libraries of all levels who have never received formal library training.   After the seminar, when they return to their own positions, they can assist their professional librarians technically ..." [3] Consequently, the subjects covered in the previous 29 seminars are all fundamental and pragmatic in nature.   In recent years, LAC found that even the library professionals suffer from limited knowledge of international library trends and new concepts which affect their daily library operations.   As a result, LAC collaborated with the Department and School of Library Science of National Taiwan University and sponsored annually a seminar on Library Automation. It also delegated to the Medical Library Committee the responsibility for holding a summer seminar on medical science.   All the participants in these two seminars are graduates of library schools, and the topics are on a much more advanced level.

PROFESSIONAL PUBLICATIONS

The publications in the library field have positively influenced and promoted the concepts of continuing education and staff development.   They provide the library personnel and students the best resources for getting to know about current events and activities within the library sphere.   These publications can be divided into four categories: 1. Newsletters; 2. Bulletins; 3. Library School publications; and 4. Scholarly Journals.

1. Newsletters
   A. *Library Association of China Newsletter*, bimonthly.
      Originated in1975 to cover LAC's current events and activities, meeting minutes, announcements of new publications, and special reports.
   B. *National Central Library Newsletter*, quarterly.
      First issued in 1978, the Newsletter includes NCL's programs, current events and activities, speeches and lectures, and new publications, and serves as an important communications link for the library profession.
2. Bulletins
   A. *National Central Library Bulletin*, semi-annually.
      An official publication of the Library, reissued in 1967.

B. *Bulletin of the Library Association of China,* annually.
   First published in 1954, and has been coming out simultaneously with
   LAC's annual conferencwe. Its contents cover papers, book re-
   views, conference activities, library activities, committee reports, and
   meeting minutes.
3. Library School Publications
   A. *Bulletin of Library Science (Shu-fu),* annually
      Published annually since 1979 by the Student Society of Library Sci-
      ence of the Department and Graduate Institute of Library Science at
      the National Taiwan University, including short articles by faculty mem-
      bers and research results by students.
   B. *Bulletin of the Department of Library Science,* annually.
      Issued by the Department of Library Science, Fu-Jen Catholic Uni-
      versity in 1972 to publish papers authored by the students and faculty
      members in the Department.
4. Scholarly Journals
   A. *Journal of Library Science,* irregular.
      First issued in 1967 by the Department of Library Science, National
      Taiwan University. So far, four volumes have been issued, including
      research papers, announcements of newly published survey reports, and
      book reviews in the library and related fields.
   B. *Journal of Library and Information Science,* semi-annually.
      First published in 1975 by the Department of Social Education, Na-
      tional Taiwan Normal University in collaboration with the Chinese
      American Librarians Associations in the U.S., this bilingual (English
      & Chinese) Journal aims to promote the development of Chinese li-
      brary and information services.
   C. *Journal of Educational Media & Library Sciences,* quarterly
      Originated in 1970, this bilingual publication is a joint effort of the
      Department of Educational Media & Library Sciences and the Tam-
      kang University Library. It is devoted to domestic and international
      studies regarding the fields of library science, information science,
      audiovisual and educational technologies.
   Except for the two scholarly journals, all the publications mentioned a-
bove are free of charge. They are of great value to library professionals
and other practitioners.

INTERNATIONAL CONFERENCES

By sponsoring or participating in international conferences, librarians

meet with national and international scholars to exchange experiences and i-
deas, to discuss possible solutions for problems encountered by libraries,
and to talk about the future trends in library development brought about by
the emerging new technologies. These conferences are a kind of shortcut
by which librarians may reach the ultimate goals of their continuing education policies. For the past ten years, government agencies and private groups
have encouraged their librarians and information specialists to attend this
type of scholarly meeting e.g., annual meetings held by oprganizations like
IFLA, ALA, and ASIS, without any reservation. Even better, these groups
and agencies often encourage or financially support domestic academic institutions to convene such conferences or seminars. Some famous examples
are as follows: the First Asian Library Cooperation Conference, held in Tamkang University in 1976; the Library Practices Seminar, summoned by National Taiwan Normal University in 1979; the 1980 Library Development Seminar, sponsored by the National Central Library; the International Conference on Library Automation for Chinese Materials, held in National Taiwan Institute of Technology in 1981; and the First Asian-Pacific Conference
on Library Science in 1983 by National Taiwan Normal University. More
than half of these conferences are sponsored or co-sponsored by LAC or NCL.
Two significant objectives of sponsoring or participating in international conferences are that it can either increase the opportunity for people and groups
at the national and international levels to exchange new concepts and ideas,
or provide library professionals and workers more chances to share the academic achievements of the world. Such conferences are undoubtedly one
of the best ways to provide continuing education to library personnel.

SURVEY AND ANALYSIS

As mentioned earlier, attending conferences has positive effects on
continuing education and staff development. However, in order to secure
even more direct and frequent results, it is wise to make the best use of human resources, mainly senior librarians and teaching faculty members in library schools, and of the equipment and facilities in large libraries to offer
continuing education programs . The main purpose of this paper is to investigate all the continuing education and staff development programs and
activities at various institutions, such as national and governmental libraries,
college and university libraries, library associations, and library schools.
Both primary and secondary data have been collected and analyzed in accordance with the objectives and levels of courses and program actvities offered, in order to interpret all modes of continuing education and staff develop-

ment for the past five years.

The survey was conducted on a selected sample of 56 large libraries that are capable of providing continuing education programs, including 21 public libraries, 30 academic libraries, and 5 special libraries. The results were not very satisfactory. Twelve libraries indicated that besides sending staff to take part in continuing education programs held by other institutions, they conducted similar programs themselves in-house. Forty-four libraries revealed that they have established policies for professional advancement, though they have never sponsored any workshops or seminars of this nature. Overall, most libraries have achieved, to some extent, the promotion of continuing education by granting time for staff to take courses, and so on.

The programs sponsored by LAC are very often the most extensive ones, with the widest participant groups. Upon analyzing their course contents, we found that basic, fundamental courses, such as Cataloging and Classification, Reference Services, Collection Development and Acquisitions, and Non-Book Materials make up 87.6%, while the rest is for the future trends courses, such as Library Automation. It is obvious that these programs are of a rudimentary, preparatory nature (shown in Table 1). The full details are well documented in the LAC Newsletter, #26-45 [4]. As for the training sessions held by library schools, these are mostly aimed at the retraining of full-time library professionals, with the exception of the Department of Social Education, National Taiwan Normal University, whose mission is to train primary and middle school libray personnel. The courses offered are more specialized and advanced, such as Library Automation, System Analysis and Data Structure. More recently, the focus has been on computer related courses such as Artificial Intelligence, Expert System and Management Information Systme (MIS). It is the responsibility of these technology-oriented courses to make sure library personnel can keep up with the trends and developments in computerized library systems. These advanced courses now comprise a major portion of all the courses offered by library schools. The percentage is as high as 92.7% (as shown in Table 2 of the appendices). As for special library groups, such as medical libraries, they cannot combine their continuing education and staff development programs with those of other libraries. Therefore, they have requested hospital libraries to plan and to arrange a curriculum for the retraining of medical library personnel. As shown in Table 3, the courses arranged for the medical library retraining programs put equal stress on the fundamental and advanced aspects of librarianship.

Despite various approaches to concerted efforts in providing continuing education and staff development programs, libraries in general still struggle with bottleneck problems, particularly technological ones. In order to overcome this difficulty, Tamkang University Library initiated a librarian exchange program with Ohio University (Athens) Libraries in 1981, and with the University of Illinois (Urbana-Champaign) Libraries in 1984, selecting one or two of the best qualified librarians each year to visit there for a period of four to six months, receiving short-term, in-service training. These exchange librarians also take the opportunity to visit many other famous libraries in the U.S. and Canada. Upon returning, they share what they've learned with their fellow librarians. Having seen the great benefits of the Tamkang University Exchange Programs, Fen Chia University Library also signed a contract with Ohio University to dispatch its library personnel to receive training abroad. National Taiwan University, National Taiwan Normal University, the Agricultual Science Information Center and the National Central Library have also jumped on the bandwagon and are sending their staff abroad.

CONCLUSIONS AND RECOMMENDATIONS

There are positive effects of providing librarians with a variety of programs and opportunities for their continuing education. However, there are points that still remain imperfect and need to be addressed:

1. The need to upgrade the levels of courses is apparent. After examining the courses offered, we discovered the majority of them are geared for preparatory education. The twenty-nine annual seminars held by LAC in the past have definitely trained a great number of library personnel, and have contributed a great deal to the development of the library profession. Nevertheless, the LAC has not upgraded the level of curriculum arrangement as yet. Certainly we have no intention here of denying the need for basic courses in the library science programs. Instead, we suggest that policies and objectives for long or middle range plans should be settled on. Only after the established goals have been reached will the need for upgrading the curriculum seem inevitable. At the current stage, the following strategies are recommended:

A. Decrease the number of fundamental courses according to trends and development of the library profession. In this information age, library automation is the inescapable trend and ultimate objective for most libraries. Each library ought to speed up in these respects and become fully automated. Currently, the National Central Library has done a great deal toward the preparation of a computerized library system. Once the information network has been established, a completely integrated library network will be realized within days. Afterwards, the need for original cataloging and classifying of library materials in a medium-sized or small library would be decreased or completely eliminated.   On the contrary, the need for computer applications in the library will be increased daily.   Therefore, it would be better for us to design a proper curriculum in advance, and implement it each year by gradual addition of higher level courses.

B. The qualification of participants should be restricted.   The librarians who have received formal pre-service education should not participate in the beginning level of staff development programs, to avoid wasting the time and money of libraries and librarians.   It can be recommended that they attend higher level continuing education programs.   In addition, the evaluation of randomly selected program participants should be conducted to access the usefulness of the courses and their applicability to actual job situations.   The result should be the support of curriculum revision in the future.

2. Continuing education seminars should be held in sections.   For the convenience of the lecturers and learning efficiency of the participants, the seminars should be arranged in sections according to the degree of difficulty and complexity.   Only those who have completed the prerequisite sessions will then be allowed to attend the advanced ones.

3. The arrangement of a curriculum should correspond with developing global trends.   It should aim at adapting the policies and strategies of other major libraries, domestic or foreign, and the courses offered at the library schools here and abroad, so as to reshape our curriculum according to practical needs.

4. The provision of summer library school programs for the existing library schools is recommended for the professional advancement of library staff and /or for those who have their library degrees.

5. The need for expanding the scope of LAC's annual meeting to incorporate discussion sections on current events should be taken into careful consideration.

NOTES

1. The term "library school" in this paper refers to the departments and/or schools of library and information sciences of colleges and universities in Taiwan.
2. Barbara Conroy, *Library Staff Development and Continuing Education: Principles and Practices* (Littleton, Colo. : Libraries Unlimited, 1978) P.xv.
3. Chien-Chang Lan, *"San Shih Nien Lai Te Chung-kuo T'u-Shu-Kuan Hsueh-Hui* (三十年來的中國圖書館學會)", *Bulletin of Library Association*

of China. 35 (1983) : 4.
4. *Library Association of China Newsletter*, 26-45 (1981-1985).

APPENDICES

Table 1. Courses Offered in Professional Training Programs
Held by LAC and Other Libraries

Courses	Frequency	%
Basic Courses		
Acquisitions Techniques	21	
Audiovisual Materials & Production	6	
Cataloging & Classification	33	
Children's & Young Adults' Literature	16	
Intro. to Library Science	20	
Library Administration	4	
Library Extension Services	2	
Library Practical Works	12	
Library Programs & Services to children	10	
Non-Book Materials	15	
Public Libraries	9	
Reference Services	25	
School Libraries	10	
Total (basic)	183	87.6
Advanced Courses		
Chinese MARC	4	
Information Science & MARC	4	
Information Systems & Services	1	
Introduction to Information Science	2	
Library Development & Future Trends	10	
Library Automation	5	
Total (advanced)	26	12.4
Total (both)	209	100.0

Table 2. Courses Offered in Professional Training
Programs by Library Schools

Courses	Frequency	%
Basic Courses		
Anglo-American Cataloging Rules	4	
Chinese Cataloging Rules	3	

Intro. to Computer Science	1
Library & Information Science	1

Total (basic)	9	7.3

Advanced Courses

Application of Micros in Library	6
Artificial Intelligence	1
Authority Files	4
Chinese MARC	7
Computer Networking	4
Data Bases	8
Expert System	1
Indexing & Abstracting	7
Information Technology	2
Input of Chinese Records	4
Introd. to Chinese Computer & Computing	11
Intro. to Information System	6
LC MARC	1
Library Automation	15
Library Network	6
On-Line Cataloging	4
On-Line Searching	3
Principles of Library Statistics	1
System Analysis, Design & Evaluation	9
Telecommunications	5
Thesaurus	3
Others	7

Total (advanced)	115	92.7
Total (both)	124	100.0

*Table 3. Courses Offered in Professional Training
Programs Held by Medical Libraries*

Courses	Frequency	%
Basic Courses		
Acquisitions	2	
Audiovisual Materials	2	
Cataloging & Classification	2	
Circulation	1	
Library Administration	1	
Periodical Management	2	

Reference Services	3	
Total (basic)	13	46.4
Advanced Courses		
Family Medicine	1	
Intro. to Chinese Medicines	1	
Library Automation in Medical Libraries	1	
Nursing Reference Documents	1	
Seminars on Medical Science	11	
Total (advanced)	15	53.6
Total (both)	28	100.0

*All library practicum, on-site visit, and seminars are not entered here (Tables 1-3).   LAC's sectional training sessions are included.

Libraries and Information Centers — Their Changing
Role in a Changing Environment

Herbert S. White
Professor and Dean
School of Library and Information Science
Indiana University
Bloomington, Indiana, U. S. A.

The traditional concept of libraries and of librarians has evolved over the years as defined by the community of library users, but as also willingly agreed to by librarians. It centers on the roles of libraries as keepers and storehouses of the world's recorded information. Such libraries can be very large or they can be small, as warehouses can be of either size as well as a whole variety of range in between. The emphasis of such organizations, and the responsibility of those who staff them, is quite simple and quite clear, even when carrying out those responsibilities can involve complexity. The task first and foremost is to acquire, and it is no coincidence that those considered great research librarians of the 19th and first half of the 20th century were most renowned for their ability to find what others could not find, and to acquire it for their own unique collections. As with museums and art galleries, the primary value system for libraries was and largely remains that of ownership. Libraries were and largely still are "measured" in terms of the size and not the content of their holdings, and libraries with 6 million volumes are presumed to be excellent, those with 2 million less so. The primary objective of library policies, if indeed such libraries can be said to have objectives, is to reach the threshold of that additional million volumes – to join the million volume club or some even more exclusive group. The example is not far fetched. Membership in that most exclusive of United States academic library groups, the Association of Research Libraries, is based on a rather complex formula, but one of the primary and probably the most significant ingredient is the number of volumes held. Other things are measured, including staff size and building size, but elements of service are not. I would include in the definition of service everything from the anticipation of information requests by compiling bibliographies before they are requested all the way down to the most mundane of criteria – how often does the telephone ring before it is answered? None of them are a part of any official measurement systems in which librarians rank their institution, or in which outsiders rank them.

Nor should it be automatically assumed that the purpose of purchase for ownership is directly related to the needs of users. There is certainly no objection to people using this material, but the primary purpose is satisfied if we have it at least theoretically available for use, that is, in the card catalog. If the material is charged out to someone else and therefore unavailable for specific use at a particular time, that is not the library's fault and the library is not to be blamed. That perhaps rather strange value system of ownership *for* use but not *of* use was documented for books by Michael Buckland[1], and confirmed for journals in a study conducted for the U.S. National Science Foundation by Bernard Fry and this writer[2]. That study confirmed that .under budgetary stringency libraries would cancel the second copies of heavily used periodicals in order to protect their ownership of periodicals which nobody used, and certainly statistics which confirmed this fact were available as early as the 1960s, primarily through the work of Richard Trueswell[3].

Libraries will of course make efforts to obtain for users specific items they do not own, or even items they do own but cannot locate or supply. However, that process has, except in special libraries, no particular urgency or priority. As Veaner has noted[4], libraries are not particularly adept at improving the speed of interlibrary loan. They are very good at convincing users that they ought to wait. Perhaps to some extent librarians can claim to be excused from the harsh judgement which is implied by the above. Libraries and librarians have been under control of their users. This is indirectly the case for public and special libraries through the budgeting control process, and here little change can be expected until the individuals who control funds perceive a greater reason to spend more money. However, for academic libraries that control has not been exercised through an administrative hierarchy but through groups of users who in one sense are nothing more than fellow employees of the librarians. This has been true in the United States, and undoubtedly even more true in other countries, where even the post of library director is generally reserved for someone considered "more important" than a librarian. This represents a political issue which is at the heart of the change which I believe must come. It will, at the same time, not be an easy task to accomplish. Power and authority, once acquired, are not readily ceded and this is particularly true in the academic community in which faculty are already paranoid about their own lack of authority and respect, and in which we have given them little indication of our insistence on regaining control over library decisions and small reason to believe that there are questions and concerns that we and not they are uniquely able to address and solve.

We have of course in large measure created this problem for ourselves, through the emphases we have given to the assessment of library services. These center on two easily quantifiable criteria: 1. the size of the collection (most often used in academic libraries), and 2. circulation from that collection (the compelling criterion in justifying the value of public libraries). To a large extent these strategies for justifying library expenditures developed, at least in the United States but to some extent also in other countries, in the more affluent (at least for libraries) 1950s and 1960s, when such strategies really worked in securing more funds.

However, this rather myopic strategy quickly becomes a double edged sword in a time of declining resources, or one in which more exacting measurements and justifications of value are demanded. The 1980s find us in both. The emphasis on public library circulation as the criterion of value is easily turned against us when such statistics are demanded to identify the least "productive" branch library to be closed during a budget crisis. Our protests at that point that circulation alone is not a valid measurement for determining the least valuable branch are probably not likely to be believed, and our dilemma is only made worse by the fact that we have not been willing to identify other criteria for making that determination.

For academic libraries, the concentration on maintaining the collection above all else becomes a significant problem in the face of several disturbing factors. These include the continuing growth in the published literature. They include also the understandable desire of university faculty to expand areas of concentration and specialization, a desire which exists quite independently of whether or not the faculty is growing or contracting. Finally, problems are affected by the rapid increase in price of published materials, an increase fueled by paper, labor, and postage costs. For those countries on the wrong side of changing international monetary exchange rates, the problem becomes even more severe.

The monster we have created and which is now running out of control is one which esteems libraries as collections and entities with a value and life of their own, and does not assume any sort of crucial role for librarians in the process. In this kind of scenario, a budgetary confrontation about how to spend scarce funds is almost invariably decided in favor of library collections at the expense of librarians. The pressure on the chief librarian is to reduce labor costs through automation so that more money can be spent on the collection. The option of reducing labor costs through automation to allow additional funds to be shifted to other labor categories so that professional services for users can be expandded receives scant attention in this discussion, and sad to say few librarians will even mention let alone press for such a reallocation.   Library materials budgets for the expansion of the collection have, as Robert Munn[5] has noted, insatiable appetites.   As long as this priority ranks first in budgetary discussions, then whatever ranks as the second priority becomes irrelevant, because we never get to the second priority.   Reshaping the value system of libraries from the present simplistic approach to one which seeks and identifies not only a broader range of criteria but also of strategies for addressing qualitative need is in my judgement the fundamental requirement that faces us if we want to develop and expand a professional role in the information age.   Ultimately that will require assertiveness as well as perhaps confrontation, but difficult as that is we must also get our arguments and facts organized.   Much of the latter part of this paper will discuss that strategy.

However, we also face other challenges.   The development of new technologies, primarily computer technologies, has spawned a new coterie of professionals who, dissatisfied with a narrow role of processing bits of data in response to instructions specified by the user community, have asserted that indeed what they do is information processing, and what they are developing are not computer processing systems but management information systems. As libraries depend more heavily on technology to carry out even the most mundane of functions, it is inevitable that these fields will come into contact and probably conflict.   In order to prepare ourselves for this confrontation we must be ready to be able to discuss to some extent what computers can do for us, and to develop some systems, hardware, and software familiarity. However, it is even more crucial that we be able to decide and articulate what it is we would like to have done, and why.   As I will note later, this initiative for change will not come from our user communities.   Our users have no particular interest in changing libraries except in making them larger in the number of things they contain.   Whatever innovation is developed must come from us.

In dealing with the rapidly growing and confident army of computer professionals who call themselves information professionals, we face problems which are not uniquely ours at all.   Other professional groups of users – be they educators, mathematicians, historians, or sociologists, are engaged in the struggle to retain control over their professional processes, to assure that what occurs is something that is convenient and efficient for them, and not necessarily and primarily for the machine.   I shared in this very clearly delineated ideological conflict while I served for six years as a board member of the American Federation of Information Processing Societies, and that struggle is far from ended. For librarians the issue has one further grave dimension. Computer professionals not only don't know about information handling in libraries – they think they do, and they think it is all very simple. As if that array of concerns were not enough, we face at least one more. Even the option of the status quo – of concentrating on purchase and supply from that collection – mundane and clerical as that process is perceived to be, is no longer open to us. There are going to be other ways to use or get around using the "stockroom." Bibliographic access to major network holdings of monographs is already available via computer terminal, and extension of that access to individual subscribers is at present foreclosed only by the lack of protocols to make this economically viable for the organization controlling the data base. For periodical data bases direct end user access has been possible for some time, through international data base packagers and distributors such as DIALOG, RECON, and BRS. Some organizations, including major societies such as the American Chemical Society and corporations such as the Institute for Scientific Information, also package their own data bases and sell or lease them to anyone with necessary funds. The only other requirement, of course, is a terminal, and access to these is growing at a tremendous rate. Individuals or organizations with terminals are therefore no longer dependent on a library to find out what exists, if that is the extent of the information request. Libraries are already·learning that the size and time constraints of their processing backlog cannot be hidden, under the premise that until we announced an item through our card catalogs others did not know it existed. The scenario of a user coming to the library with knowledge that a book exists, and that it has already been processed by national data bases, will recur with increasing frequency. It will be difficult to tell such individuals that they will have to wait weeks longer, let alone months.

At the present time individuals still have to come to the library to obtain such items, and some librarians take such an unnatural pride in this routine and clerical function that there are articles in the professional literature which express our pleasure at the development of information centers which handle information intermediation and analysis because as a result libraries increase their circulation[6]. It is a startlingly narrow view of professional status, but even this role will no longer be automatically ours. Increasingly, data base suppliers have recognized that bibliographic access without document access leads only to frustration, just as librarians have known that if you can't supply or obtain an item it may be better not to suggest its existence, because then individuals work with other and often totally acceptable options. Many bibliographic data base services, particularly as these include periodical articles, now include a document order option, free of copyright implications.

For many disciplines particularly in the physical sciences, the periodical lite-rature is the prime literature of communication, and the combination of bibliographic and document access and delivery can completely foreclose a library role, *IF* that is all the library does.   All that access to these dependable and rapid document delivery systems requires is money.   Although that can be a significant barrier for some, it must be reognized that within the overall budget context of a corporation or even a university, the $6 or $10 cost of receiving an article in this manner is trivial, if there clearly is a need.   For those librarians who would think to retreat from the information age to the presumed "safety" of the delivery business, that safety will no longer be there.

Despite all of these dangers and challenges which I have sought to define and describe, I do not agree with the doomsayers who predict a demise for our profession.   At least, I disagree to the point of arguing that not only can such a fate be avoided if we recognize the dangers, but also that we now face an opportunity of breaking out of a mold which has never served us well and which has not earned us prestige or reward, to a newer role which at least promises both.   The reason for my optimism is the recognition that this changing information environment has also increased the opportunities for individuals to work effectively in providing assistance in its identification, analysis, selection, and use.   It has already been suggested that the profession of dealing with information as defined in its broadest terms may be the largest economic sector in the industrialized world.   In countries where this has not happened as yet, it is likely to begin to occur in the next generation as routine manufacturing and agriculture require fewer and fewer people, and as we shift from a production to an information society.

That there will be a growing role for information professionals appears to be an unquestioned certainty, despite the efforts of data base developers and software producers to make their products more "user friendly." Even to the extent to which they succeed, growing complexity will outstrip their efforts.   There are many reasons for this rather certain prediction.   The growth of literature continues unchecked, and as this information becomes increasingly available, the public's sense of feeling overwhelmed will increase even further.   Beyond this growth, estimated by Anderla for the field of science at 8%/year,[7] there are two additional phenomena.   Educational specialization is becoming narrower, while problems we face as a society become even more interdisciplinary.   We know more and more about less and less, while the problems we are expected to address require that we know more and more about more and more.   No level of educational preparation any longer suffices, and intense knowledge of a narrow discipline encompassing 100 monographs and 50 journal titles leaves one hopelessly inadequate.   The difficulty becomes greater when the key piece of information is contained in a work which not only we have not read, but which we haven't even known existed.

Of course, information ignorance does not have to be admitted, and we know from the very early work of Calvin Mooers[8] that the willingness to pretend to having complete information is far-reaching when an admission of ignorance is either threatening or inconvenient, when it interferes with a conclusion already reached, or when it pressures a time schedule. The very fabric of library and information center use depends on a willingness to admit that there is something we do not know, and the wide fluctuation in library development between countries is related in part to how acceptable such an admission is in the national character and value systems.

To some extent, this is a problem which librarians cannot deal with directly. However, it is important that we not place further strains on the information seeking process by appearing to be critical and judgemental when individuals seek information. The work of social scientists has already told us that many people feel uneasy in libraries, and have felt uncomfortable since childhood. To a considerable extent, this explains why so many people stop using libraries when they leave school, and why even those forced to use information prefer to use an intermediary such as a secretary. Brinberg[9] has told us that there are different kinds of information users, with different needs and preferences. Libraries, to a great extent, treat all of them as though they were scholars or would-be scholars, intent on doing all selection and analysis themselves. There are such individuals, to be sure, but we cannot even be certain that researchers prefer this approach as a method of information access. We give them no choice but the monolithic system we have devised for one kind of perhaps largely mythical user. If individuals avoid using libraries, or if they are drawn to nonthreatening information systems developed by the for-profit information industry, it is because at least to some extent we drive them away. We know from Brinberg that different users have different information preferences. He suggests that researchers prefer raw data for their analysis (and I would caution that perhaps only some of them do), that engineers and sales personnel seek specific answers, and that managers are looking for a range of acceptable options. The proper people-oriented library information system deals with each of these types on the basis of its own needs and preferences. Some people want books, others prefer condensations, still others would rather read reviews. Are we qualified to judge their decisions and motives? I think not. Do we have the right to do so? Certainly not.

One thing which can be said with some certainty is that if librarians do not develop the flexibility of dealing with needs and preferences through a whole range of options and preferences, then others will do this instead of us, and there will be very little if anything left for us.   However, this need not and ought not to happen, if librarians affirm their position, authority and responsibility, through a combination of reassurance, interested inquiry, and assertiveness, in claiming the responsibilities which are ours.   In the vernacular, such claims to unique territory are known as demands for "turf."

We should be in the best position to make this claim and to establish its validity, because of our experience and our education.   Users should be served on the basis of their individual needs , but those needs cannot be established simply by asking them what it is they would like or would prefer.   The answers elicited through this process will only be a restatement of what has taken place in the past, and no growth or progress will occur.   The negotiation process to determine real need and optimum information service is an interactive one, involving both users and librarians, and each with a unique expertise to contribute.   The user obviously knows better the purpose of his inquiry, but only the librarian can fully understand the options which are available. We know enough about question negotiation to recognize that asking the wrong question (or an incomplete question) will often lead to an incorrect or misleading answer.

The field of information intermediation will grow rapidly despite any attempts to develop direct user-friendly approaches, and despite the fact that the elimination of intermediaries is obviously to the advantage of those who sell information packages.   It will grow because of the complexity already mentioned, but even to a greater extent because of a growing reliance on experts and specialists in everyday life.   The reliance on information specialists parallels our reliance on experts in all areas of activity.   This is the largest growing sector of the economy, and it is to this growth that Daniel Bell refers.[10]

The field will not be ours automatically.   There is a growing argument that librarianship is somehow a part of a larger profession, and some schools of library education have been merged with computer science, telecommunications, or journalism.   The relationship with those disciplines is obvious and important, but we are not a part of what they do any more than they are a part of what we do.   Merger in that sort of context can only lead to the disappearance of our profession, and it is ironic that this attempt should be taking place only shortly after librarianship has begun to emerge from behind the shadow of programs of education, of which they were for many years an illfitting part.   The desire to wed library science to other disciplines is understandable, because there is an almost irresistible urge to merge smaller units until ultimately we end up with groups of almost equal size. The strength of our profession is in a uniqueness which is nevertheless closely related to other disciplines through alliances. At Indiana University we have developed a large number of such cooperative programs with Music, Journalism, Art History, Chemistry, and the History and Philosophy of Science for library science/subject competencies which must appear obvious. Others perhaps warrant an explanation. Our cooperation with educational programs in History is designed to produce qualified archivists, because we believe that in this case neither educational base can suffice without the other. Our cooperation with the School of Public and Environmental Administration is designed to prepare individuals for work in libraries which must justify their existence in a sector of competition and approval of governance at the local or national level, or within a university hierarchy. Our cooperation with the School of Business concerns records management, because we recognize that in corporate activities all information functions are likely to be merged under one administrative unit, and it is quite proper that this occur. When the search for needed information crosses the line of format and includes books, periodicals,patents, technical reports, internal memoranda, and laboratory notebooks, it is important that this profession be ready to accept this broadened responsibility.

There are those who suggest that other formats of electronic communication will in a short time replace the printed word as stored in books and periodicals.[11] I consider these arguments simplistic even as they do correctly describe a general trend. They are simplistic because, as we know, computers are excellent producers of paper output, which are stored even as the digitized information is equally available. Electronic journals have appeared, but they have not replaced published journals. They are an additional and not a substitute form, and they just give us one more variant with which to deal. The argument is irrelevant in any case, because our profession has never been format-dependent. The printed book as we know it only goes back half a millenium, and libraries go back a lot further. Just as there were libraries of parchment scrolls and perhaps stone tablets, so collections stored in bits and bytes change our responsibility not at all.

If we are to succeed, then we must make our services available and publicized to the entire spectrum of the user community, and we do this by pointing out how good we are and certainly not how cheap we are. Library costs are a highly visible and emotional topic, but this is only because of a complete failure to identify and hold accountable other methods for incurring and then hiding costs when access to the library is made difficult. It is not difficult to argue that the more library costs are reduced beyond a critical level, the greater the risk that overall even more money will be spent, because it will be spent by those not competent to work efficiently in this field, and because the real costs will quite effectively be hidden from view.

It is for this reason that our profession must seize its area of responsibility, its "turf."[12] This means that either we are given the resources and authority to perform, or that the task doesn't get done at all. We have never been good at creating crises, only at avoiding them. All that has gained us is the reputation for accepting any sort of inconveniences, and somehow still muddling through. The ability to operate under declining resources without a visible impact earns us only the assurance of further declining resources. Why would any manager stop a process which appears to work so well?

Librarians have not done well in tying their idealistic goals into specific and finite objectives, and in articulating these as programs with strategies and resource requirements for which those who supervise and control us are responsible. They are not "required" to provide resources, but they are required to accept responsibility for what service dilutions take place in the absence of resources.

In all of this, of course, our users can be and should be our most effective allies. However, in order to be able to establish this concept we have to let our clients know what we can provide for them, or at least what we could provide for them. Publishers know all about the advantages of trial subscriptions, but librarians know very little about the marketing strategy involved in trial services or products, which, if successful, now provide a source of pressure on higher management to provide support, or risk the wrath of the newly deprived user community. This is a process which in an earlier article I referred to as "ingratiated irreplaceability."[13] That is a somewhat strained phrase, and perhaps a former student put it into a much better context. Hired for a temporary one year position in a corporation to undertake on-line bibliographic searches, she had been clearly told that this position was only funded for one year and could not be extended. And yet, when I asked her whether or not this caused her concern, she stated that it did not. "After a year," she confided, "they will be unable and unwilling to exist without me." And, of course, she was right.

The information profession provides for us almost limitless opportunities to increase our scope and our importance. However, this will only happen if we make our clients understand what we are ready to provide for them. If we wait for them to ask us, either nothing will happen, or some other group, less qualified but more assertive, will step in to fill the gap. If we fail because of this, we will have nobody but ourselves to blame for our demise.

REFERENCES

1. Michael K. Buckland, *Book Availability and the Library User* (New York: : Pergamon Press, 1975).
2. Bernard M. Fry and Herbert S.White, *Publishers and Librarians: A Study of Scholarly and Research Journals* (Lexington, Mass. : D.C. Heath, 1976).
3. Richard W. Trueswell. "Some Behavioral Patterns of Library Users: The 80/20 Rule," *Wilson Library Bulletin* 43 (Jan. 1969): 458−61.
4. Allen B. Veaner, "1985 to 1995. The Next Decade in Academic Librarianship, Part I," *College and Research Libraries* 46 (May 1985): 209−229.
5. Robert F. Munn, "The Bottomless Pit, or the Academic Library as Viewed from the Administration Building," *College and Research Libraries* 29 (Jan. 1968): 51−54.
6. Masse Bloomfield, "Role of One Technical Library in Support of an Information Center," *Special Libraries* 57 (Jan. 1966): 39−44.
7. J.G. Anderla, "The Growth of Scientific and Technical Information − A Challenge," *Information* 2−3 (1974): 1−52.
8. Calvin N. Mooers, "Mooers's Law, Or Why Some Retrieval Systems Are Used and Others Are Not," *American Documentation* 11 (July 1960):204.
9. Herbert R. Brinberg, *The Contribution of Information to Economic Growth and Development*. Theme Paper at the 40th Congress of the International Federation for Documentation. Copenhagen, Denmark: Aug.18, 1980.
10. Daniel Bell, *The Coming of Post-Industrial Society; A Venture in Social Forecasting* (New York: Basic Books, 1973).
11. F. Wilfred Lancastter, *Toward Paperless Information Systems* (New York: Academic Press, 1978).
12. Herbert S. White, "Library Turf," *Library Journal* 110 (Apr. 15, 1985): 54-55.
13. Herbert S. White, "Organizational Placement of the Industrial Special Library and Its Relationship to Success and Survival," *Special Libraries* 64 (March 1973):141−44.

The Future of American Library Education —
Return to Basics?

Tze-chung Li
Professor and Dean
Graduate School of Library and Information Science
Rosary College
River Forest, Illinois, U.S.A.

American library schools are having a difficult time. They are confronted by the problems of declining enrollment, changing modern technologies, and a shrinking market for their graduates. From 1979 to 1983, the number of students enrolled in library science master's degree programs dropped from 9,180 to 8,139, a decrease of 12.8 percent.[1] Take Rosary, for example. Its library school has been able to maintain a stable enrollment since 1982, but that enrollment is less than half of what it was in the peak year of 1972 when 449 students were enrolled in one semester. The over-all decrease in enrollment has already claimed casualties among library schools.

Changing modern technologies have had a serious impact on library operations. Practically all librarians are required to have basic knowledge of, and skills in, the library application of modern technologies. In talking about information technology and the traditional library, De Gennaro states that library objectives must, among other things, include the implementation of an integrated system with an online catalog and appropriate internal and external network interface, as well as access to resources elsewhere by means of modern technologies.[2] Library science curricula must incorporate the use of modern technologies or library functions may be lost to other units that can provide the same information more efficiently and effectively.[3]

Enrollment is directly proportional to the market. American colleges and universities conferred a total of 3,979 master's degrees in library science in 1982/83, a significant decrease of 42 percent in five years and 48 percent in 10 years.[4] The library market which can use library science graduates each year is estimated to be 110,000.[5] It is further constrained by the fact that many professional positions in libraries are not filled by library science graduates.   For instance, some 30 percent of the federal library professionals at all levels did not have a master's degree in library science.[6]

A thriving market for library science graduates exists outside of libraries. The business sector alone has over 4 million corporations of which 160,000 are listed in the *Million Dollar Directory*.[7]   The corporations listed in the directory, including the top 50,000 companies with net worth exeeding $1.85 million each, transact over two-thirds of the national volume of sales and employ 40 percent of all workers in the United States.   If library schools can exploit this market by teaching their students in the management of information in the business sector, employment opportunities for library science graduates may double.

Library schools are now struggling for survival and aggressively looking in new directions for vitality.   One noticeable direction is the extension of their programs to information science at both undergraduate and graduate levels.   From 1979 to 1983, while the number of graduate students in library science is down, the number of undergraduates in library and information science has increased substantially, from 1,290 to 2,349, a comfortable jump of 82 percent.[8]

With the scope of the program broadened to include information science, new courses not existing in the 1960s, such as database management, microcomputers, programming languages, and online searching, have been developed and integrated into the regular library science curriculum.   A comparison of 1976 and 1982 course offerings indicates a substantial increase of course offerings in these five categories: library automation, information storage and retrieval, systems analysis, interactive computer systems, and programming.[9]   To underscore the new directions, many library schools have changed their titles.   Of the 56 ALA accredited library schools, 27 use "information science," 12 "information studies," and 5 "educational/ instructional technology," "information service," and "information management," respectively.[10]

To justify this movement toward the information science field, Daniel identifies three types of information worlds: literature, document, and machine-readable data.[11]   The world of libraries and archives deals with knowledge in recorded form and it focuses on the historical time frame and the book/periodical storage medium.   The second world is represented by paper-work or records centers.   The last refers to computers, telecommunications, and automated information systems dealing often with numerical information.   These three worlds, according to Daniel, can be brought together organizationally and the new breed of librarians must penetrate into the third world.   As stated emphatically by Fosdick, information science is now critical to library science education.[12]   The significance of developing information science courses is two-fold: to help produce a "new breed of librarians" and to enable library science graduates to seek employment in other sectors, such as the information industry.

It must be noted, however, that this change of direction comes not from the strength but the weakness of library schools.   The juxtaposition of library science and information science courses and the recent movement toward information science, though not a desperate strategy, show diminishing confidence in the foundation and role of traditional librarianship.

In commemoration of the Special Libraries Association's 75th anniversary, the Association's Illinois Chapter produced *Information and Special Libraries in 2009.*[13]   Fifty-six contributors expressed their views, noting the changes in the library profession caused by technological developments. The bottom line is that librarianship, having its roots in tradition, deals not simply with media but with messages in the media.   Knowledge of the subject matter of the messages is essential to providing effective library services.

For the effective use of government publications, for instance, a basic knowledge of government structure and functions is required.   Vertrees and Murfin reported that students learned more by studying not only government publications but also the legislative process, including the relationship between Congress and the President and the executive branch agencies.[14]   In the use of legal resources, McCallum suggested that "essential to helping a library user find the law is some understanding of what constitutes the law."[15]   It is preferable that an area bibliographer have first-hand knowledge of the area.[16]   Obviously, the ability to handle information resources in a discipline is largely dependent on how thorough the librarian's knowledge of that field is, regardless of what form the sources are in — electronic, paperless, or optical.

Historically, the development of three literature courses in the humanities, the social sciences, and the sciences was intended to stress the contents of subject disciplines.   These courses, as mentioned by Shove, are "to provide a knowledge and understanding of the basic ideas, concepts, objectives, and current trends in the humanities, the social sciences, and the sciences."[17]   Linderman supported this view stating "there seems to be a distinct advantage in the literature course which, in studying any one subject, such as Sociology or Political Science, considers at the same time the development of the discipline, the classic writing in the field... "[18]

According to the INFROSS (Investigation into Information Requirements of the Social Sciences) survey, social scientists tended to underuse the services of librarians.   This was said to be the most significant finding of the survey.[19]   A scientist spent four hours repeating an experiment, but, in fact, only thirty-six minutes were required for a librarian to locate the information.[20]   In these cases, users did not delegate their research activitiess − including bibliographic searching − to librarians.   They may not be aware of the availability of library services or they may not have confidence in the librarian's ability to find information.   The latter possibility should move library schools to seriously reevaluate their programs.

Librarians have in general a distinctive role to play.   American librarianship has progressed through at least three stages of development, from bookmen to technicians and from technicians to professionals.   An important force in the development has been the teaching role of librarians. In 1876, the Bureau of Education stated that librarians should not only understand their primary duties as purveyors of library supplies to the people, but should also realize their high privileges and responsibilities as teachers.[21]   This concept was further explored by John Cotton Dana, reiterated by William S.   Learned, and strongly advocated by Alvin Johnson.[22]   Johnson's advocacy had particular significance in the 1930s when the adult education movement reached its highest pitch.

Since the 1960s, however, the importance of the librarians' teaching role has shifted to the informational function.   To some, the real future of library service lies in the direct provision of information; instructing the user in the technique of information-searching is an important, but secondary, goal and is not necessarily a reference function.[23]   It is encouraging to see the recent array of advocates for the librarians' teaching role.

In response to *A Nation at Risk,* a report by the National Commission on Excellence in Education,[24] the Department of Education produced *Alliance in Excellence*, stressing skill and proficiency in finding and using information effectively, a function in which libraries play an essential role.[25] It considers libraries to be an integral part of the overall educational system and consequently "the librarian must be considered an educator as well as a librarian."[26]   The American Library Association also responded with a statement noting, in particular, the teaching role of librarians.[27]   "Librarians are teachers, and they serve both students and teachers."[28]   The reaffirmation of the teaching role of librarians makes it clear that they should have knowledge of subject fields as well as of information technology.

Present library education tends to stress skill and proficiency in providing information *as it is*.   Familiar teaching modes, such as treasure hunting and pathfinders, rarely teach students to process information into more useful information.   Rush defines information processing as "the manipulation of data so as to reveal or highlight salient characteristics, features or properties of data, or relationships among various data elements or classes of data elements," and criticizes library schools for not teaching such a process.[29] It will be hard, without subject knowledge, for students to work effectively on even simple information processes, such as distinguishing various information pros and cons available on a subject, choosing the most appropriate sources of information, and interpreting the information so as to make it more useful to patrons. Although the undergraduate program mentioned earlier may make the FTE more presentable in the budgeting process, it doesn't offer a sufficient background in the liberal arts and sciences. Nor does it offer a subject concentration, so it is not the kind of program with which library schools should educate professionals.

Developing information science courses is essential to strengthen traditional library science. Library science education must be "state-of-the-art technologically."[30] New courses are particularly important if library schools intend to expand their market to any sector other than libraries. Library science students are now required to take courses in traditional library science and also courses in modern information science. It is, however, not feasible for any student to grasp well both fields in one year's studies, the general program structure of most library schools. The result will be that students take fewer courses in traditional library science and receive a superficial education in information science.

One solution is to prolong the period of study as some library schools have already done. The problem is that the extended period of study will not make the graduates more marketable in the library profession.[31] If one year's curriculum is adequate for entering the library profession, why do we need a two years' program? It would be more useful, however, to extend the period devoted to studying the subject content of a discipline.

The relationship between library science and information science is similar to that between library science and business administration. These programs may enrich each other, yet each has its distinctive purpose. Many library schools offer courses geared toward business administration, such as personnel management and managerial finance. They are useful, but not essential to librarians, simply because library schools educate librarians, not business managers. Likewise, courses in information science are useful, such as database management, programming languages, and systems analysis, but librarians can function competently without having studied them. A survey of eight groups of libraries revealed that courses in traditional library science are essential to anyone who wishes to be hired.[32] Courses in library automation, computer programming, and systems analysis and design are generally considered desirable but not essential.[33]   A survey of the largest public library systems on library competencies has a similar finding, though some computer-related courses are considered essential in the future. [34]   According to a survey of Rosary graduates from 1980 to 1984, only 27 of the 106 respondents consider computer programming a necessary competence for librarians.[35]

The hybrid program, mixing library science and information science, may not result in a bonanza.   It can very well adversely affect the foundation and role of librarianship.   The future of American library science education does not lie in mere application of modern technologies, but in returning to basics to strengthen traditional library science.   Emphasis must be placed on the knowledge of the subject discipline required of librarians.   Rush has criticized current library and information science education because "courses deal with media, but not with messages," and "courses deal with sources but not their content."[36]

To make librarianship a viable, respected profession, library schools must restore confidence in traditional library science, stress the librarian's competence in using resources effectively, and reaffirm the librarian's teaching role.   They must chart a course for the future of library education in the following directions.   First, stress the importance of knowing subject content and see to it that students are taught to *process* information as well as to *provide* it.   Second, reaffirm the distinctive functions of librarians, with particular reference to their teaching role in most types of libraries.   Third, integrate information science courses into traditional library science courses.   If there is a need for separate courses, they should be developed in such a way that they do not encroach upon library science education.   Fourth, develop a full-fledged information science program, stressing managerial aspects.   This should exist side by side with the library science program, and should aim at producing a different professional species.

FOOTNOTES

1. Association of American Library Schools. *Library Education Statistical Report*, 1980-1982; Association for Library and Information Science Education. *Library and Information Science Education Statistical Report*, 1982-1984.
2. Richard De Gennaro, "Shifting Gears: Information Technology and the Traditional Library."   A lecture delivered at the University of Pittsburgh, 1983, pp. 9-11.
3. JoAnn Segal and John Tyson, "The Library's Changing Role in Higher

Education," *Library Journal* 110 (1985) :45
4. "Fact-file: Degrees Conferred by U. S. Colleges and Universities, 1982-83," *The Chronicle of Higher Education*, October 9, 1985, p.22.
5. National Commission on Libraries and Information Science documents released on May 22, 1985.
6. John Berry, "New Threats to the MLS?" *Library Journal* 110 (March 1985):23-4.
7. "Introduction," *Million Dollar Directory* (1985).
8. See note 1.
9. Howard Fosdick, "Trends in Information Science Education," *Special Libraries* 75 (October 1984): 301.
10. *Graduate Library Education Programs*, October 1985. Chicago: American Library Association.
11. Evelyn Daniel, "1980's Forecast: Special Librarian to Information Manager," *Special Libraries* 73(April 1982): 97-98.
12. Howard Fosdick, "Trends in Information Science Education," *Special Libraries* 75 (October 1984): 292-302.
13. Special Libraries Association. Illinois Chapter. *Information and Special Libraires in 2009: Informed Speculations.* Chicago: Special Libraries Association Illinois Chapter, 1984
14. Robert L. Vertress and Majorie E. Murfin, "Teaching the Legislative Process: An Evaluation of Classroom and Library Instruction and a Legislative History Exercise," *Government Publications Review* 7A (1980):505-7.
15. Sue Vest McCallum, "Legal Research for Non-law Librarians," *Government Publications Review*, 6 (1979) : 264.
16. Beverly J. Brewster, "Area Bibliography Programs in U. S. Library Schools," *International Library Review* 9 (Jan. 1977):8.
17. Raymond H. Shove, "Objectives of Adult Literature Course and Their Place in the Library School Curriculum," in Association of American Library Schools, *Report of Meeting*, Minneapolis, June 24, 1954, p. 46.
18. Winifred B. Linderman, "Changes in the Literature Courses in the New Library School Programs," in Association of American Library Schools, *Report of Meeting*, Minneapolis, June 24, 1954, p.49.
19. Maurice B. Line, "The Information Uses and Needs of Social Scientists: An Overview of INFROSS," *Aslib Proceedings* 23 (1971): 416.
20. Albert H. Rubenstein and others, "Search Versus Experiment the Role of the Research Librarian," *College and Research Libraries* 34 (1973) :280-8.
21. U.S., Bureau of Education, *Public Libraries in the United States of*

America (Washington, D. C. : Government Printing Office, (1876),p. xi.

22. John Cotton Dana, *A Library Primer* (1896); William S. Learned, *The American Public Library and the Diffusion of knowledge* (1924); Alvin Johnson. The Public Library; A People's University (1938).

23. Anita Shiller, "Reference Service: Instruction or Information," *Library Quarterly* 35 (1965) :52-60.

24. National Commission on Excellence in Education, *A Nation at Risk*; *The Imperative for Educational Reform* (Washington, D.C.: Government Printing Office,1983); National Commission on Libraries and Information Science, *Annual Report*, 1983-84 (1985), pp. 13-7.

25. U. S. Department of Education, *Alliance for Excellence; Librarians Respond to A Nation at Risk* (Washington, D. C.:Government Printing Office, 1984).

26. *Ibid.*, P.4.

27. American Library Association, Task Force on Excellence in Education, *Realities: Educational Reform in a Learning Society*. (Chicago: American Library Association, 1984).

28. *Ibid*, p. 4.

29. James E. Rush, "The Challenge of Educating Library and Information Science Professionals: 1985 and Beyond," *Technical Services Quarterly* 3 (Fall/Winter 1985-86): 97.

30. "A Conversation with Tom Galvin," *Technicalities* 4, no.11 (1984) : 4.

31. *Statistical Data From Questionnaires Collected by Indiana University School of Library and Information Science*, n.d.

32. *Ibid*.

33. *Ibid*.

34. Nathan M. Smith and others, "The Public Library Director's View of Library Education," School of Library and Information Science, Brigham Young University, n.d.

35. "Alumni Questionnaire, 1980-1984." Rosary College Graduate School of Library and Information Science, 1985. Unpublished.

36. James E. Rush, "The Challenge of Education Library and Information Science Professionals: 1985 and Beyond," *Technical Services Quarterly* 3 (Fall/Winter 1985-86): 102.

Future Trends in Library and Information
Science Education in Japan

Yoshinari Tsuda
Professor
School of Library and Information Science
Keio University
Tokyo, Japan

INFORMATION SCIENCE EDUCATION

For many years, practicing librarians have been complaining that library schools are not producing the kind of graduates who can be used in the actual library works right away.

To this criticism library and information science educators have been replying by claiming that the educational aim is to equip students with sound theoretical knowledge, so that they can cope with any kind of library work in a variety of situations with understanding of their meanings.

However, recent development of electronic information technology and its increasing rate of adoption and implementation in library and information works seems to make this reply of educators less convincing than it used to be.

Are library schools really producing the kind of students who can meet new requirements in changing environments of library and information service fields? At least, in Japan, we can not say with confidence that we do. Today's graduates of library schools need to be prepared better than before in various skills and knowledge in information sciences.

As early as in 1968, when keio University library school added to its undergraduate library science program, a new two-years Master's program, it was decided that all the traditional library science subjects were to be taught in the undergraduate program and the graduate program was to be concentrated on information science oriented subjects. And when students with non-library science undergraduate education seeked to apply for the graduate program, then, they were asked to spend one extra year to take undergraduate basic subjects before they started their graduate studies. This decision is even now followed so that students can study information oriented subjects more fully.   But the trend of library schools to go into information science education is not so strong in Japan, and even now, there are only three library schools that are using the term "library and information science" for their name.

According to the 1982 survey conducted by the Japan Library Association (JLA) there were 133 colleges and universities and 100 junior colleges that have library science courses.[1] However, the majority of these schools were offering a very limited number of traditional library science subjects. As the license of librarianship in Japan is issued by the Ministry of Education and candidates are requested to finish only 19 units of subjects for Shisho (librarian) and 8 units for *Shishokyoyu* (teacher librarian), most schools offer just that many units of subjects.

To see how much of the recent world trend of offering information related subjects along with traditional library science subjects penetrated in library science education, this survey of JLA (1982) was examined.   This revealed the fact that only 73 out of 233 universities, colleges, and junior colleges which have library science courses, were offering some kind of information science subjects.   Among these 73 schools, 61 of them had only one introductory subject.   Ten were offering 2 to 6 subjects.   And only two were offering more than 30 subjects.   These two were Keio University and National University of Library and Information Science.

Even though this trend of teaching information related subjects in the library science education is not so flourishing, a steady increase of these subjects among library science courses is observed, and on the other side the number of schools that are offering library science education itself is decreasing slightly.

The previous JLA survey in 1977 reported that 141 colleges and universities and 101 junior colleges had library science courses.   That means that 9 of them had stopped offering library science courses during these 5 years between 1977 and 1982.   And as in 1977, there were 64 colleges and universities that offered at least one subject in information science, that means that during these same 5 years of period, nine new colleges and universities started to teach information science subjects.

The most popular course among them is "Joho Kanri" (information management).   But the content of this course differs from school to school, because the background of teachers who are teaching this particular subject differs a great deal.   Some of them call themselves documentalists, some are computer specialists, and some are librarians who are involved in some kinds of information works such as on-line searching.   And even such librarians who belong to old traditional library science are sometime assigned to teach this course.

Besides this "Joho Kanri," more than 60 schools are offering a course on communication.   And a fairly large number of schools are teaching social survey as a part of library science courses.   But except these three subjects, others are all very traditional ones such as "school librarianships," "classification and cataloging," "reference service," "history of books and libraries," "library administration," etc.

CURRICULA OF SCHOOLS OF LIBRARY
AND INFORMATION SCIENCE

Keio University in Tokyo changed the name of its School of Library Science to School of Library and Information Science in 1968.   But this example was not followed by any other schools for a long time.   This was partly because that most of other schools were (and even now are) offering only the minimum number of subjects barely satisfying the government requirements for professional librarians or teacher librarians, which consist of very traditional library science subjects.   And because of that there is no margin left in their curricula to change into or to add new information course.

When the library school of keio University was started with five American faculty members in 1951, it very much took after the American pattern of library education.   The first major curriculum change occurred in 1972. Then, the undergraduate curriculum was grouped into five categories.   They were "fundamentals," "recorded materials," "organization of materials," "information systems," and "miscellaneous."

In 1984, the next major curriculum revision took place.   During these 12 years, from 1972 to 1984, the school had been trying to meet the changing demands of emerging information society by adding new information related subjects, such as "bibliometrics," "on-line searching," "office automation," "business information analysis," "medical information," "user study," etc. to the miscellaneous group.   And this practice of simply adding new subjects to the miscellaneous group eventually created a problem of unbalanced distribution of subjects among these five groups.   This was the reason that the school took the trouble of reviewing the old curriculum and revising it thoroughly.

The new undergraduate curriculum consists of 6 groups of subjects.   They are "information," "information retrieval," "reference materials," "organization of materials," "information systems and management," and "information processing technology."   And besides them, an introductory subject on library and information science and seminars are offered.   All the subjects except selective ones are grouped into these six categories as either core or distributive requirements (D.R.).   The idea of this grouping was based on professor Saracevic's presentation at the First Asian Pacific Conference on Library Science held here in Taipei in March 1983.

The master's course curriculum is also divided into six but slightly different groups that follows.

Group 1   Information Science and Technology
          Information Science and Technology, Seminar
Group 2   Structure of Information, I-II
          Structure of Information, Seminar
Group 3   Information Systems
          Information Systems, Seminar
Group 4   Information Media
          Information Media, Seminar
Group 5   Information Storage and Retrieval, Advanced I-III
          Information Storage and Retrieval, Seminar
Group 6   Mechanization in Information Handling
          Mechanization in Information Handling, Seminar
          and Research Methods I-II.

The Ph.D. curriculum is grouped into 3 categories. They are "information systems," "information media," and "information processing."

Next to Keio University, the National University of Library and Information Science developed an extensive education for information science. This school started in October 1979 in Tsukuba with only an undergraduate program, but added a Master's program in April 1984.   They have now about 60 faculty members, and nearly half of them are computer oriented persons.

Their undergraduate curriculum consists of 5 groups of subjects. They are "basic courses of library and information science," "information and society," "information media," "organization of information," and "library and information systems."   They are heavily slanted to computer science and are offering such subjects as "data structure," "database structure," "file structure," "database management," "systems analysis," "pattern processing," "artifical intelligence," "computer systems," "library automation," etc. besides ordinary programming courses.

Their graduate course curriculum is categorized into 8 different groups. They are "basic courses of library and information science," "cognition of information," "construction of information," "relationship of information to society," "information media," "organization of library and information systems," "use of information machineries," and "library information retrieval."

As there are not many information scientists in Japan, the faculty of this school is made up mainly of two distinctly different groups of traditional librarians and computer scientists. And apparently they need some more time till they can be intermixed to form a desired group of information scientists.

The third school of library and information science only started this April at Aichi Shukutoku University in Nagoya. Their course curriculum is divided into 6 groups following the pattern of Keio University. But more stress was placed on the "information" group with its DRs of "user study" and "communication," and such, and also on "information processing technology" group with its DRs such as "information processing," "office automation," and "library automation." Besides these subjects the school is offering a group of elective subjects such as "information evaluation," "business information," "searching theory," "construction of databases," "bibliographic information network," "mass communication," etc. And a special emphasis is placed on these two: online searching and office automation.

As for the computer facilities of these schools, while Keio University is using the university computer center, National University of Library and Information Science and Aichi Shukutoku University are using their own computer facilities.

INFORMATION EDUCATION IN OTHER DEPARTMENTS

Even though there are only three schools in library science education which call themselves schools of library and information science, there are 38 other courses in other departments that use the term "information" as a part of their names. Recently, the number of these new courses are increasing rapidly. And every year new ones are being proposed to the Ministry of Education for approval (Table 1).

Table 1. Number of "Information" Courses in Other Departments
(Based on a record of the Ministry of Education)

Information Engineering	21	4	25
Electronic Information Engineering	4	1	5
Electric Information Engineering	2	0	2
Information Processing Engineering	1	1	2
Information Communication Engineering	1	0	1
Information Control Engineering	0	1	1
Information Systems Engineering	0	1	1

Information Mathemtics	5	0	5
Information Science	1	1	2
Business Information	1	4	5
Information Management	1	1	2
Information	1	0	1
Total	38	14	52

Most of these courses belong to schools of engineering, and some belong to schools of economics.   Compared with already existing courses, a fairly large proportion of them are now being proposed.   That means that teaching "information" in these schools is somewhat a new trend but they are increasing in number much faster than in library science education.

As there is a general tendency of calling computer science infor- ·mation science in Japan, some of these courses given in schools of engineering might be just that.   However, it can not be denied that there is a strong trend of increase of information related courses in either departments of engineering and economics.

Because a low standard of professional librarianship in Japan is forcing the graduates of full scale schools of library and information science in seeking positions in libraries to compete with a great number of graduates from more than 200 other schools that offer minor courses in library education, many of the graduates of full scale schools have to look for employment in various business firms and industries.   And there, they have to compete with graduates of these information courses in other departments.   This means that the graduates of schools of library and information science should be equipped with more skills and knowledge in handling information in not only library situation but also in these office environments.

CONCLUSION

The situation in Japanese library science education can be summed up as follows.

1. Most library science education is offered on the undergraduate level, and only four universities (Keio, Tokyo, Kyoto and National University of Library and Information Science) are offering graduate programs.
2. At least two years of study is required to finish a Master's program in Japan.   And in the case of Keio University, if a student does not have previous library science education, he will be requested to spend one extra year to study core subjects of undergraduate library science course.
3. Ph.D. programs are offered only by Keio University, Tokyo University

and Kyoto University, and the number of their students is very limited.
4. Accordingly, there is a very small number of qualified teachers in library science courses.   And in many cases, teachers of these courses have only 19 units of very traditional, very limited library science education.
5. More than 200 universities, colleges, and junior colleges are offering some kind of library science courses but the number of subjects being taught is very much limited to barely meet the government requirements for the licenses of professional librarian or teacher-librarian which are far lower than that of other developed countries.
6. Many of the students who come to the graduate program for library and information science have other than a library science background and a science background is not uncommon among them.
7. Only three of the schools that are teaching library science named themselves as schools of library and information science.
8. Only 73 out of more than 200 schools which are offering library science courses are teaching also some information related subjects. And though the three schools of library and information science have fairly extensive information science courses, they are exceptional cases. In most other cases only one subject is being taught.
9. Information related subjects are being taught more in courses of other departments than in library science courses and the largest number of courses are taught in engineering departments.
10. In Japan, there are many traditional librarians and also many computer scientists, but very few information scientists.

By taking into account the above mentioned situations in library science education, the following things can be predicted.
1. The increase in the number of information related courses offered in colleges and universities will be accelerated, but more in computer science and business administration and less in library science.
2. Opening of many new graduate courses in library and information science can not be expected.
3. Over-production of licensed Shisho (professional librarian) will continue at least for a while.   And there will be not much chance of raising the quality of these Shisho in the near future.
4. Graduates of schools of library and information science will keep seeking jobs in business firms and industries as well as in libraries.   And the schools should aim to equip their students with a kind of skills and knowledge that can be useful in finding information to solve various problems encountered in these work situations.

5. Demands for qualified information science teachers will increase more in the future as the pressure toward information oriented education becomes greater.

REFERENCES

1. Japan Library Association. *List of Teachers in Library Education*: 1982 survey. Tokyo: J. L. A., 1983.
2. Japan Library Association. *List of Teachers in Library Education*: 1977 survey. Tokyo: J. L. A., 1978.

Future Trends in Library and Information Science Education in North America

Norman Horrocks
Professor and Director
School of Library Service
Dalhousie University
Halifax, Canada

Library and information science education in North America today encompasses many activities and at differing levels. There are programmes in colleges and universities leading to formal qualifications at technician, undergraduate, graduate, advanced certificate[1] and doctoral level. There are Continuing Education activities which may or may not lead to a formal credential or some form of certification. These Continuing Education opportunities may be offered by colleges and universities but are not their exclusive province. Library associations, libraries and increasingly, the private sector,* are all providing Continuing Education experiences.

At the first professional level, still generally referred to as the MLS degree (i.e. Master of Library Science, although the name does vary across the various graduate schools offering it), there is a distinction between those programmes which are accredited by the Committee on Accreditation (COA) of the American Library Association and those which are not. The fact that increasingly Schools are changing the name of their first professional degree, the MLS, reflects an even greater change in that many programmes are now seen as preparing their graduates for careers in information handling not necessarily linked with a library as such.

At the present time, there are 63 programmes in North America which carry COA accreditation. Although they share accredited status implying some degree of commonality, there are some significant differences. The most obvious is that 56 are located in the United States and seven in Canada. In addition, in one of the Canadian schools, the language of instruction is

---

* e.g. The Institute for Scientific Information, OCLC, UTLAS and the many data base providers.

French and not English. There are also differences in the length of time required to obtain the MLS degree. In Canada, the MLS requires four academic terms which in six of the seven schools calls for attendance for two full academic years. In the United States the great majority of schools enable the student to complete the programme in one calendar year. These differences may support the belief that the COA *Standards for Accreditation* are contained in a flexible document.

Perhaps more obviously apparent to an outside viewer than the duration of the programme has been the change in nomenclature. The titles of what were once simply referred to as "library schools" now very commonly include the word "information". At first it was "library and information science" but now "information studies" or "information management" can be found and in some cases the word "library" does not appear at all. The .significance of these changes of name will vary from School to School. It may represent a change in philosophy by those who believe that "information science" is a discipline which can be taught alongside "library science". In others it may be the belief that the two form a natural complement as two points on the one continuum. Where some word other than "science" is added to "Information" in the School's title it may reflect a belief that the graduates of the programme are being prepared for careers not only in libraries but also in other occupations involving the handling of information. However, it should also be pointed out that a change in name may not in itself be commensurate with a change in the programme. Conversely, Schools which have not changed their titles may nonetheless have made significant changes in their programmes.

What does appears to have been universely accepted, with or without a name change, is the integration into the curriculum of "information science". This means that the general, introductory courses in reference work, cataloguing, selection and the like, now have built into them appropriate content relating to various aspects of automation and machine applications. There seems also to be a growing realization that there are machine applications to be studied in management as libraries grow in size, become more complex and increasingly are under pressure to demonstrate their cost effectiveness. While all of this may be true of those Schools offering the MLS degree it is interesting to note that there are other approaches being considered and implemented in the information science/information management areas, both at Schools with the MLS and elsewhere and at both undergraduate and graduate level.

In the United States, the University of Pittsburgh is the best known institution which has diversified its approach. For many years now its MLS programme has operated alongside an interdisciplinary programme in Information Science which offered both masters and doctoral degrees. Since 1981, it has added an undergraduate programme in information science. Unlike the MLS which has taken as its standard the four year undergraduate liberal arts or science degree for its admission standard, the bachelors programme is a purely technical offering for those working with computer based systems. Although it is perhaps too early to be definitive there is no evidence at present that this bachelors degree is seen as an entry to the MLS programme. A slightly different approach is that being followed elsewhere in Pennsylvania at Drexel University. Its library school is now the basis for a College which offers the bachelors, MLS and doctoral degrees. The bachelors degree is in information science, again with no clear relationship to the MLS. A third U. S. university, Minnesota, has taken a deliberate decision to phase out its MLS programme in favour of an academic department which will offer degrees in information science at the bachelors, masters and doctoral level. In adition a number of Schools call for undergraduate courses as pre-requisites for admission to their MLS programme.

In Canada there are two slightly different approaches. Toronto, which currently offers the MLS and Ph. D., is proposing the introduction of a Masters in Information Science. This will be offered alongside the MLS but at the present time it is not planned to seek COA accreditation for the MLS programme. In the same city, the Ryerson Polytechnical Institute has phased out its library technician programme in favour of a Certificate Programme in Information Studies.[2] This programme is aimed at the information handling area but is not clear at this time where its graduates will find themselves employed. Indeed some of its current students seem to be regarding the programme as a form of Continuing Education to be added to their existing MLS.

Although the area of information science/management may have attracted the most attention in the literature there are other subject areas which are offered alongside or in conjunction with the MLS degree. These may take the form of joint degrees, specializations within the MLS programme itself or separate programmes in their own right. The major subject fields involved have been archival management or law librarianship with health sciences/medical librarianship also offered but to a lesser amount. Generally speaking, the emphasis has been on specializations or joint degrees.

Meanwhile education for those working as librarians in schools remains a concern of those Schools offering the MLS and those in Faculties, Schools or Departments of Education. In both Canada and the United States a qualification in education allied to courses or a degree in Library Science are expected of those who increasingly see themselves as Teacher-Librarians. In this role the emphasis is on the educational function to be carried out. A recent report published in the U.S. has underlined the need for the improvement of staffing in school library and media programmes.[3] ALA's division, the American Association of School Librarians, established in 1984 a Library Educators Discussion Group to seek solutions in this field. Earlier in Canada, CLA's division, the Canadian School Library Association, published a three-tier approach for education of those involved in school situations.[4] Two Canadian Library schools introduced a Masters degree for Teacher Librarians alongside their MLS but low enrollments forced the dropping of these new programmes. It seems fair to say that neither country has yet found the right balance for practitioners in this branch of the profession.

Allied to these concerns for specialist areas — information science, law, medicine, archives, schools, etc. — there remains the status of the basic MLS itself. Should it seek to be a generalist degree or should it offer opportunities for specialization within what is still in COA's words "a first professional degree". A degree at the Masters level should represent mastery of the subject itself, in our case library/information science. In addition many would argue that there should be a common "core" of knowledge to be expected of all those seeking to demonstrate mastery of the field. Yet virtually a century after Melvil Dewey opened his Library School at Columbia College in New York, there is still dispute over whether there is in fact a common core and what it contains. One of the most telling arguments in favour of a lengthened programme of study has been that it should provide opportunities for a certain amount of specialization beyond a "core" in the MLS programme, an opportunity either limited or not possible in the U. S. one calendar year programme.[5]

There are many related and unresolved issues surrounding the curriculum beyond the specialization/generalised approaches which do not relate to the length of the programme itself. There is still discussion on whether or not library schools should regard themselves as "training" or "educating" their students.[6] The Schools, operating in an academic environment, have leaned towards the latter despite pressures from employers to emphasize "training". Not all employers take this limited view. In fact, some would support the view that for certain major research libraries a good subject degree is more important than the MLS.[7] These sometimes broad generalizations tend to overlook that North American schools, operating graduate programmes, commonly recruit students who have subject specializations at honours bachelors, masters or doctoral level before they enter the MLS programme.

Whatever the motivation, there is evidence in both the U. S. and Canada that employers are taking an increasing interest in the Library Schools and their operations. Possibly the closing of a number of U. S. schools in recent years has served to focus attention in this area. Possibly the Schools themselves have devoted more effort to explaining just what it is they seek to do and why. It could also be that outside forces, most noticeably the Federal governments in both the U. S. and Canada although operating separately and independently, have forced the profession to better define what its particular competencies and skills are. So it is that in place of individual carping criticisms based on real, or imaginary or outdated perspectives of Library Schools we are seeing today organizations within the profession making known their collective views based on their greater awareness of the current state of library education.

The most noteworthy example of this was the Invitational Conference on accreditation held in Chicago in September, 1984.[8] Organized by the Association for Library and Information Science Education and with the cooperation of the Committee on Accreditation of ALA, representatives from many associations and employer groups came together to discuss the present accreditation process and how it might be changed in the future. Although accreditation is a voluntary process, the American Library Association is the body recognized by the Committee on Post-Secondary Accreditation to carry out this task in the United States.[9] The seven Canadian library schools have chosen to seek accreditation from ALA in the absence of any such system in their own country.[10] What emerged from the ALISE Conference was the announcement of a major study by the COA, funded by the U.S. Department of Education of the future administration of the accreditation process. Specifically the study is examining how other professional associations such as the American Society for Information Science, the Special Libraries Association, the Medical Library Association, etc., might become involved along with ALA itself.[11] What underlies this is the interest and concern of those sections of the profession represented by these Associations in seeking to have their views taken into account by the Schools, especially in the area of curriculum. The early signs for continued dialogue with the Schools seem promising although some difficult decisions lie ahead. Independently, a similar trend of dialogue between employers and the Schools has been seen recently in Canada.[12]

While the employers' concerns with the graduates of the MLS programs are understandable and welcome, it has to be realized that they are not always at an altruistic level. Employers are almost all facing financial pressures forcing them to examine carefully just what it is that the MLS holder does and for which a professional salary has to be paid. It has to be recognized that with increased automation many of the tasks once performed by professional librarians can now be carried out effectively by technical or indeed clerical staff.[13, 14, 15] Library technician programmes are attracting an increasing amount of attention as sources of supply for staff at this level. It is too early to say whether Schools which have introduced undergraduate programmes, or are considering doing so, are seeking to cater for a perceived need at this level or responding to what they see as a changing market within the information profession. Library Schools are not immune from the problems of balancing enrollments within academic institutional budgets.

Equally, Library Schools are not immune from the problems and challenges facing the society in which they operate. The literature is full of forecasts of how life will change in what is surely now only the early stages of the computer revolution. As librarians we have seen our adjustment to the changing environment with our card catalogues giving way to on-line access. We have coped with first print and now microcopies and will be able to handle electronic communications also. The role of the library and information centre may change but we have a record of adjustment. But in any case, our role is not just information handling. We have traditionally provided service to children and young adults. As people in North America change jobs more frequently than in the past, many retire from formal employment earlier and live longer, there are life-long learning, retraining and recreational roles for our libraries. As we see the still high illiteracy rates in North America, as well as the continuing immigration into the continent, then the need for libraries and librarians should remain. The challenge in all of these areas is to ensure that this need is recognized and met.

FOOTNOTES

1. J. Periam Danton, "Between M.L.S. and Ph.D.: a Study of Sixth-year Specialist Programs in Accredited Library Schools." Chicago: ALA, 1970.
2. Barbara Shainbaum, "Ryerson Winning with Information Studies", *Quill & Quire* 51 (1985): 75-76.
3. U. S. Department of Education. *Alliance for Excellence: Librarians Respond to a Nation at Risk* (Washington, DC: USDE, 1984).
4. Canadian School Library Association. *A Recommended Curriculum for Education for School Librarianship.* Ottawa: C.S.L.A., 1981.

5. For a discussion of the issues see "Two Year Library School Programs: Useful Extension or Waste of Time?"; Robert M. Hayes, "Allows Specialization and Apprenticeships Without loss of Basics"; F. William Summers, "Longer Programs Mean Higher Costs with No Proof of Benefits", *American Libraries* 14 (1983): 619-620.

6. Herbert S. White, "Education vs. Training: A Problem of Definition," *Journal of Academic Librarianship* 10 (1984): 198-199.

7. Patricia M. Battin, "Developing University and Research Library Professionals: a Director's Perspective" *American Libraries* 14 (1983): 22-25.

8. See the special issue on Accreditation, *Journal of Education for Library and Information Science* 25 (1984).

9. See Russell E. Bidlack, "Accreditation," *ALA World Encyclopedia of Library and Information Services* (Chicago: ALA, 1980), pp. 18-21.

10. The Canadian Library Association currently has a committee looking into the question of a Canadian system of accreditation. See the January, 1984 and subsequent issues of *Feliciter*.

11. For the background see Robert M. Hayes, "The American Library Association — U.S. Department of Education Grant," *Journal of Education in Librarianship and Information Science* 25 (1984): 141-144.

12. The First Symposium on Library Education held in Calgary, Alberta, October, 1985. Proceedings are to be published.

13. Norman Horrocks, "What Does It Take to Run a Library: the Future of the M.L.S.," Manitoba Library Association *Bulletin* 14 (1984): 7-10.

14. Allen Veaner, "Librarians: the Next Generation," *Library Journal* 109 (1984): 623-625.

15. Jose-Marie Griffiths, "Our Compentencies Defined: a Progress Report and Sampling," *American Libraries* 15 (1984): 43-45.

Appendix
Conference Program

國立台灣大學舉辦
圖書館學與資訊科學教育
國際研討會

INTERNATIONAL CONFERENCE ON LIBRARY AND INFORMATION SCIENCE EDUCATION

November 29-30, 1985

NATIONAL TAIWAN UNIVERSITY

PROGRAM

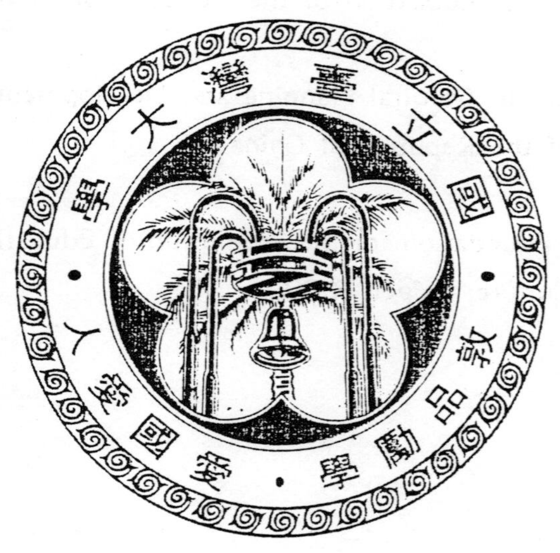

國立台灣大學圖書館學系暨研究所

DEPARTMENT AND GRADUATE INSTITUTE OF LIBRARY SCIENCE, N. T. U.

Taipei, Taiwan, R. O. C. Tel:(02)396-2859 • 351-0231 Ext. 2296

Acknowledgment

We are grateful to the following agencies for their generous grants which made this Conference possible:

Ministry of Education of the Republic of China

Council for Cultural Planning and Development
of the Republic of China

China Foundation for the Promotion of Education and
Culture, Taipei, R.O.C.

Conference Program
Contents

Theme: Library and Information Science Education

Topics: The Present Role of Library and Information Science in the Information Age

Current Status and National Trends of Library and Information Science Education in the East and the West

Assessment of Current Library and Information Science Curricula

The Integration of Library Science and Information Science

Future Trends in Library and Information Science Education

Conference Agenda

Friday, November 29

Registration 08:00 — 09:00	Chien Shih-liang Memorial Hall National Taiwan University
Opening Ceremony	Welcome Address Dr. Chen Sun
09:00 — 09:30	President, National Taiwan University

Introduction of Delegates from Abroad
Dr. James S. C. Hu
Secretary-General of the Conference

09:30 — 10:00   Refreshment Break

Session I   Chairperson: Professor James S. C. Hu
                                    National Taiwan Univeristy

10:00 — 12:00   1. The Art and the Science of Library and Information
Science

   Speaker: Professor Charles H. Davis
                  University of Illinois at Urbana-Champaign,
                  USA

2. Professional and Academic, the Recognition of the
Library and Information Science Education

   Speaker: Professor Josephine Yu Chen Sche
                  Tamkang University, ROC

3. The New Technology and Its Potential for Information
Professionals and the Effects on Library and Information Science Education

   Speaker: Professor Ching-chih Chen
                  Simmons College, USA

12:00 — 14:00   Luncheon

Session II	Chairperson: Professor Chen-yung Fan National Taiwan University

14:00 – 16:00

1. Library Education in the Republic of China

   Speaker: Professor James S. C. Hu
National Taiwan University

2. Problems Confronting Library Science Education in the Republic of China

   Speaker: Professor Harris B. H. Seng
National Taiwan University

3. Library and Information Education Today: from the British Point of View

   Speaker: Professor Peter Havard-Williams
Loughborough University of Technology, England

16:00 – 16:20 Refreshment Break

16:20 – 17:40

4. The First Professional Step; the MLS in Library and Information Science in the United States

   Speaker: Professor Harold Goldstein
The Florida State University, USA

5. Stability and Change: Library and Information Science Education in the United States, 1985

   Speaker: Professor Edward G. Holley
University of North Carolina at Chapel Hill, USA

Saturday, November 30

Session III	Chairperson: Professor Lucy Te-Chu Lee National Taiwan University

08:30 — 10:30

1. The Management of Libraries: an Assessment of Library and Information Science Curricula

    Speaker: Professor Robert M. Hayes
    University of California at Los Angeles, USA

2. The Role of Practical Work in Library and Information Science Curricula

    Speaker: Professor Rupert Hacker
    Bavarian Civil Servants' College
    Federal Republic of Germany

3. Design of the Curriculum for a 2-Year Library Technical Assistant Program in Recruitment Plan of the Republic of China

    Speaker: Professor Chien-chang Lan
    Fu Jen Catholic University, ROC

10:30 — 10:50   Refreshment Break

10:50 — 12:00

4. Education and Training for Online Use of Databases in the Republic of China

    Speaker: Professor Lucy Te-Chu Lee
    National Taiwan University

5. Continuing Education and In-Service Training for Librarians in the Republic of China

    Speaker: Professor Shih-hsion Huang
    Tamkang University, ROC

12:00 — 13:30   Luncheon

Session IV	Chairperson: Professor Harris B. H. Seng National Taiwan University

13:30 – 16:00

1. Libraries and Information Centers — Their Changing Role in a Changing Environment

   Speaker: Professor Herbert S. White
   Indiana University, USA

2. The Future of American Library Education — Return to Basics ?

   Speaker: Professor Tze-chung Li
   Rosary College, USA

3. Future Trends in Library and Information Science Education in Japan

   Speaker: Professor Yoshinari Tsuda
   Keio University, Japan

4. Future Trends of Library and Information Science Education in North America

   Speaker: Professor Norman Horrocks
   Dalhousie University, Canada

16:00 – 16:20   Refreshment Break

16:20 – 16:30   Closing Remarks
Dr. Yen Chu
Dean, College of Liberal Arts
National Taiwan University

Participants

Administrative Officers of the National Taiwan University

Sun, Chen 孫　震
President
National Taiwan University

Lo, Tung-bin 羅銅壁
Dean of Academic Affairs
National Taiwan University

Chou, Tao-chi 周道濟
Dean of Student Affairs
National Taiwan University

Huang, Ta-chou 黃大洲
Dean of Business Affairs
National Taiwan University

Chu, Yen 朱　炎
Dean, College of Liberal Arts
National Taiwan University

Delegates from Abroad (in alphabetical order)

Chen, Ching-chih
Professor & Associate Dean
Graduate School of Library and Information Science
Simmons College
U.S.A.

Davis, Charles H.
Professor & Dean
Graduate School of Library and Information Science
University of Illinois at Urbana-Champaign
U.S.A.

Goldstein, Harold
Professor & Former Dean
School of Library and Information Studies
The Florida State University
U.S.A.

Hacker, Rupert
Professor & Director
Department of Librarianship
Bavarian Civil Servants' College, Munich
Federal Republic of Germany

Havard-Williams, Peter
Professor & Head
Department of Library and Information Studies
Loughborough University of Technology
England

Hayes, Robert M.
Professor & Dean
Graduate School of Library and Information Science
University of California at Los Angeles
U.S.A.

Holley, Edward G.
Professor & Former Dean
School of Library Science
University of North Carolina at Chapel Hill
U.S.A.

Horrocks, Norman
Professor & Director
School of Library Service
Dalhousie University
Canada

Li, Tze-chung
Professor & Dean
Graduate School of Library and Information Science
Rosary College
U.S.A.

Tsuda, Yoshinari
Professor
School of Library and Information Science
Keio University
Japan

White, Herbert S.
Professor & Dean
School of Library and Information Science
Indiana University
U.S.A.

Delegates from the Republic of China (in alphabetical order)

Chang, Chung-tao 張仲陶
Professor of Electronic Engineering and Technology
National Taiwan Institute of Technology

Chang, Daniel T.C. 張東哲
Director of Library
National Tsing Hua University

Chang, F. W. 張奉文
Professor and Director of Library
National Central University

Chang, Grace Y. D. Yu 兪雨娣
Associate Professor of History
Soochow University

Chang, Peter Pi-te 昌彼得
Deputy Director
National Palace Museum
Professor of Library Science
National Taiwan University

Chang, Yi-ting 章以鼎
Head, Library Extention Department
National Central Library Taiwan Branch

Chang-Wang, Teresa Y. C. 汪雁秋
Head, Bureau of International Exchange of Publications
National Central Library

Chen, Ho-chin 陳和琴
Associate Professor of Educational Media & Library Sciences
Tamkang University

Chen, Lawrence H. 陳興夏
Director of Libraries
National Taiwan University

Cheng, Andrew Teh An 鄭得安
Professor and Director of Library
Tunghai University

Cheng, Chi-nan 鄭吉男
Director
Taipei Municipal Library

Cheng, Feng-shen 鄭鳳生
Special Assistant to Chairman
Chinese Maritime Transport, Ltd.
Associate Professor of Library Science
National Taiwan University

Cheng, Heng-hsiung 鄭恆雄
Head, Technical Services Department
National Central Library Taiwan Branch

Chiang, Fu-tsung 蔣復璁
Academician
Academia Sinica
Former Director
National Palace Museum

Chin, Chiu-cheng 靳久誠
Director of Library
National Taiwan Normal University

Chou, Nancy Ou-lan (Hu) 胡歐蘭
Head, Acquisitions Department
National Central Library

Chow, Tsin-fu 周駿富
Professor of Library Science
National Taiwan University

Chu, Tar-song 朱大松
Director
National Central Library Taiwan Branch

Chou, Josephine Y. T. 卓玉聰
Head Librarian
Veterans General Hospital Library

Fan, Chen-yung 范承源
Research Fellow
Institute of American Culture, Academia Sinica
Professor of Library Science
National Taiwan University

Hou, Chien 侯　健
Professor of English Literature
National Taiwan University

Hsieh, Ching-chun 謝清俊
Research Fellow
Academia Sinica

Hsieh, Hsiang-chi 謝祥圻
Professor of Information Engineering
Feng Chia University
Professor of Library Science
National Taiwan University

Hsu, Monica Chien-hua　鄭建華
Head, College of Medicine Library
National Taiwan University

Hu, Chia-yuan　胡家源
Associate Director
Tunghai University Library

Hu, James S. C.　胡述兆
Professor, Chairman & Director
Department and Graduate Institute of Library Science
National Taiwan University

Huang, Jing-huei　黃競慧
Teaching Assistant
Department of Library Science
National Taiwan University

Huang, Jack Kai-tung　黃克東
Professor & Director
Department of Computer Science
Ming Chuan College

Huang, Shih-hsion　黃世雄
Director of Libraries
Professor
Department of Educational Media & Library Sciences
Tamkang University

Huang, Sophia H. C.　黃鴻珠
Associate Professor of Educational Media & Library Sciences
Tamkang University

Juang, Fang-rung 莊芳榮
Section Chief
Council for Cultural Planning and Development
Executive Yuan
Associate Professor of Library Science
National Taiwan University

Ko, Shu-ling 柯淑齡
Director, University Library
Chairperson, Department of Chinese Literature (Modern Literature Section)
Chinese Culture University

Ku, Karl Min 顧　敏
Director
Legislative Yuan Library

Kuo, Li-ling 郭麗玲
Instructor of Library Science
National Taiwan Normal University

Lan, Chien-chang 藍乾章
Professor & Chairman
Department of Library Science
Fu Jen Catholic University

Lee, Bosco Wen-ruey 李文瑞
Professor of Agricultural Extension
National Taiwan University

Lee, Huei-chung 李惠中
Instructor of Library Science
Fu Jen Catholic University

Lee, Lucy Te-Chu 李德竹
Professor of Library Science
National Taiwan University

Lee, Mei-yueh 李美月
Director of Library
National Sun Yat-sen University

Lee, Michael 李　炎
Director
Bureau of International Cultural and Educational Relations
Ministry of Education

Lee, Thomas C. 李　瞻
Professor and Dean
Graduate School of Journalism
National Chengchi University
Professor of Library Science
National Taiwan University

Lei, Shwu-yun 雷叔雲
Chief, Government Documents Section
National Central Library
Instructor of Library Science
National Taiwan University

Li, Pei-lieh 葉佩莉
Head, College of Law Library
National Taiwan University

Lin, Kuang-mei 林光美
Head, College of Engineering Library
National Taiwan University

Lin, Mei-ho 林美和
Professor of Library Science
National Taiwan Normal University

Lin, Mong-jenn 林孟眞
Associate Professor of Library Science
National Taiwan Normal University

Lin, Phyllis C. F. 林志鳳
Chairman
Department of Library Science
The World College of Journalism

Lin, Shao-hsun 林少薰
Instructor of Library Science
National Taiwan University

Ling, Shau-yuin Hsu 許小雲
Head, Acquisitions Department
National Taiwan University Library

Liu, Chang-po 劉昌博
Member of the Council
Library Association of China

Liu, Hao-ying Fang 范豪英
Director of Library
National Yang-Ming Medical College

Lu, Ho-sheng 盧荷生
Associate Professor of Library Science
Fu Jen Catholic University

Lu, Yu-hsing　陸毓興
Instructor of Library Science
Fu Jen Catholic University

Ma, Kuang-heng　馬廣亨
Director
Taiwan Provincial Taichung Library

Ma, Tao-hsing　馬道行
Director
Science & Technology Information Center
National Science Council

Mao, Ching-chen　毛慶禎
Instructor of Library Science
Fu Jen Catholic University

Pan, Mei-yueh　潘美月
Professor of Library Science and Chinese Literature
National Taiwan University

Sche, Josephine Yu Chen　陳　豫
Associate Professor of Educational Media & Library Sciences
Tamkang University

Seng, Harris B. H.　沈寶環
Professor of Library Science
National Taiwan University

Shaw, Shiow-jyu Lu　盧秀菊
Instructor of Library Science
National Taiwan University

Soong, Chien-cheng 宋建成
Head, Department of General Affairs
National Central Library

Sun, Yo-yu 孫又予
Chief Librarian
Main Library
Chung Shan Institute of Science & Technology

Tang, Chen Pi-yung 陳碧蓉
Head, Reader's Service Department
National Taiwan University Library

Tang, Shiuann 湯　絢
Teaching Assistant
Department of Library Science
National Taiwan University

Tien, Sieu-mai C. 鄭雪玫
Associate Professor of Library Science
Fu Jen Catholic University
National Taiwan University

Wang, Chen-ku 王振鵠
Director
National Central Library
Professor of Library Science
National Taiwan University

Wang, Chung-i 王中一
Director of Library
Soochow University

Wang, Fuh-hwa　王復華
Teaching Assistant
Department of Library Science
National Taiwan University

Wang, Min-hsing　王民信
Head, College of Liberal Arts Library
National Taiwan University

Wang, Nancy Ching-hung　王景鴻
Director of Library
National Palace Museum

Wang, Pu　王　璞
Curator, Department of Books & Documents
National Palace Museum

Wang, Shih-fong　王士峯
Instructor of Library Science
National Taiwan University

Wang Tseng-tsai　王曾才
Professor of History
National Taiwan University

Wang, Wen-chuan　王文泉
Instructor of Library Science
National Taiwan University

Weng, Hweifen　翁蕙芬
Teaching Assistant
Department of Library Science
National Taiwan University

Wu, Liu-li 吳瑠璃
Instructor of Library Science
National Taiwan Normal University

Wu, Ming-der 吳明德
Associate Professor of Library Science
National Taiwan University

Wu, Tsu-shan 吳祖善
Head, Cataloging Department
National Taiwan University Library

Yang, Chen-chau 楊鍵樵
Associate Professor of Electronic Engineering
National Taiwan Institute of Technology

Yang, Chia-lo 楊家駱
Professor of Library Science
National Taiwan University

Yang, Kuo-shih 楊國賜
Professor, Chairman & Director
Department & Graduate Institute of Social Education
National Taiwan Normal University

Yang, Mei-hwa 楊美華
Associate Professor & Director of Library
Feng Chia University

Yang, Zu-zan 楊日然
Professor of Law
National Taiwan University

Organizing Committees

Ad Hoc Committee

Chen Sun 孫　震
President
National Taiwan University

Yen Chu 朱　炎
Dean
College of Liberal Arts

James S. C. Hu　胡述兆
Chairman and Director
Department & Graduate Institute of Library Science

Executive Committee

James S. C. Hu　胡述兆
Committee Chairman

Harris B. H. Seng　沈寶環
Professor of Library Science

Chen-yung Fan　范承源
Professor of Library Science

Lucy Te-Chu Lee 李德竹
Professor of Library Science

Ming-der Wu　吳明德
Associate Professor of Library Science

Shiow-jyu Lu　盧秀菊
Instructor of Library Science

Secretariat

James S. C. Hu 胡述兆
Secretary-General

Ming-der Wu 吳明德
Executive Secretary

Shiow-jyu Lu 盧秀菊
Deputy Executive Secretary

Secretaries:

Fuh-hwa Wang 王復華

Shiuann Tang 湯　絢

Hweifen Weng 翁蕙芬

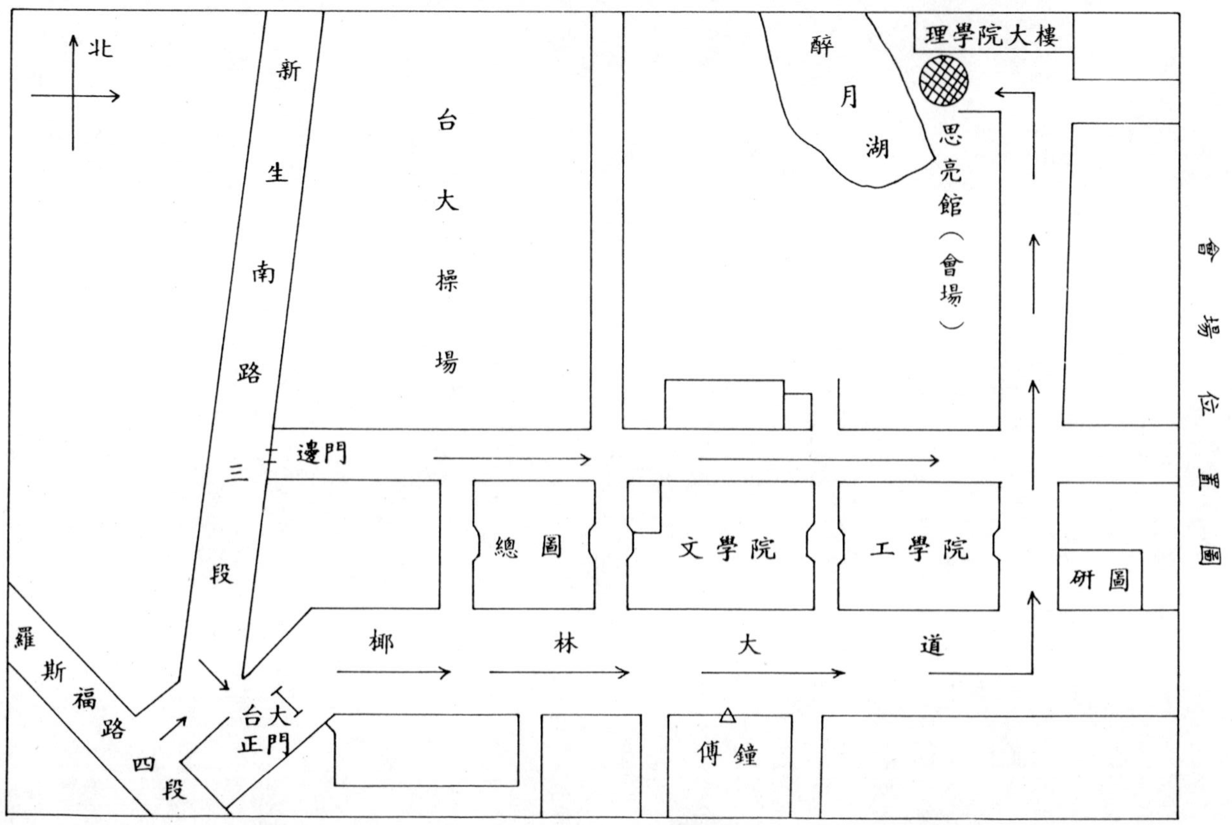

會　場　位　置　圖
北
理學院大樓
醉月湖
思亮館（會場）
研圖
台大操場
總圖
文學院
工學院
邊門
椰　林　大　道
傅鐘
新生南路三段
羅斯福路四段
台大正門